Understanding Child Development

RUDOLF STEINER'S ESSENTIAL PRINCIPLES
FOR WALDORF EDUCATION

Angelika Wiehl and Wolfgang-M. Auer, editors

Translated from the German by Margot Saar

WALDORF EARLY CHILDHOOD
ASSOCIATION OF NORTH AMERICA

Understanding Child Development
Rudolf Steiner's Essential Principles for Waldorf Education

First English Edition

© 2020 Waldorf Early Childhood Association of North America.
All rights reserved. No part of this book may be reproduced without the written permission of the publisher, except for brief quotations embodied in critical reviews and articles.

ISBN: 978-1-936849-53-6

First published in German by Beltz Juventa,
Werderstrasse 10, 69469 Weinheim, Germany.

Editors: Angelika Wiehl, Wolfgang-M. Auer
Translator: Margot Saar
Graphic Design: Lory Widmer

Published in the United States of America by
Waldorf Early Childhood Association of North America
285 Hungry Hollow Rd.
Spring Valley, NY 10977
www.waldorfearlychildhood.org

Visit our online store:
store.waldorfearlychildhood.org

This publication was made possible
by a grant from the Waldorf Curriculum Fund.

Contents

5 Source Texts (S): Rudolf Steiner on the anthropology and education of childhood – Angelika Wiehl and Wolfgang-M. Auer

7 The future of childhood – David Martin and Silke Schwarz

Preface

This selection of study materials on the theory and practice of Waldorf education is the result of the editors' many years of experience in Waldorf schools, Waldorf kindergartens, and in teacher training.

The heart of the book consists of a collection of extracts or "source texts" taken from Rudolf Steiner's writings and lectures. Much of what Rudolf Steiner said about Waldorf education was noted down during his lectures and is therefore, while not conducive to textual critique, well suited to comparison and deepening. Given that childhood is the main focus of this publication, we have only included those extracts from the original texts that reflect central thoughts on particular topics and facilitate the study of specific themes in Waldorf education: an approach tried and tested in teacher education. For a deeper understanding of the context in which Rudolf Steiner presented his thoughts on anthropology and education it is, however, essential to study the full texts. The Source Texts are presented here under specific headings, each with a short introduction. They are embedded in essays on child anthropology and education that introduce the reader both to the most recent research and to the thinking of Waldorf education.

The authors would like to thank all the students of Waldorf education whose contributions and questions during our training seminars led us to make this selection of texts available in book form. We also thank the Association of Waldorf Kindergartens in Germany and the Helmut-von-Kügelgen Foundation for promoting our research and making this publication possible.

Angelika Wiehl and Wolfgang-M. Auer
November 2018

1 Introduction

ANGELIKA WIEHL, WOLFGANG-M. AUER

There have never been as many endeavors and as many institutions aiming to protect childhood as in the early twenty-first century. And yet, many children today are exposed to hazardous and unhealthy living conditions. Lack of time, poverty, war, migration, media consumption—there is a long list of reasons why children don't grow up in a more healthy way. While modern lifestyles, society and families, public awareness, and schools do what they can to promote a healthy and joyful childhood, children continue to suffer from neglect and the violation of their human rights. The image that went around the world in 2015 of the lifeless body of three-year old Aylan Kurdi, who drowned in the sea between Syria and Greece, is a deeply shocking document. But children today are not only endangered by war and displacement; in the Western world we have increasingly also the inescapable influence of digital media, the education systems that are guided by economic interests, and the attempted or actual overprotectiveness of parents, all of which leave children little scope for the individual development that is so essential. Children typically develop in phases, first from infancy to the middle of childhood, then into adolescence and later into adulthood, educating themselves as individuals according to their intentions or "inner forces," as Wilhelm von Humboldt[1] suggested (Humboldt 1792/2015). In order to develop with dignity, children have always relied on the loving and protecting support of adults, because only in adolescence will they gradually acquire the ability to take responsibility for shaping their own lives.

If the family can no longer provide a nurturing education and home for a child, then others—relatives, friends, or educational institutions—must take on this task and assume responsibility. The child support and protection that indigenous or rural communities may still provide "instinctively" must be achieved in new ways in modern Western societies. We need to (re-)find an understanding of what makes us human

---

1 Wilhelm von Humboldt, (1767-1835), German linguist, philosopher, and educational reformer.

that ensures children are no longer seen as either a blessing or burden, as substitute partners, or even prestigious objects, but as fully respected individuals with their own aims in life and their own rights. It is, however, not a small number of educated adults, educators, teachers, physicians, or institutions for the protection of childhood that will bring about the necessary changes; society as a whole needs to rethink childhood and make it a priority. From puberty, that is to say from the moment when young people become themselves able to have children, they must be able to understand that they, too, are responsible for humanity, and that the qualities that make us human need nurturing. Adolescents and young adults must be prepared for this task today, regardless of whether or when they start a family and have children of their own. Living conditions in the Western world provide all that is needed: parents can prepare themselves early on for having children, and they receive medical, social, and educational support in bringing them up. All that is needed to promote child development is in place, but it is up to each of us to decide how to make use of this. We each have the responsibility to take an interest in childhood and to attend to the individual child.

Rudolf Steiner's Waldorf education can provide valuable guidelines for an educational attitude that takes its first cue from the individual child's destiny, an attitude that needs to be developed by parents and by professionals in day nurseries, children's homes, schools and other educational institutions. Starting in the 1960s, numerous books have been published on early years and school education, focusing on a variety of aspects and establishing specific concepts derived from Steiner's anthropological and educational ideas. Among the authors of these publications, Karl König and Bernhard Lievegoed deserve special mention for elaborating the anthroposophical principles of child development in the realm of special needs education and medicine. Their books continue to be newly published and have become fundamental study material in Waldorf teacher trainings (König/Soldner 2017; Lievegoed 2016). They explore and develop Rudolf Steiner's anthroposophical and pedagogical thoughts, providing practice-based access to the sources of Waldorf education.

In 1971, a first selection of source texts on the anthropology of Waldorf education, edited by Elisabeth Grunelius and Helmut von Kügelgen, was published as study material by the German Waldorf Kindergarten Association (*Das Wesen des kleinen Kindes*) and by the International Association of Waldorf Kindergartens (*Understanding Young Children*). This compendium remains unique in that it brings together in one volume Rudolf Steiner's many statements on childhood and on the first seven years in particular, which are usually dispersed across many lectures and some written works, and makes it possible to study the subject-matter in context. This publication is, however, not widely used in German, and is no longer being distributed in English, because it lacks the introductions and explanations of concepts and contents specific to anthroposophy that one would expect to see today in such textbooks. Moreover, modern studies in developmental psychology reveal that the phases of childhood and youth cannot be as strictly divided into seven-year periods as the literature on Waldorf education tends to imply. There are indications—for instance in the longitudinal studies conducted by Remo Largo (2017)—that developmental phases are increasingly individual and that seven-year periods can at best be seen as an ideal. While Rudolf Steiner described human development as unfolding in seven-year stages, he also refers to transitions such as the Rubicon, for instance, which children typically experience around their ninth or tenth year, when they become more conscious of their relationship with the world (Föller-Mancini/Berger 2016). Waldorf teachers see this crucial moment as representing the end of the first phase of childhood that is then followed by the middle of childhood and early puberty. The source texts from Steiner's work included here (Chapter 5) were specifically selected for their relevance to the age up to the ninth or tenth year and they, along with the other contributions in this book, therefore relate to both preschool and early school education.

Understanding Child Development was published for the specific purpose of making such fundamental study materials available for use—in addition to primary Steiner texts on anthropology and (Waldorf) education—in teaching seminars and study courses. The selection of anthropological and educational topics presented is of particular relevance to today's discourse on child education because they refer to lesser-known aspects which are explained in the framework of essays into which these source texts are embedded. The source texts themselves are based on Steiner's anthropology (his view of the human being and of human development), and need to be seen in their contemporary context.

Chapter 2 gives an introduction to the "anthropology of childhood from the point of view of Waldorf education." In preparation for the study of the source texts (Chapter 5) three main themes that are essential for an understanding of Waldorf education are introduced: the concept, or knowledge, of the "I," the idea of reincarnation, and Steiner's theory of the fourfold human organization. The section on child constitution looks at children as beings of body, soul, and spirit and includes experiences from pedagogical practice.

In Chapter 3, Wolfgang-M. Auer outlines the "development and education of the senses" on the basis of Steiner's concept of the twelve senses, which has been studied from various perspectives in the past but newly researched by Auer (Auer 2007). Looking at the twelve senses anthropologically yields not only diagnostic possibilities but also a wealth of inspirations for early years and school education. The study and care of the senses, for which educators and teachers need special training, affect all the basic skills children need to develop.

In chapter 4 Angelika Wiehl presents an overview of the anthropology and education of the imitating child. Rudolf Steiner marks out imitation as the predominant learning disposition in the first seven years of childhood. By including the findings of fields of knowledge such as aesthetics, sociology, and neurobiology it can be demonstrated that imitation is a faculty that is essential not only in childhood but throughout life because it allows us to take possession of the world, develop and transform ourselves, and be creative. It is therefore essential to create conditions both in educational institutions and at home that facilitate imitative, person-to-person learning in a natural way.

Chapter 5 forms the heart of this publication. It offers selected source texts on child anthropology and education taken from various phases in Rudolf Steiner's working life. The texts, or extracts, feature specific aspects of Waldorf education in childhood and present them in subchapters each with an individual introduction. The entire chapter provides study material for use in teacher training and professional development. The selections include aspects of childhood as presented by Rudolf Steiner in his works. While these aspects are being applied in the pedagogical practice and referred to in the relevant literature, they have so far not been made available as a separate body of study materials.

Chapter 6 provides ideas for the study and practice of Waldorf education, some of which relate to text study and others to the actual teaching practice. In addition to a theoretical foundation, Rudolf Steiner's anthropology also includes guidelines on how to put the theory into practice. Rather than providing instructions on how to work, however, Steiner offers sources of inspiration for an individualized approach to child education.

In Chapter 7 David Martin and Silke Schwarz look at the future of childhood in the twenty-first century. Drawing on their own research and experience as medical practitioners they call attention to a series of modern phenomena that can either hinder or promote healthy child development. Their approach to enhancing child development and child health in the age of digitalization and acceleration is rooted in the insights of anthroposophy that were introduced in the previous chapters and documented in the source texts.

For reasons of space the bibliography is limited to the sources that have been used and cited in this publication. It is not a complete list of literature available on the topic of Waldorf education. Rudolf Steiner's works, if they are not special editions, are cited with their GA number (the number assigned to them in the German-language catalog of collected works) and referenced in the text as "Steiner GA" followed by the corresponding number.

2 An anthropology of childhood

ANGELIKA WIEHL AND WOLFGANG-M. AUER

2.1 Introduction
2.2 The miracle of childhood
2.3 The child as a spiritual I-being
2.4 Child constitution and education

2.1 Introduction

The anthropology of Waldorf education is the result of Rudolf Steiner's years of study in the humanities and natural sciences, extended and deepened through meditation and spiritual science. The lectures he gave in the First Teachers Course (GA 293), complemented in subsequent seminar sessions (GAs 294 and 295), have always been seen as fundamental to the theory and practice of Waldorf education. To the content of this course of 1919 he continued to add over the following years in numerous lectures on education. Steiner's "educational anthropology" is unique in that it describes the physical, mental, and spiritual dimensions of the human constitution phenomenologically—dimensions that are clearly apparent to the interested observer—then evaluates their relevance to the pedagogical practice on the basis of his own anthroposophical, or spiritual-scientific, studies, recommending finally that teachers undertake their own meditative studies. He critically discusses but does not restrict himself to findings established by the natural sciences or developmental psychology.

While, in the twentieth century, anthropology became the subject of various scientific disciplines that have also informed it, today's image of human nature is essentially based on a natural-scientific, empirical, and mechanical understanding that we find reflected in the current endeavors to understand and change the human being. Recent studies, often referring to Maurice Merleau-Ponty's *Phenomenology of the Body* (1966), focus on "embodiment" (or incarnation) in an attempt to demonstrate that the mind needs a physical foundation for its realization and the soul self-experience (Storch et. al. 2017). At the same time, the proponents of transhumanism, a philosophy that by now has an impact on many disciplines, promote "the universal technological optimization of physical and mental performance" of human beings and unlimited "prolongation and quality of life" (Benedikter 2017). Serious efforts are invested in transferring human intelligence to robots that will then take the place of humans. To equate mental faculties and consciousness with mere physical or embodied experiences or artificial intelligence means to take an increasingly mechanistic view of the human being that fails to explain the origin or essence of spirit and soul. The attempts of neuroscientists at locating mental processes in the brain are not convincing either since their imaging research methods only record biophysical processes. Their usual conclusions, though widely accepted in the field of education, apply only to brain development, however; they cannot explain the origin of consciousness and of mental processes (Wagemann 2010).

Apart from the views mentioned, educational anthropology cites mainly sociological and social factors in relation to human development and formation. The multi-dimensional representation of human nature as put forward since ancient Greece in ever-new philosophical and anthropological variations is hardly considered in education. A recently published study on educational anthropology by Christoph Wulf and Jörg Zirfas (2014) discusses a variety of themes in essays such as "Ways of Access," "The Body," "Social Issues," "Time," "Space," "Culture," "Subjects," "Boundaries"—all of them ultimately aspects of how we inhabit the world. The image of the human being they present cannot, however, accommodate human qualities such as self-determination and self-knowledge. We witness instead how, in the twentieth and twenty-first centuries, every discipline—be it education, philosophy, psychology, medicine, anthropology, behavioral biology, paleontology, or ethnology (Kluge 2003)—offers one particular way of looking at the human condition. This is why Rudolf Steiner's attempt at establishing a holistic but differentiated image of the human being is unique. For him the human being is constituted of body, soul, and spirit, in accordance with earth and cosmos, and "destined to lead an ethical existence for the purpose of realizing good intentions based on insight, freedom, and love" (Stoltz/Wiehl 2019).

Spread across many different writings and lectures rather than summarized in one particular context, Steiner presents an image of the human being from three different perspectives, that of soul, spirit, and body, detailing each of them individually. This approach of dividing the human being and then considering the individual aspects in a new context is consistent, but alien to the modern way of thinking that tends to focus on isolated events. Steiner's process-oriented and fragmentary way of thinking that also includes insights gained in spiritual research requires methodical preparation. It is crucial today that we learn to "read Steiner in a new way" (Kiersch 2014, p. 9ff.) and investigate his anthropological insights in the light of modern spiritual-scientific and natural-scientific research in order to unlock their potential as a source for education. It was not Steiner's intention to develop a universal educational anthropology. His aim was to provide, as a foundation for the Waldorf school, a comprehensive image of the human being that was not informed by natural-scientific insights alone, but verifiable through methodical spiritual research (ibid.; Steiner GA 21). It was for this purpose that he continued to develop his research method and his insights, as Kiersch and others have illustrated (Demisch et. al. 2014).

There are numerous publications that rephrase Steiner's anthropological foundations of Waldorf education in detail (Leber 2002) or develop them further (Loebell 2004, Kranich 1999, Rohen 2009). In addition, there have been critical works, mostly from the 1980s, that question in particular the anthroposophical or philosophical underpinning of Waldorf education (Prange 1985/2000; Ullrich 1986/1991, 2015) because it is not accessible to the (natural-) scientific research methods they employ. While this conflict needs to be mentioned it cannot be further discussed. It should be possible today to develop an educational anthropology, as Remo Largo has done on the basis of his own developmental research (Largo 2019), that assigns to each individual the possibility for self-realization in a life suited to them. On the strength of its implementation in Waldorf schools and kindergartens across the world alone, Rudolf Steiner's approach should be included in any comprehensive anthropological anthology.

Steiner's view of humanity is not based on functional or social criteria; it is neither Darwinist nor does it see humans, as the Bible suggests, as the crown of all creation. According to Steiner, humans are essential to earth evolution, a view that is diametrically opposed to the thinking prevalent today of human existence depending on that of the earth (Pleger 2013, p. 11). In Steiner's spiritual-scientific anthropology, human and earthly as well as cosmic evolution go hand in hand (Steiner GA 13). One can criticize this human-centered approach but it is mirrored in today's questions regarding human, earthly, and cosmic existence and in the current discourse because we are, as humans, responsible for humanity and for the earth.

The following sections provide insight into aspects of Rudolf Steiner's anthropology that inform the theory and practice of Waldorf education today and can therefore be read in preparation for the source texts in Chapter 5. Starting from current anthropological thinking, we will introduce the concepts of reincarnation, of the "I" and I-knowledge that are fundamental to Steiner's educational anthropology and that form the essence of his image of the human being in general. Taking recent research results into account we will then outline Steiner's theory of the human constitution or of the fourfold human organization from which insights can be derived into child development and the corresponding pedagogical practice. Examples from the classroom will illustrate how an understanding of the human constitution and of human development can provide orientation for teachers in their daily work.

2.2 The miracle of childhood

The birth of every child is like a miracle, even if modern prenatal investigation methods inform us long before whether it is a boy or a girl who wants to come into the world, and despite the possibilities of genetic engineering and medicine to manipulate child development. The gaze of a newborn child is enchanting and we feel awed by the special atmosphere created by his or her presence. We sense the individuality that tries to express itself and that will have to find its path through life, relying on our care and protection until it has reached independence. These qualities of the newborn are interestingly perceived less and less as the child grows older. Adapted as we have become to modern lifestyles we forget that children don't embark on this earthly life as physical beings only but that they come with a spirit-soul that provides the forces for their future development.

Lisa Miller, who has conducted extensive studies worldwide into "children's spiritual intelligence" (Miller/Barker 2015) concludes that we all have a natural connection with the spiritual world but that we allow this connection to fade away and consequently lose the ability to relate to the spirituality of young children. Miller interprets spirituality as an "inner sense of living relationship to a higher power (God, nature, spirit, universe, the creator, or whatever your word is for the ultimate loving, guiding life-force" (ibid., p. 6). Miller's empirical research into adolescence confirms that spirituality is not linked to "religion or choice of religious denomination" (ibid., p. 7), but is experienced as a universally human capacity of spirit and soul and as a profound personal relationship with the transcendent. According to Miller, the quality of feeling connected to a higher spiritual dimension in childhood has important implications for adolescence through to adult life. It is, Miller points out, the best preventative against addiction, drugs and depression. She therefore advises parents in particular to learn to appreciate their children's spiritual disposition rather than persuading them against it, and to seek access to the spiritual dimension themselves. Miller's global scientific research confirms previous assumptions that spiritual faculties play a significant part in human development.

Miller builds a bridge to Rudolf Steiner's understanding of childhood and of human nature in general. Instead of empirical studies Steiner employed spiritual-scientific, phenomenological research methods and a meditative approach in order to prove the reality of the transcendent or spiritual. Without going more deeply into the "meditative path of inner development" proposed by Steiner—there are plenty of very good publications on this[1]—the following sections describe Steiner's ways of observing the human spiritual dimension and I-being as well as the exercises he recommends for gaining access to them.

Steiner sees the "I" as the inner essence that determines our destiny; a spiritual entity that, in addition to changing daily between waking and sleeping, or between a waking and a sleeping consciousness, also alternates between incarnation and excarnation, or between earthly and spiritual life. Waking up in the morning is like a birth, going to sleep at night like a death, and—similar to the ancient Egyptian worldview—this cycle of reincarnation continues as part of human evolution between earthly and spiritual existences (Steiner, GA 9, p. 72ff.). While we inherit our physical body, our spirit being has an individual biography that cannot be explained by social influences alone but is a result of our previous actions. Steiner suggests an exercise that can help us to understand this phenomenon as a purely spiritual process:

> To observe these relationships correctly, we must learn to perceive that some impressions in human life work on the soul's potentials in the same way that standing before something still to be done works on what we have already practiced repeatedly in physical life. Rather than affecting abilities acquired through practice in the course of this life, these impressions affect potential abilities of the soul. If we achieve insight into these things, we arrive at the idea of earthly lives that must have preceded this one. In thinking about it, we can no longer be content with assuming that *this* life is preceded only by purely spiritual experiences. (Steiner, GA 9, p. 46f.)[2]

---

1 On Rudolf Steiner's meditative path of self-development cf. Demisch et. al. 2014; Zimmermann/ Schmidt 2016; Smit 1996.
2 English translation in Rudolf Steiner, *Theosophy*, Hudson NY 1994, tr. C. Creeger, p. 75

We need to become aware of the "soul's potentials" or gifts that seem like abilities we have acquired through practice, but that were not acquired in this present life but in a previous existence. For Steiner the thought of reincarnation follows logically from the natural-scientific theory of evolution (Steiner GA 34, p. 67ff.) that is also the basis of his educational anthropology. He uses a metaphor to describe reincarnation as a transformative process that occurs in the alternation of earthly and spiritual existences (Steiner 1907, p. 331f.): Just as an entirely new being emerges when the caterpillar spins a cocoon, dissolves into it and reappears as a butterfly, we are transformed through death and rebirth, or from one life to the next. When the spirit-soul, or the I-being, assumes a spiritual existence after death, the earthly body dissolves; and like a butterfly emerging from its cocoon, the spirit-soul frees itself from its earthly existence. A new physical body is then prepared for the next incarnation and enlivened by the incarnating spirit-soul that seeks to take on its future earthly tasks. Death and rebirth are transitions between purely spiritual and earthly modes of being, in which the human soul evolves in different ways. It carries the experiences gained in earthly life into the world after death where it prepares its tasks and intentions for a new incarnation. That children do not come into the world as "blank slates" but as intentional beings is clearly apparent: in the way they express their own will, in their ingenuity, and in their urge to learn in the world and from other people. According to Steiner it is more important to observe this fact, the birth aspect in particular, in order to gain an understanding of the child's developmental needs than to focus on death and immortality or an unlimited earthly life, because our task as educators in physical life is to continue "the work higher beings used to do before birth" (Steiner, GA 293, p. 21), in other words, the activity carried out by spiritual forces in an existence that preceded physical life. These events are what we see reflected in the "soul's potentials."

2.3 The child as a spiritual I-being

In his life's work Rudolf Steiner presented ways of gaining an understanding of our I-nature and of achieving I-knowledge through the consistent observation of thinking as a "spiritual exercise" (Wiehl 2015, p. 82ff.; Ziegler 2015, p. 114ff.). He distinguishes between the "I" we experience in our everyday consciousness and the "true I," pointing out that the former can be experienced like any "ordinary empirical content of consciousness," while the latter can only be perceived "intuitively" through the meditative practice of thinking (Steiner GA 12, p. 12; Steiner 2007).

Steiner introduced the idea of the true or higher "I" early on in his philosophical treatise *The Philosophy of Freedom* (GA 4, first published in 1894), where he proposed that we can gain a concept of this higher "I" by observing our own thinking, the difference to ordinary conceptualization being that in the moment when we know our own "I" intuition and concept merge into one. I-knowledge is, in this sense, an intuition and therefore an insight gained in purely spiritual experience, in thinking. The "I" can know itself as an "I" in thinking, while I-consciousness "is based on the human organization" (ibid., p. 148f.) and therefore distinct from the purely spiritual, self-knowing "I." It is our capacity for intuitive knowing that allows us to perceive ourselves as I-beings and understand the spiritual foundations of our existence and that of the world.

"The meaning of human existence is connected with thinking, morality and love, and knowledge is understood as a part of life. The deepest essence of all things can be conceived through intuitive thinking as creations of the free human spirit." (Stoltz/Wiehl 2019).

In his book *Spiritual Guidance of the Individual and of Humanity* (Steiner GA 15, Q 6) Rudolf Steiner introduces an exercise that can lead to awareness of our spiritual existence and I-being in a concrete experience that supports his educational anthropology. Practicing self-reflection, he points out there, can help us "to realize that, in addition to the self we encompass with our thoughts, feelings, and fully conscious impulses of will, we bear in ourselves a second, more powerful self" (ibid., p. 9).[3] By reflecting on actions we performed years ago, we discover that much of what we did and said then we only fully understand now, many years later. From this we can conclude that there is a power guiding us, a "benevolent power presiding in the depths of our own being" (ibid., p. 10). We realize that we are not alone in the world but live embedded in a wider spiritual context. We can think right back to the moment of our first memory, which is also the moment when we began to feel ourselves as I-beings and when we first said "I" when referring to ourselves. Everything that occurs in life after this moment can potentially be remembered, while the three or four years of earthly life preceding it are concealed from us. In memoirs this significant moment of I-awakening is often described as an experience of "I am an I" or that "suddenly the world stood visibly before me."

Steiner speaks of important developments that occur in us in these first three to four years of life and that these are caused by the spiritual powers we can become aware of when we practice the kind of recalling

---

3 English translation in Rudolf Steiner, *The Spiritual Guidance of the Individual and Humanity*, Hudson NY 1992, tr. S. Desch, p. 9

mentioned earlier. This "work on our own body is guided from a perspective that is wiser than anything we can achieve later with our full consciousness" (ibid., p. 11). It promotes brain development, orientation in space including standing up and learning to walk, as well as speaking and thinking. According to Rudolf Steiner these activities, rather than being caused by heredity or the environment, are rooted in the spirituality that was already at work before we were even born. They originate in these spiritual forces but need for their development a setting where other people serve as role models and their actions and attitudes as inspirations. Even purely physical processes such as the forming of organs or the change of teeth require a human environment that promotes healthy development, although they are not influenced in the same way by spiritual forces but occur more independently. This distinction between the effect of spiritual forces and that of biological-genetic dispositions in child development is fundamental to Waldorf education which sees children as beings who are not merely products of heredity and social influences but self-determined individualities seeking to realize themselves in an enlivened body and in a particular environment.

An interesting experience we had in various teacher training seminars was that our students, when asked to draw their understanding of Steiner's presentation of the child being, chose to express this in the form of concentric circles, with the outer circle representing the "I" in its environment. Their impression of the human organization was that the "I" is not at the center but a force that envelops the child being. This observation supports the impressions described earlier that children are surrounded by an aura, by a higher part of themselves that gradually, as they grow older, emerges as I-experience and then I-consciousness. Steiner describes in this context that with young children, before they achieve I-consciousness, this universal connectedness with the spiritual world withdraws into their inner being in order to make I-consciousness possible as children learn to establish their own "relationship with the outer world" (ibid., p. 15). It is this transformation that allows us to become free and independent beings, able to withdraw from and reconnect with the world.

2.4 Child constitution and education

With his anthropology Rudolf Steiner introduced a theory of the human constitution or fourfold organization that, in accordance with the classical picture, sees the human being as consisting of body, soul, and spirit. For Steiner the body is the physical dimension that gives us access to the physical world around us, that allows us to perceive and interact with the things in the world and to express ourselves toward other beings. The soul is for him the mode of being that enables us to experience pleasure or desire in relation to things and events, or feelings such as joy or discontent. The spirit is what allows us to gain knowledge of the phenomena in the world and relate them to each other (Steiner GA 9, p. 21). These three domains are not strictly separated, however, but interlinked in multiple ways. Our physical state can influence our mental condition and vice versa. Soul experiences can form the foundation of spiritual insights, and our spiritual faculties rely for their realization on the dispositions and possibilities of soul and body.

Closer observation reveals a much more differentiated view of the human being that Steiner first presented in 1904 (Steiner GA 9), developing it further in 1907 in an essay entitled *The Education of the Child in the Light of Anthroposophy* (Steiner 1907). This more evolved differentiation is also known as Steiner's theory of the fourfold human organization. It is particularly relevant to human development in childhood and adolescence through education and teaching. The four constituents of the human organization Steiner distinguishes are:

1. The "physical body," which is more or less identical with the material body described in anatomy and biology;

2. The all-permeating "life body" or "ether body" which encompasses all the life processes that form the basis of our soul faculties;

3. The "sentient body" or "soul body" which is the domain of drives, desires, emotions, feelings, and sensations but also of reason, in other words, the realm of the natural soul being;

4. The "I" which is self-aware and forms the center of each individual.

Each of these constituents has, as we shall see below, its own specific character and faculties and provides particular conditions and possibilities for learning and development.

The physical body is the individuality's concrete manifestation, its physical form. Everything we absorb into our physical body has lasting character. Once we have learned how to climb stairs as children we have imprinted into our physical body certain movements that will be available to us through life. We will not forget these skills as long as our physical functions are intact. Wrong body or hand movements imprint themselves too and are therefore not easy to correct. If we aim to imprint something into the physical body, that is to say, if we want children to learn something physically, we need to observe certain conditions. There needs to be clarity as to what we are aiming for, be it upright walking, climbing, or cycling. The movements and skills that will be required for performing the activity in question well have to be practiced daily, starting with easier steps and moving on to the more challenging ones. The results achieved are usually better the earlier we begin with such training. This is how children, or adults, learn how to walk, do somersaults, climb, cycle, and high-jump, but also how to scoop up sand with a shovel, use a knife for carving or a pen for writing. Autonomy, that is, the capacity to be open to every new and unfamiliar situation and approach it with confidence, is not developed in this way. It is not a physical skill that can be acquired through training.

Autonomy, just like sociability or a sense of rhythm, belongs to the qualities that are subject to the principles of the life body (Auer 2017, p. 51ff.). The life body represents life, the life forces, and the organism's diverse life processes. All life processes are rhythmic and repetitive and always active. They unfold in harmony with the entire organism, as long as this organism is healthy. The life body evolves and learns through repetition and rhythm, but also through metamorphosis, which is also crucial to the development of autonomy.

Children do *not* gain autonomy through training, that is, by being permanently exposed, from an early age, to situations that require them to be autonomous or that prove that they can do something independently. The results of attachment research over the last decades show something else (Grossmann/Grossmann 2017). Securely attached children will leave their mother sooner, walk away from her and explore the world, even crawl into an adjacent room where they can no longer see their mother. As they grow older, they easily enter into new situations without holding on to their mother's hand. Later on, they approach new and unfamiliar situations calmly and confidently. Securely attached children are able to enter into new relationships because they experience their mother or another attachment figure as the safe haven they can always return to.

The certainty thus acquired is a prerequisite for autonomy or independence. The situation is very different for insecurely attached children. They either conceal their insecurity behind an apparent calmness and normality (the insecure-avoiding type) or they show their insecurity and fear by holding on to their mother and never leaving her side (the insecure-ambivalent type). Both types will not dare to explore the world on their own and will later be unable to meet new and unknown situations autonomously (ibid., p. 140). This shows that autonomy cannot be trained but that it is acquired through transformation or metamorphosis. Securely attached children don't display independent behavior at first because they *are* dependent on their attachment person, but this dependence, which is a necessary precondition for feeling secure later, allows them to develop autonomy later, when they are between two and five years old.

Around the first year, children, as they imitate older children or grown-ups, try to discover the world, by sitting up, standing up, starting to walk, or by exploring what lies hidden in drawers and cupboards. However often they fail, they never stop trying, day in, day out. This persistence is owed to the forces of the sentient or soul body. The desire or wish to do what others are doing, or the curiosity to find out what is concealed inside a drawer, are soul-body qualities. Desire, wish, curiosity, the joy of discovery, and, above all, interest are essential motives for learning and require a diverse and experiential learning environment, because learning must be sufficiently stimulating so that children and adolescents devote themselves wholly to it. The following examples from a Waldorf classroom illustrate ways of stimulating the soul body:

A teacher wanted his students to take on classroom chores such as sweeping, cleaning the blackboard, or looking after the plants. His colleagues warned him of possible difficulties: if one talked to the children about the necessity of such chores and prepared a roster for them, they would start off enthusiastic but soon lose interest, because there was no motivation. The situation is different, however, if the teacher calls on the forces of the soul body. The teacher in question began by sweeping the classroom himself, which he always did with cheerful devotion with the children present. After a week or two one of the children asked to be allowed to take on the sweeping. The teacher declined in a friendly but firm manner. After a few more weeks, several children asked, but the teacher still made them wait. Only once he had the impression that the desire awakened in the children was strong enough did he give in and entrusted the task to them. This works with other tasks too. The desire that arises in the children is highly motivational and it lasts for a long time. Years later, these students continued to be committed to the communal needs of the class. The example illustrates the sustainability of educational measures if the forces of the sentient or soul body that develop in the first years of school are involved.

The same forces of the soul body can be called on when we teach intellectually. If you want to get students interested in subjects and tasks, it is best not to present everything to them ready-made in the lessons. If you explain everything in one day, answer all the questions, and reveal the solutions, you will take away the children's joy in learning. It is better to plan the lessons so that important questions are left open, possible solutions hinted at but not yet supplied. Only on the following day, when the contents and tasks have been repeated and deepened, will the students find the answers and solutions together in class. This kind of approach sparks curiosity and interest in the lessons and in subjects. This interest is transformed desire. With a similar approach or method we can get children to read books, play an instrument or develop enthusiasm for literature, music, and art. In all these situations that are about contents and conscious attitudes, it is the soul body that makes the forces available which are needed for learning.

According to Rudolf Steiner, the "I," or fourth dimension after the physical, life, and soul bodies, is not a construct of consciousness (chapter 2.3), nor is it, as today's neurosciences suggest, a conscious function of the individual (Wiersing 2015, p. 252). Steiner describes the "I" as a real spiritual entity that lives in each of us, that comes from an existence before birth and brings with it the results of an earlier life in the form of dispositions and individual characteristics. Readers may be open to the following arguments even if they don't wish to commit to the idea of reincarnation. The "I" joins itself to a physical body, a life body, and a soul body and develops, in conjunction with these, the basic human capacities of moving, walking upright, speaking, feeling, and thinking. For this to be possible the "I" needs role models from whom these and other faculties can be imitated. The "I" rejoices in self-learning and develops best when it can learn out of its own forces. In the first years of life in particular, children only follow their own will impulses (Steiner GA 303, p. 120f.) and therefore need "little in terms of methodical and reflected pedagogy" (Wiersing 2015, p. 235).

The four constituents of the human organization are noticeable from birth. Each of them needs its own time to mature and unfold specific powers, dispositions, and capacities. When the physical body is born, its entire potential is available. In order to realize this potential, infants need to be active, enjoy plenty of movement, and have the chance to apply themselves (Auer 2007, p. 34ff.). The more children can do physically at this age and the less is done for them, the stronger and more mobile they will become, but they need adults as role-models for movements, gestures, and activities, for walking upright, speaking, feeling, and thinking. Without role models worth imitating children cannot develop these human faculties. Children learn intensively when the adults around them carry out meaningful everyday activities. There is nothing we adults have to teach children at this age, because they learn by themselves.

The life body develops in the first six to seven years of life. Fostering the life body is the main task of education at this age. The life body needs regular day-to-day rhythms. We must not forget that children have to first enter and live themselves into an unknown world and that they first need to gain confidence. They can do this best when they find something they already know every day and when they can have the experience that a certain order prevails in the world. In addition, the life body needs repetition: the same story, finger game, ritual every day at the same time over a longer period of time. Anyone who has experience of young children knows that they demand this: they enjoy repetition and don't need something new every day. A caregiver who looks at a picture book with a child while waiting for the mother to arrive, has to repeat this every day. Repetition also enhances memory formation. The life body also needs rhythm, for instance the rhythmic alternation of free play and guided activity. It needs proximity, affection, and attachment possibilities, time for free play so that the children can process what they experience in their own way, and opportunity to practice activities and behaviors, following the child's need for self-learning. In addition, the life body needs opportunities for developing imagination, which it can do best if children can play with unspecific materials and unfinished toys (S 19-21). It falls to educators to create the right conditions for all this to happen. When children reach the age of six or seven the life body is born (Steiner 1907, p. 19f.). By then, all the faculties arising from the forces of the life body—autonomy, memory, imagination, and the ability to practice—are available and need to be employed in order to develop further.

The sentient or soul body develops between the ages of seven and twelve to fourteen. Up until puberty, the qualities of the soul body require a protected atmosphere in order to unfold. After that, at around the age of 14, they are ready to be born. Up until the age of eleven, the development of objective feeling is one of the big themes in education. Steiner points out that while thinking and will develop basically by themselves through the experiences we have in life, this is not the case with feeling. Feeling has an important role to play, however, because it links thinking and will (Steiner GA 307, p. 79f.). If this link is missing, we may see extreme behaviors and actions, caused by a lack of feeling-based judgment or empathy. We can support the development of feeling with songs and poems, folktales and imaginative stories because they offer children the possibility to perceive and experience a feeling world and bring it to artistic expression. The sentient or feeling life is generally best developed through artistic perception and activity, through painting, writing poetry, music-making, and playacting.

In the first years of school, children need adult authority figures to look up to and revere. In order to avoid misunderstandings, it needs to be pointed out that this feeling relationship originates with the child and has nothing to do with authoritarian behaviors on the part of the adults. Children long to be shown access to the world by a revered person. They long to know how adults experience and understand the things and beings of the world. School children initially mainly seek access to the world through feeling. Teachers have therefore the task to speak to them about the world in a way that allows this feeling access to happen. One way of doing this is by telling imaginative stories about plants, animals, and other phenomena in the world. Moreover, according to Steiner, children should first encounter the world through feeling at this age and only then through thinking because this will enable them later to gain a deeper understanding of the world (Steiner 1907, p. 29).

When the children reach their twelfth year, it is time to work on developing the thinking. At this age the children or adolescents begin to discuss and argue in ways that can become quite challenging for adults. But their arguments are not yet rooted in reality. This is the time when the thinking needs to be given opportunities to develop and this is best done using a phenomenological approach based on exact observation. An example of how teachers can prepare themselves for teaching seventh grade can be found in Michael Faraday's 1860 lectures on the chemistry and physics of a candle (Faraday 1964).

We conclude this outline with a brief glance at the third developmental stage: adolescence. The "I" has actively participated in the development of the other three constituent bodies. Any drive for development originates in the "I." But the "I" now needs its own time to develop and prepare itself for its task of guiding and shaping the future biography. Young people test their "I" when they claim their right to self-determination, isolate themselves, or take risks. The big question that is crucial for young people is whether or not they can see a purpose in life, or in school for that matter. This is why three specific experiences are more important at this age than any teaching contents, and it falls to adults to enable young people to have these experiences. The first experience is "I can understand the world"— even its negative and bad aspects. Discussions on historical topics, current affairs, and politics can help with this. Second, "There is something in the world that interests me." Offering a wide range of subjects and meaningful topics kindles personal interests. Third, "I can make a contribution to the world; I am needed" (Zech 2018, p. 278ff.)—an experience young people can have when they do work experience and projects, or when they engage in social initiatives.

Much in young people's future life depends on these three experiences. The wholesome effect they have points to the three principles of salutogenesis: comprehensibility, meaningfulness, manageability (Antonovsky 1997). I-development is further enhanced by engaging with philosophical questions, by receiving guidance in self-education, through self-directed tasks such as year-projects or drama projects, and by adults be-

3 Development and education of the senses

WOLFGANG-M. AUER

3.1 Introduction

Our senses are our gateway to the world. This oft-cited image is fitting because only through these sensory gateways do we have access to the world and to others. Everything we know of the world we know through perception. Each gateway shows us a certain segment and enables us to have a specific experience. Through one gateway we hear what is audible in the world; through another we see what is visible; through yet another we have olfactory or tactile experiences of the world. When we read or hear other people speak this also happens through one of our gateways of perception. If one of these gateways is closed we cannot perceive what lies behind it. One of our ways of accessing the world is missing and as a consequence that part of the world does not exist for us. For the blind the visible world does not exist. While they can find access to the things of the world through other gateways, such as hearing, smelling, or touch, the gateway of vision remains closed to them.

The question as to how many senses human beings have is still answered in various ways today and this will not change as long as one approaches the question from various angles. If we only acknowledge the senses that have visible organs, we restrict ourselves to the classic five, the senses of seeing, hearing, smell, taste, and touch, and exclude any others. The Greek philosopher Aristotle (384-322 BCE) already mentioned these five senses in his treatise *On the Soul* (Aristotle 2018) and they continue to form part of the scientific standard today, including in the literature on education. But they merely represent one particular selection.

If we approach the question by looking at the function of the sensory receptors, the answer will be a different one. The number of senses increases because one needs to differentiate within the kinesthetic system the senses of movement, force, and position, and within the haptic system the senses of touch, vibration, and gravity (Zimmer 2012, p. 53ff.) The answer is different again, if one distinguishes, as we do here, the senses according to their respective perceptual range. In education it is not the difference between the sense organs or sensory receptors that is of importance but the varying perceptions and experiences conveyed by the individual senses. The approach is not new but was introduced by Charles Sherrington (1857-1952) when he singled out body perception as a separate experience to which he referred as "proprioception" (Sherrington 1906). His theory was then further developed by the French scientist Maurice Merleau-Ponty (1908-1961) in his *Phenomenology of Perception* where he examined the experiential range of the body- and the world-related senses (Merleau-Ponty 1966). Steiner presented his sensory theory three years after Sherrington, introducing first ten (Steiner GA 115) and later twelve senses (Steiner GA 170, p. 238ff.). He assigned proprioception to the four "body senses" (touch, life, movement, balance), added the sense of warmth to the world-related senses, and introduced the perception of speech, of conveyed thoughts, and of the "I" of other people to the list of senses. The latter three senses in particular have hardly been considered although their perceptual scope and their disorders (such as visual agnosia, phonagnosia, prosopagnosia, aphasia) are known to scientists (Auer 2007) and have even been made famous by Oliver Sacks's case studies (Sacks 2002).

Steiner expounded his theory of the senses primarily in lectures, first to members of the Theosophical Society and later to members of the Anthroposophical Society and to teachers, but never in public. The concept was so important to him, however, that he decided, in 1910, to devote a book to its detailed description. This book has remained unfinished and has been published as a fragment (GA 45). In the following decades a number of publications on Steiner's theory of the senses appeared,[1] explaining the concept in non-scientific terms. The first scientific discussion—and for many years the only one—came out in 1977 (Scheurle 1984), followed in 1996 by the first scientific monograph on the sense of language (Lutzker 1996). In 2007, Wolfgang-M. Auer published a comprehensive scientific study of all twelve senses (2007), followed in 2008 by guidelines for the education of the senses in kindergartens (Auer 2015).

---

1 Aeppli 2013; König 1971/1986; Lehrs 1973/1982; Soesman 1991.

It is probably due to its delayed public reception that Steiner's concept of the senses is little known and that it has to this day never been seriously discussed publicly or within the human sciences. One exception is Renate Zimmer's *Handbuch der Sinneswahrnehmung* (handbook of sense perception) that at least mentions Steiner's concept of the twelve senses, although Zimmer ultimately dismisses it as unscientific (Zimmer 2012, p. 55). This is unfortunate given that today's research largely confirms the sensory and perceptual domains described by Rudolf Steiner (Auer 2007), which means that a scientific exchange could be fruitful for both sides.

Steiner presents the twelve senses in varying categories, for instance divided into day and night senses (S 11), that is to say, into senses we use more consciously and senses we use more unconsciously. In another context he divides the senses into three groups: first, the senses for self-perception, second, the senses for the perception of outer nature, third, the senses for perceiving others and their expressions. Steiner allocates these three groups to the soul forces of thinking, feeling, and will. He never expressed a preference for any particular system. The latter has been more widely received, with users introducing the unfortunate and ambiguous terms "lower," "middle," and "upper" senses for the three categories. (König 1971/1986; Aeppli 2013). The three groups of senses are:

sense of "I"	the other person
sense of thought	thought senses
sense of language	("upper" senses)
sense of hearing	
sense of warmth	outer nature
sense of vision	feeling senses
sense of taste	("middle" senses)
sense of smell	
sense of balance	oneself
sense of movement	will senses
sense of life	("lower" senses)
sense of touch	

Table 1 (based on Aeppli 2013 and König 1971/1986)

A different classification (table 2) has recently proved helpful, particularly in relation to education. It divides the senses first into two groups—the *body senses* with which we perceive our own body, and the *world senses*, which we use to perceive the world. The world senses are again divided into the two subgroups of *communicative senses*, on the basis of which we develop language, and the *guardian senses* that encompass the senses of taste, smell, and warmth which, in addition to their specific perceptual tasks, also assume a guardian function. The following diagram is based on this second classification.

BODY SENSES	WORLD SENSES			
	COMMUNICATIVE SENSES			GUARDIAN SENSES
sense of touch	sphere of hearing	sphere of sight	sphere of touch	sense of taste
sense of life	sense of hearing	sense of vision	sense of touch	sense of smell
sense of movement	sense of language / sense of form			sense of warmth
sense of balance	sense of thought / sense of meaning			
	sense of "I" / sense of individual style			

Table 2 (Auer 2007, p. 14)

We will now submit the three groups of senses to closer scrutiny, including not only descriptions of what they perceive, but also the experiences they convey—which is the more important aspect when it comes to childhood education. We will then outline the Moving Classroom concept that is used in Waldorf schools to allow children's often underdeveloped senses to still mature during the lower grades. To conclude this chapter we will briefly look at the development of the senses after the seventh year and the need for research in the realm of the senses.

3.2 Development of the body senses

Perception through the sense of touch requires us to make contact with a part of the world and experience its many qualities: is it large or small, smooth or rough, hard or soft, wet or dry, and so on. There is one aspect of this sense that stands out from the others and this aspect is of particular interest in this context. Whenever we touch something, when we make contact with a piece of the world through our sense of touch, this piece of the world also touches us. Our contact with it also lets us perceive ourselves, in the place where we are being touched. Experiences of touch tell us that we have a body and where this body is. We have a general idea of where our back is, but we only experience its actual surface when is touched by someone or something. Thanks to the thousands of tactile perceptions children experience in various places, they gradually develop an image of their body, a "body schema." To a certain extent this body schema develops even before birth (Grunwald 2017, p. 42ff.), but most of its development occurs in the first two to three years of life, and it needs to be renewed and updated again and again throughout life. Getting to know one's own body with its form and dimensions really well from the inside is one of the most essential preconditions for a successful life. Our body surface is, on the other hand, also an important boundary that separates our inner from our outer life, our self from the world. This is the next important experience children have: I am inside and the others are outside. The quality and presence of this experience determines whether or not children identify with their body, whether they feel at home in their body, and how they relate to others (Auer 2007, p. 23ff.). Children who did not have enough such experiences or who associate negative memories with them, can develop insecurities, aggression, and restlessness (hyperactivity), a fact that proves how crucial it is that we enable children to have these experiences.

With our sense of life we perceive all the life processes in our body. On the whole, the sense of life does not convey every detail of our wellbeing but rather an overall impression. When someone asks how we are, we can say "I'm fine" or "I'm not feeling very well today." It is when the balance of the life processes is disrupted that the sense of life makes itself felt, through pain for instance. Our perceptions are more precise and above all more conscious in some areas, and they have to be because we need to control the processes in those areas. We sense when we are hungry or thirsty, exhausted or weak, when we need a break, but also when our strength returns again. And we sense when we need to sleep, and after sleeping, we sense whether our sleep has been restorative. These perceptions always swing to and fro between too little and sufficient. Children have to learn from adults how to evaluate these perceptions and above all how to respond to them in the right way. The two most important aspects to consider here are firstly, that children should only be given food when they are really hungry, and secondly, that eating, drinking, and sleeping should have regular times that coincide with the rhythms of the day and of the individual child. All life processes are regular and rhythmical because they depend on regularity. A regular daily rhythm will therefore strengthen our life processes, and our health in general, and enable the sense of life to develop in a healthy way. But there is another side to the sense of life. Soon after children start standing securely on their legs they are keen to apply their strength by carrying, pulling, or pushing things around, and by climbing onto chairs or ladders. Once they have done this, and only then, will they know that they can do it. It is important for children to experience that achieving goals is tiring. Success makes them feel happy and proud. Many kindergartens have introduced forest days with long walks. Such activities offer children plenty of opportunity for testing themselves. Children who have this experience again and again learn to know their strength and possibilities, and this knowledge gives them self-confidence (Auer 2007, p. 34f; Lang 1995, S.17). For older children and adolescents, adventure education can provide the required experiences.

With the sense of movement we perceive every movement and the position of our body and our limbs, not by observing them from the outside vision but by sensing them from inside our body. The sense of movement develops as we move. Initially, infants can't do much more than kick their legs and perform sucking movements with their mouth. But because they can perceive every movement, they learn to change, differentiate, and above all control their movements. Reflexes are increasingly replaced by self-guided movement and the children learn to move in a way suited to their environment. The first climax in the development of movement is achieved when children can stand up and walk independently, for walking upright lets them face the world and other people as the hands become free of the task of carrying the body around and are available for creative, cultural activity (Steiner GA 306, p. 34ff.; S 4).

Certain preconditions need to be in place, however, for this to happen. Children need role models to orient themselves on. The significance of such role models is apparent in "feral children" or "wild children" who have grown up among wolves or other animals and adopted these animals' way of walking (Malson et. al. 1972; Singh 1964). These children were very apt at walking on all fours, but unable to walk upright because they did not have the corresponding role models. In addition, children need space and an environment that inspires a multitude of movements in them. In a surrounding where there are thresholds, inclines, and stairs children acquire different movements than they would in a room without all these challenges. If children get much movement outside in the fields and woods, they gain a different kind of confidence than children do whose experience is restricted to wooden floors and asphalt. If children are to learn how to climb stairs, all they need are stairs. The stairs alone teach the child how to climb.

Among the possibilities we have for movement, we can distinguish four qualities we need in life and they can already be stimulated in childhood (Auer 2007, p. 47ff.). The first is mobility. Children acquire mobility when they are given sufficient space and encouragement to move, when they play with other children, when they skip, jump, run, bend over, stretch, turn around, do somersaults, and later through swimming and other sports. This makes the children mobile and able to carry out and control movements. Mobility is also the foundation that determines the extent to which the other qualities will be achieved.

The second quality is that of "joining in with movement." What does that mean? Think of a situation where two adults are turning a rope and children jump into the rope, one after the other, each skipping until they get entangled and then making space for the next child. When you observe the children who are waiting in line you see how most of them copy the rhythm of the rope with their whole body. When it is their turn, they will jump into the rope without getting entangled because they have absorbed the rhythm of the rope into their movement organism. Those who don't have this preparation tend to get stuck. Adults should try this, too. But this is just one way of practicing joining in with movements. Children learn it whenever they hold hands and run through the kindergarten, forming a long snake, when they take part in circle games, play ball, make music, dance, or do eurythmy. It requires them to let go, to not move as they would like but join into a pre-existing rhythm that they do not determine themselves. This is about entering into an outside movement and moving with it. This movement quality can later give rise to empathy, to the ability to work in a team, to enter into dialog, to communicate, and to be ready to join into processes. All these skills are needed often in life. Children already need them in school.

The third movement quality, dexterity, is promoted by working with materials, objects, tools, instruments. In order to use a certain tool skillfully—one could also say correctly—we have to adapt our movements entirely to the requirements of the material or tool in hand. The same applies to musical instruments. In order to be able to play the cello, you must first learn to move your arms, hands, fingers in the way demanded by the cello and the bow. Dexterity is therefore also the ability to adapt to existing situations and conditions, to identify with them. Kindergartens offer plenty of possibilities for developing dexterity as long as the children are included in all the practical activities.

The fourth quality of movement is that of expression. Self-expression or communication always happens through movement. Whether we speak or write, sing or paint, use facial expressions, gestures, miming, music, or drama as ways of expressing ourselves, they always involve movement. From people who are paralyzed from head to toe we learn what self-expression through movement really means. After suffering a stroke, the French journalist Jean-Dominique Bauby can no longer move any part of his body apart from his left eyelid. He lies in bed like a sack of potatoes, all limp and without expression. Only with his left eyelid he can express himself if someone helps him. This other person goes through the alphabet and when they come to the right letter Bauby moves his eyelid. Then the helper starts again. Letter for letter, word for word, sentence for sentence, a message emerges. Bauby was able to dictate an entire book, *The Diving Bell and the Butterfly,* in this way (Bauby 1997). This book tells us something important about how someone feels in such a situation. "Paralyzed from head to toe, the patient, his mind intact, is imprisoned inside his own body, but unable to speak or move. In my case, blinking my left eyelid is my only means of communication" (ibid., p. 12). Without movement, and therefore without the means of self-expression, one experiences oneself as imprisoned in one's own body. From which we can conclude that being able to move conveys a sense of freedom and independence. The ability to express oneself through movement overrules the sense of being constricted and builds a bridge to others. Children who have not sufficiently developed this ability unconsciously experience the wall that separates them from others and develop aggression as a means of destroying this wall. The movement of expression also needs to be learned and developed from an early age. This happens when adults read or tell stories, when they speak and sing, and accompany their songs, rhymes, and ring games with gestures. It also happens in eurythmy and role play. But it always needs the inspiration by a role model.

All movements involve the sense of balance, because even the minutest movements change our body balance and this requires subtle corrections, often in several other places. We can easily observe how subtle the perceptions of the sense of balance are if we close our eyes and move our whole body slightly forward, backward, and then sideways. The lightest deviation and its direction are registered precisely, as is the moment when we are vertical again. The sense of balance already develops before birth. Each time the mother moves, walks, turns, stoops, and straightens herself, sits down and gets up again, the spatial position of the unborn child changes. The sense of balance registers and learns from this and is then well prepared for life after birth.

We register three things with our sense of balance: the first is the direction in which we are moving, which means we always know where we are going. The second is the effect of gravity, which means we always know where above and below are, and we can orient ourselves vertically, stand upright and walk. Once children have learned to walk, they learn to enter into the forces of gravity and stay upright in any situation. This, too, needs plenty of practice through movement. Children who are carried a lot and pushed around in a buggy are prevented from gaining confidence in this respect. They need challenges such as uneven or sloping surfaces, steps, swings, ropes for swinging and climbing, tree trunks and stilts for balancing on. A bit of walking is not sufficient for standing confidently on one's feet.

There is another aspect that is often forgotten. The sense of balance registers when body and head are moving and, in response, the muscles of the body move in order to keep the body upright. But this response does not only involve the muscles in the body, but also those in the head and even in the eyes. The eyes, too, respond to any positional changes. If children move a lot, this strengthens the ocular muscles as well as the synchronization of the muscles in both eyes, which is, in turn, an important precondition for reading (Hannaford 2013, p. 137ff.; Ayres 1992, p. 99ff.). The third advantage we gain through the sense of balance is related to this. Take the following example. If you read and at the same time shake your head, you are still able to read. If you hold your head still, however, and shake the book at the same speed, reading becomes impossible, or at least much more difficult. This has to do with the sense of balance that registers the movement of the head but not that of the book. Whenever the sense of balance is involved, the eyes are performing compensatory movements, holding on to the image they see. We experience this in other situations, too. If you focus your eyes on a chair or any other object and move your head left and right, up and down, you will notice that the object remains in its place because the eyes respond by compensating for the moving of the head. They only do this, however, if our sense of balance and its cooperation with the eyes are well developed. Whenever we move, turn around, sit down and get up, or when we drive, the images of what we see move across the retina in the opposite direction. This movement is fast and confusing and would throw us off balance if the eyes did not balance this out and hold on to the images. This is how we gain an important capacity, namely that of keeping our calm and balance despite outer movement. Children who were unable to develop their sense of balance sufficiently in this way are insecure in their uprightness. They are constantly engaged in establishing both their balance and upright position and become stressed when asked to focus on other things such as listening to a story or paying attention in the lesson (Ayres 1992, p. 96ff.). As a way of compensating for this shortcoming, such children move constantly, run around, and spread restlessness. They need help with training their sense of balance and we have to make sure that they have, in addition to what has already been mentioned, plenty of opportunity for skipping and jumping, walking on stilts, using a scooter or bicycle, and performing activities, including writing and painting, whilst standing up. Movement games that require quick responses are also helpful.

The perceptions of these four body senses form the foundation for all other experiences (Auer 2007, p. 70ff.) and accompany every other perception. Whether we observe a bird, read a book or listen to another person, we always perceive our own body and where it touches something, its life processes, our posture and movements as well as our state of balance. The gateways of these senses cannot be closed at will. Because they constantly accompany all other perceptions, they constitute the continuum of our self-experience. I always know that it is I who sees the bird, reads a book, listens to another person. This conveys to each of us, adults and children, a basic sense of security in life. The first step of this should be achieved by the age of six or seven, when children start school. If this is not the case we must create possibilities for the required maturing to still happen so that the children can gain school-readiness. The concept of the Moving Classroom in Waldorf schools aims to support this development (Auer 2017). More on this later.

3.3 Development of the communicative senses

All senses connected with speech and language are communicative senses (Auer 2007, p. 79ff.). Aside from the senses of hearing and language or form, thought or meaning, and "I" or individual style, they include also the senses of vision and touch because their domains are also affected by speech (see table 2). These senses, too, are present from the beginning of life and need developing. This happens from day one, through perception. Due to a misinterpretation of certain passages in Steiner, Willi Aeppli disseminated the view that the senses of language, thought, and "I" are only developed in later years and that they are not available until then (Aeppli 2013, p. 43 ff.). This view does, however, not stand up to either closer scrutiny of the Steiner texts in question or the scientific facts.[2]

We will start with the sense of hearing and a concrete example. A baby has just been fed and is content and sleepy. The mother puts him in his cot, pulls up his blanket, says a few worlds, and smiles. Then she leaves the room and is no longer visible to him. He can hear certain sounds, however, her steps on the carpet, on the wooden floor, out in the hallway, her activities in the kitchen. He falls asleep. After two hours he wakes up,

---

2 Auer 2017, p. 36 and www.forschung-waldorf.de/publikationen/detail/das-bochumer-mod-ell-des-bewegten-klassenzimmers/

is hungry, and starts crying. Again, he hears particular sounds and then his mother appears again. This repeats itself. He doesn't know yet where the sounds are coming from. But they soothe him, give him confidence that his mummy is there even if he can't see her. Later, when he can crawl and walk and explore the world, he learns to understand this wider context.

It is part of young children's exploration of the world that they try out what things sound like. This is why they hit first the wooden floor with a stick, then the carpet, then a lid, and then an upside down pot, listening to all the different sounds they create. They repeat these actions again and again in order to gain certainty. Or they scrunch and rip up pieces of paper. Strong paper sounds different from thin paper, tearing sounds different from crumpling sounds. They pile building blocks into a saucepan and close the lid. That sounds different from what it sounds like without the building blocks. So they do it again. Such simple explorations teach children how each material or activity has its own sound and that one can even hear whether a saucepan is full or empty. This is how children get to know the physical world; they learn to allocate sounds to the things and processes and gain trust in their surroundings. Such experiences are important for the child's hearing which is being trained by subtly different sounds and noises. This enables children to distinguish speech sounds and to hear, for instance, whether someone is talking about a beetle or a beagle (Auer 2015, p. 30ff. and p. 83f.).

Parallel to the sense of hearing, children develop the senses of vision and touch. Everything children pick up in order to investigate its sound, they also touch and see. They perceive the many color nuances and how the colors change depending on the light. Children hold different objects in their hands, such as saucepans or building blocks; they take in their weight and shape, and what they feel like. If children have opportunity to explore the world themselves, the senses of hearing, vision, and touch will develop together and will enable the children to have a saturated, multisensory, and therefore real experience of the world.

When we listen to someone speaking, our sense of language lets us perceive the sound of the language and of the words, the accent and intonation of the speaker. As part of this process we pick up everything the other person, consciously or unconsciously, expresses, including their feelings and emotions. If we try to stop a ten-month old baby from clambering up the stairs and say, in a calm and friendly tone so as to not frighten her, "no, not up the stairs!" the child will keep climbing. Infants don't understand the meaning of words, they don't understand concepts, but they hear the intonation which, in this case, comes across as positive and encouraging. If we say "uh uh" instead, in a slight staccato, with falling intonation, the child will stop climbing because her sense of language will pick up the negative expression conveyed in the intonation.

The sense of language or form is available from birth and develops simultaneously with hearing and vision. Children understand their mother's smile as much as the loving expression in her voice (Gopnik et. al. 2000, p. 46ff.). Soon they also understand her gestures and body language and learn to express themselves in the same way. In their third year, children are quite secure in their perception of other people's feelings and they enjoy expressing their own feelings through speech and facial expressions. Soon they use this capacity very cleverly in order to get what they want from adults. It is important to foster this development, because by perceiving the feelings of others children develop their own feelings. We often forget that our feelings are not naturally given to us. Nature only furnishes us with a few basic, undifferentiated emotions such as joy, fear, anger, sadness, disgust, surprise (Ekman 2004, p. 82). They first have to be refined and developed into feelings and this happens primarily through adults expressing feelings that are audible and visible to the children. Feelings are audible in our intonation, when we tell folktales and stories, and in the jolly or sad mood of the tunes we sing to children. They are visible in our facial expressions and body language, but also in a picture, work of art, or nature table. Children explore and consolidate these feelings through play and communication.

In the child's second year the sense of thought or meaning awakens and with it an understanding for the conceptual content of speech. Children first learn that everything has a name and then that one can express everything by joining words together, first two and then more. They perceive how adults and older children do this and copy them. If what they say is understood by others, then it was correct. This is how children learn grammar and syntax. This development, too, unfolds simultaneously in vision and hearing. Visible language includes gestures such as pointing and waving, symbols such as arrows, emoticons in text messages, or pictograms like the one designating an emergency exit. Visible language is immediately comprehensible without explanation and replaces the corresponding words. Words, sentences, even whole stories can be made visible through miming or a picture, and of course also through script. Sign language is the visual equivalent of the spoken word for the hearing impaired. It, too, has emotional and intellectual levels. For children who grow up with deaf parents sign language becomes the mother tongue.

When language has developed to this level the thinking also increases. In order to develop their thinking children need people around them who communicate their thoughts. When children hear others talk, when they perceive how others tell or explain something—including through miming or signing, drawings and images—they perceive the thoughts that are conveyed to them and, as they think along with others, they develop their own thinking. We can observe how children then try these thoughts out for themselves and test them when they play or in their daily activities. The folktales and stories grown-ups tell children are an important source for the perception of feelings and thoughts. It is important to know that children need to hear good language, language of a high standard, to inspire their speech development.

After birth, children recognize their mother's voice, and it will not be long before they also recognize her face. Other persons, father and siblings, then follow. Later they know people not only from their voice but also from the way they form sentences, in other words from their style of speaking. This is how we later recognize poets, writers, or composers from their particular linguistic or musical style. At the visual level, we perceive a person's individual character in their movements. We recognize their way of walking, their gestures, their handwriting, or, in artists, their style of painting. When we know someone well we also experience their individual style in the way they express their feelings or from the way they think. These perceptions belong to the sense of "I" or individual style. What exactly is it that we perceive with this sense? We perceive the individual way in which a person's "I" expresses itself in thought, feeling, and movement. Children need to perceive this in order to unfold and realize their own personality. Genie—a girl who grew up locked into a dark room, with no toys and hardly anything to train her perception on, no one to speak to, not cared for by anyone—was unable to unfold her personality (Eliot 2001, p. 516f.). When she appeared in public at the age of twelve her developmental age was that of a one-year old and this did not change for the rest of her life. Here senses were intact, but she had no opportunity for developing these senses or any of the talents she had brought with her, nor could she develop her feeling and thinking as children usually do by perceiving role models. There is not much human beings can do well from birth. The most important faculties and qualities first need to be developed. Upright walking, speaking, feeling, and thinking, all the faculties we bring with us, even our own personality must be developed and this we can only do when we have role models. Language—not only spoken but all forms of language—plays an important part in child development, because without language children cannot develop their feeling, their thinking, or their personality.

Does this mean that children who cannot hear or see are excluded from any kind of development? It does not, because the domain of the sense of touch includes its own form of language that allows all these faculties to unfold. Biographies of deaf and blind people illustrate this impressively. The best known of these biographies is that of Helen Keller (1880–1968). Serious illness left her blind and deaf when she was 18 months old. She learned to master the new situation she found herself in and was soon able to move around the house and the garden and participate in family life. She perceived what others did by feeling their position and movements with her hands, most of all by placing her hands on theirs and performing their actions with them. This is how she learned how things are done and was able to help around the house and garden. When Helen was almost seven years old, the family employed a private tutor who taught her how to communicate by signing. Helen learned to write and read and even to speak acoustically. Later she went on to read literature at university, gained a doctorate, wrote several books, and travelled all over the world.

In her autobiography she describes the day of her teacher's arrival. She did not know what was going on and no one was able to enlighten her, but she was aware that something important was about to happen. Looking back she wrote:

"On the afternoon of that eventful day, I stood on the porch, dumb, expectant. I guessed vaguely from my mother's signs and from the hurrying to and fro in the house that something unusual was about to happen, so I went to the door and waited on the steps." (Keller 2016, p. 22)

Her mother was excited and maybe washed and dressed her differently or did her hair in a different way. Helen may have felt the tension and expectation in her mother's touch. Why was everyone running around the house? Not only her parents, the servants too were preparing for the event and moved about the place differently. Helen picked this up from the way the floor vibrated, from the mood, the hurrying, the excitement. Touch and vibration are two important perceptual dimensions. Other people's emotions become perceptible as they are mediated through the sense of touch. The third perceptual dimension involves the feeling of people's facial expressions, gestures, body language, movements, and form. Audible speech can be experienced by feeling the movement of a person's mouth and perceiving the vibration that accompanies it. Some photos show Helen "listening" with her hands on the piano or on the violin. String players know how every tone and pitch causes a different vibration. This perceptual sphere corresponds to the sense of language or form.

The sense of thought or meaning can also be found in the sphere of touch where it allows us to perceive, for instance, the purpose of objects or the function of tools. Both are important in honing this sense, whether or not a child can see. (Mescerjakov 2001, p. 137f.; Auer 2007, p. 187ff.). Children learn to comprehend objects and tools by touching them and feeling what they have in common. This is how they find the concept, the words that designate them they then learn from other people. There is interesting research that confirms how much conceptual language depends on touch. In various studies (Kiese-Himmel 2001, p. 117ff.) it has been possible to establish that in children with developmental language disorders touch and recognition—in other words their tactile comprehension of one- or multidimensional objects—tend to be impaired, too. We can therefore conclude that developmental language disorders can be overcome by supporting and promoting tactile perception.

Deaf-blind people can communicate using gestures and miming, but best of all by using a specific sign language. In 1881, the Austrian writer and columnist Hieronymus Lorm (1821-1902), who became deaf in his youth and blind at the age of sixty, invented an alphabet for the deaf-blind known today as the Lorm Alphabet. He used it to communicate with his family and friends. It was made public by his daughter after his death in 1908[3] and has been used ever since, mostly in the German-speaking realm. Individual letters are conveyed by the specific way in which the finger of the "speaker" touches the hand of the "listener." It was possibly a similar kind of finger language, capable of expressing everything that the spoken or written language can convey, which enabled Helen Keller to learn the names of things, concepts and designations, even grammar and syntax. Using this language perceived through touch Helen's teacher read books to her, taught her, and translated for her.

The sense of "I" or style also accommodates perception through touch. Those who depend on touch such as the blind or deaf-blind recognize others by the way they touch them. In children who are entirely open to all kinds of perception, this is natural. When we shake someone's hand or greet them with a hug, we also perceive something of their "I." When teachers shake hands with the children or adolescents in the morning they can get a sense of their I-presence.

The communicative senses constitute the central and most important group of all the senses. Education and development depend on them. In the first six to seven years a number of faculties need to be developed, and among these faculties language—not only spoken language but also language that is perceived visually or through touch—is a central one. Language is more than a means of communication. It is essential to our

---

3 Online under: https://de.wikipedia.org/wiki/Hieronymus_Lorm

humanity and we can therefore not do enough to promote its development. We can do this best by practicing not only speaking and listening with children but by letting them experience singing, music-making, painting, eurythmy, dancing, role play, theatre, puppet shows, everyday chores in house, kitchen, and garden, by letting them touch objects, use tools, look at picture books, and so on. What children learn and develop through these activities is based on their own direct experience of them and this needs active living role models, joint activities, and an inspiring environment, including spoken language accompanied by facial expressions, gestures, miming, and tactile experiences.

3.4 Development of the guardian senses

The three senses of this group—taste, smell, and warmth—are important but not as vital as the senses of the other two groups. They, too, need developing before we can perceive with them. Our everyday consciousness does not usually distinguish between taste and smell. When we are enjoying a delicious meal and tell our host how good it tastes we really mean that it smells good. We hardly notice what we perceive with the sense of taste. The sense of taste registers four different qualities: sweet, sour, salty, and bitter. The verdict is still open on a possible fifth quality, known as "umami." We taste these qualities with the tongue where each of them has an area of optimal perception. (Hatt 1997, p. 318f.). We only taste liquids. Everything that is dry, solid, or airy must first be liquidized before its flavors become perceptible. In order to find out what something tastes like we need to put it into our mouth or touch it with our tongue. The mouth is the gateway not only to the sense of taste but also to the digestive organs. Everything we ingest has to pass the sense of taste which is therefore like a guardian watching over what we take in and even rejecting it if necessary. It can, however, only do its job if its ability to distinguish is well developed. The sense of taste can develop well when children have a great diversity of taste experiences, when they can experience the subtle flavors of natural foods such as fruit, vegetables, cereals, and milk products where not one particular taste, such as sweetness for instance, covers everything else. It is also important for children to experience that particular tastes are connected with certain fruits, and so on.

We can only smell substances that are air-like, because only air can stream past our organ of smell and penetrate to the nasal mucosa and olfactory receptors (Hatt/Dee 2008, p. 39ff.). Odors that are hidden in solid or liquid food need to evaporate before we can smell them. If we take yesterday's delicious food out of the refrigerator it does not smell of anything until we warm it up again (Auer 2007, p. 235ff.). Humans are able to distinguish around 10,000 different smells. Everything living, liquids included, has a certain smell. For children it is important to learn through their own experience what the leaves, blossoms, and fruits of plants smell like, the wood and resin of trees, or different animals. Even the decomposing of living things has its particular smell, as we notice when they go moldy, decay, putrefy, ferment, or burn. All these experiences help children orient themselves in the living world, but unfortunately children today don't necessarily have access to them. And yet, we rely on this orientation for our sense of smell to carry out its guardian function. As the air we breathe in streams past the sense of smell we perceive and evaluate odors. When we register an unpleasant or dangerous smell, we cannot stop breathing but we can quickly move away and escape the potential danger.

Now to the sense of warmth. When we touch various objects in the room—the wood of the desk for instance, the pile of paper, the faux leather of the diary, the carpet, the metal on the chair, the marble window sill—we notice that some feel warmer and others colder. The paper feels slightly warmer than the desk, the faux leather and carpet even warmer, the marble and metal rather cold. And yet, all these things have been in the same room that has had the same temperature for some time. They don't have different temperatures; what differs is their ability to absorb and conduct warmth. My hand is permanently giving off warmth. If I place it on the carpet, not much warmth is absorbed or conducted. This is what we experience as warmth. If I place my hand on the marble, some of the hand's warmth is absorbed into the stone and passed on quickly, drawing more warmth from the hand. This we experience as cold. We consequently don't perceive temperature with our sense of warmth but we register whether heat streams into or is drawn away from our body. We have different thermoreceptors in our skin that respond to either increasing or decreasing temperature (Campenhausen 1993, p. 38ff.). The sense of warmth allows for two kinds of experience: the first one is that it conveys to us how objects absorb warmth. In order to develop this quality it is important that children get to experience different materials when they play or carry out practical activities. The second is that it allows us to establish whether our own body warmth is lost or whether we absorb warmth from outside. It is vital for us to know this because humans can only live as long as they maintain a certain body temperature. The sense of warmth therefore acts as a guardian. This sense needs a long time to learn and develop. Some seven- or eight-year old children are still unable to gauge the temperature situation around them. They play outside without a coat and don't notice how their body cools down. Even at that age, they need the help of adults to assess the temperature correctly and tell them to dress appropriately. Learning to register temperature changes is also important. Children learn this best if they spend much time outside whatever the weather, with plenty of exercise and suitable, non-insulating clothing that allows them to perceive changes in temperature.

3.5 The Moving Classroom

When we discussed the body senses we pointed out how important it is that these senses have reached a certain maturity by the time children start school and that the children have been able to have particular experiences with these senses. If not, they may develop a lack of faculties such as mobility, coordination, concentration, adaptability, expressiveness, and social skills. While the way children live today often does not allow them to practice these faculties, they need them in order to have a meaningful learning experience at school. It is the presence of these faculties that signifies school readiness and their absence leads to learning, behavioral and developmental disorders (Ayres 1992, p. 71ff.). The concept of the Moving Classroom in Waldorf schools has been developed especially to help children with such disorders (Auer 2017). Some mainstream schools have similar concepts that also aim at more movement in lessons and during recess (Thiel et. al. 2006).

The Moving Classroom in Waldorf schools provides possibilities for the body senses to mature and for the corresponding skills to develop. This includes daily movement games that promote movement-related qualities such as agility, dexterity, expression, as well as exercises and games that support the senses of balance and touch. The stimulating space and environment needed for this is created by replacing the desks and chairs in first and second grade by benches and large cushions. Sitting on chairs weakens the back muscles by not exercising them sufficiently and armrests prevent movement (Zimmer 2002). Some [German] mainstream schools also experiment with movable furniture and chairs without back rests as a way of promoting mobility and exercising in particular the sense of balance (Landau/Sobczyk 2001). Benches and cushions are much more versatile, however. The children can jump over them or crawl underneath, they can turn the benches upside down to balance on, and much more. Every morning, the furniture is set up as an obstacle course that allows the body senses and the faculties connected with them to be exercised (Löffler 2017). Movement is essential to learning and is used in Waldorf schools for teaching writing, math, and foreign languages. The kind of round dances and circle games that children used to play outside are also part of this concept (Magin 2017). Because the furniture is movable it can be quickly changed around to accommodate various working and teaching styles (Wiehl 2015, p. 65). This ensures, moreover, that the children alternate frequently between sitting, standing, and moving, which is essential because sitting for long periods of time is anything but healthy (Jochem/Leitzmann 2018). The approach has proved successful so far in that it has allowed many children to achieve the necessary maturation of the senses and to develop the faculties connected with them. Other faculties, too, are promoted in the Moving Classroom, such as the forming of relationships, independence, social skills, and a sense of time. Their development is enhanced, among other things, by the presence of the grade teacher, the shared breakfast, a reliable daily routine, and a gathering at the end of the school day where children learn how to deal with conflicts together (Auer 2017, p. 62ff.).

3.6 Looking ahead

When children reach the age of six or seven, an important developmental phase draws to a close. All the senses have matured to a certain level that can be built on in the following years. The faculties acquired in this early phase will be needed in later life. It depends on the quality of this first developmental stage and on the kind of experiences children were able to have whether the next stages will be easier or marked by difficulties and challenges.

Sensory development does not stop when school starts. Body senses and mobility need to be further developed through sports and games, and activities such as walking, swimming, climbing, and cycling, but also through craft activities, social games, dancing, music making, and acting. They are activities that allow children to unfold their individual strengths. The communicative senses can best develop between the early school years and adolescence, through artistic activities, singing, music making, poetry writing, painting, and sculpting. They are also strengthened when the students' perceptive faculties are honed through the contemplation of art (Auer 2015) and the exact observation of natural phenomena.

Sensory development is an essential aspect of early childhood education. Many guidebooks on early intervention and kindergarten education quite rightly emphasize the important role of the senses. Scientific research is lagging behind however for, apart from a few experts, there is no such thing as a "sensory research" discipline although this would be urgently needed, particularly in early childhood and kindergarten.

4 The child's imitative capacity

ANGELIKA WIEHL

4.1 Introduction

Imitation is a specific mode of learning typically developed in the first years of life. In the twentieth century, various sciences began to investigate the phenomenon and have since elaborated a range of diverse aspects.

Imitation is a primal faculty that enables us to get to know other people and world events, to transform ourselves and shape our life. It occurs in every moment of life, in favorable as well as unfavorable conditions. This is why children, from the moment of birth, need a protective environment that is worth imitating, where they can develop in the best possible way, physically, emotionally, and cognitively, and gain the ability to lead autonomous, responsible lives. Not only in infancy but particularly also in the first years of school we observe how children learn from taking in their environment, from how people behave and act around them, and from events that move them; and how they process their experiences in their own individual way. Imitative learning ranges from direct imitation and repetition of actions that have been perceived, to artistic innovative creations, creative acts, and changes in behavior, to less conspicuous developmental episodes. Imitation is possible due to the faculties of empathy and sympathy, innate in every child and adult, that allow us to open up to the world around us, enter into encounters, and process impressions inwardly. Imitative experiences inform the way children play and perform imaginative and artistic activities. In playful-creative activities children try out and appropriate the behaviors and attributes they observe in others.

Imitation—Greek tradition refers to it as *mimesis*—has been scrutinized empirically and theoretically ever since antiquity, first in the context of philosophy and aesthetics and then, in the twentieth and twenty-first centuries, above all in developmental psychology, the cognitive sciences, and neurobiology, but also in philosophy, educational anthropology (Gebauer/Wulf 1992, 1998, 2003; Wulf 2014b, 2017) and art education (Glas et. al. 2017). The concept of *mimesis* as a basic anthropological dimension that, as illustrated in Gebauer and Wulf's extensive studies, encompasses philosophical and aesthetic as well as social aspects, will form the foundation of the following examination of the concept of imitation in the anthropology of Waldorf education. Waldorf education sees imitation, or mimesis, as an essential basis for development and as a learning disposition present in infancy up until the ninth or tenth year of age (Wiehl 2015, p. 170ff.). In this view, imitation unfolds primarily in response to a child's attachment figures and direct environment. While the scientific disciplines mentioned above study, on the one hand, the behaviors and encoding of the imitative process and, on the other, the subsequent creative activities, the anthropology of Waldorf education focuses on the role imitation plays in the formation of the child's body and organs and how it supports the unfolding of essential faculties. This anthropological interpretation does not contradict the present research. Steiner's essential but scarce indications regarding imitation in childhood will be complemented and expanded here beyond Peter Selg's introduction (Selg 2017), as we explore aspects of imitation that have hardly been considered so far.

The approach we take below and the resulting findings illustrate the crucial part imitation, as an elementary learning disposition, plays both in childhood but also throughout life, its potential for creativity and self-education, and as a general foundation for cultural learning. The abundance of scientific studies on mimesis available in sciences such as philosophy, aesthetics, or anthropology, proves that this concept, which goes back as far as ancient Greek times, extends far beyond our usual notion of imitation or copying (Metscher 2004; Gebauer/Wulf 1992; Wulf 2014b). We therefore first examine the dimensions of *mimesis*—a term used by various disciplines ever since Plato and Aristotle—that may be relevant to the concept of imitation applied in Waldorf education. We will also highlight the importance of imitation in practical teaching and as a basic learning ability in the changing cultural conditions of our time.

4.2 The connection between imitating and learning

Imitation and learning take place at every age and in every situation, and they develop perpetually from birth into adulthood. Education commonly takes a result-oriented approach in that it regards learning as the transforming and augmenting of skills and knowledge. In school education in particular, learning is seen as functional and determined by learning outcomes, which is why its representatives speak of an effective "process of acquiring specific knowledge and skills" (Göhlich/Zirfas 2007, p. 181). In cultural history learning appears as a comprehensive "process of appropriating the world, of self-education, and transformation" (Wiehl 2015, p. 168) that is rooted in the original human need to appropriate "the reality of life as culture" (Fichtner 2008, p. 11ff.) and to self-transform through active experience (Meyer-Drawe 2012, p. 16). Independently of the specific form of imitative learning, human learning in general is part of the elementary faculties of self-development and self-education through meeting and interacting with the world around.

As an educational "key concept" learning is defined in ever-new ways, depending on the cultural and social milieu or the scientific discipline in question. The term goes back to the Indo-Germanic stem *lais* meaning furrow or track. Learning is consequently associated with "leaving a track" or "pursuing a cause." Today, learning is seen as related on the one hand to "self-formation that occurs through metamorphoses in the appropriation and memorization of life and learning contents" (Wiehl 2015, p. 246), and on the other hand to the "tracks" that a learning process leaves in the learner as well as in the learner's social and cultural surroundings. Learning, in this view, is therefore not result-oriented but above all process- and action-oriented, since a much wider framework is assumed for learning than the one usually implied in kindergarten and school education, and imitative learning is included in this framework.

A closer look at the history of terms such as copying, imitating, and mimesis reveals interesting semantic aspects. "Copying" goes back to the Latin word *copia* meaning "abundance, plenty." In the Middle Ages *imitatio* was used in the sense of "recreating an original" (Gebauer/Wulf 1992, p. 90). The Latin noun *imitatio* and the corresponding verb *imitari* have the same roots as *imago* (image)—a reference to the inner pictorial nature or the picture encoding that occurs in the imitative process. Gebauer and Wulf illustrate that the Greek word *mimesis*, translated in English as imitation, has been used since Plato and Aristotle in a wider sense as the ability to copy, present, or express things (Gebauer/Wulf 2003, p. 83). Imitating, or the mimetic process, is consequently not just a mere copying, or doing as others do, but signifies, as Karl Philipp Moritz explained "the formative reproduction of beauty [...] in experiencing the active force that produces the work" (Grimm/Grimm 1852–1960, vol. 13). The literature on learning culture and subsequently on education extends the meaning of mimesis by defining it as a "human condition that is essential for human beings to unfold their individual personality (Gebauer/Wulf 1992, p. 9). Gebauer and Wulf propose that in the mimetic process the recreating of original actions overlaps with the creating of new ones, and that this explains the capacity of imitative learning in which the human learning culture is rooted.

4.3 The emergence of a learning culture through imitative learning

People have been conscious of imitating and learning as far back as we can follow the records and testimonies of human culture. It was only with Greek philosophy, however, that reflection on these capacities began and it is still ongoing, for instance in the discourse on the concept of mimesis (Metscher 2004; Gebauer/Wulf 1992, 2003, Wulf 2017). Anthropology does not see imitation as mere copying either, but rather recognizes its creative and progressive dimension, which extends far beyond appropriation and mimicking. This dimension marks the original way of learning as the foundation of all human and cultural evolution. We find its traces in the most ancient artifacts where they appear as the result of repeated practice and creative imitation, making it possible for us to evaluate their anthropological significance. The original form of imitative learning is the beginning as well as the archetype of human and cultural formation.

Tools, small sculptures, and rock paintings are among the earliest testimonies of the human learning culture. Around 2.5 million years BCE an important revolution took place in Africa, as humans produced the first tools, worked with them and developed them further. Migrants from Africa to other continents took these skills along with them and continued to produce and use these tools (Kuckenburg 2001) wherever they went. The development of early tool-making techniques can exemplify a learning development that goes back more than two million years and continues to this time. This development began with the use of simple stone implements, which were then worked on further by striking larger and smaller flakes in order to produce increasingly differentiated and refined tools. The hand axe is one example, its even and elaborate form suggesting a certain degree of imagination in its creator. Hand axes were produced in the same way over the world. Then, around 40,000 years

BCE, astoundingly finely hewn blades, scrapers, spearheads, and needles appeared, used for specific purposes in the hunter-gatherer cultures (Parzinger 2015, p. 62f.). Interestingly, the transition from the production of the rougher to the more refined utensils was not seamless. Modern research talks of a sudden change and specialization (Lumley/Lumley 2011, p. 109ff.) that coincided with the appearance of early *Homo sapiens*: new, more delicate stone blades and pointy spears made of bone point to the emergence of a new aesthetic and material consciousness (ibid., p. 114ff.).

In addition to these new implements, the first artistic creations emerged not only across Europe but also all the way to Siberia, in Africa, and other parts of the world. Aside from the important cave paintings in France and Spain, striking ice age artifacts have been discovered in recent decades in the Swabian Alps of Southern Germany (Conard/Kind 2017). The countless portable art objects dug out in caves and under rock shelters—for instance the 4 to 6 cm tall, true to life, and richly decorated horses, mammoths, and lions—are assumed to have been symbols of cultic rituals rather than utensils for everyday use (ibid., p. 48f.). The animal sculptures, the so-called "lion-man," and similar figurines bearing human features are of striking simplicity and expression. They are seen as evidence of a symbolic thinking and imagination that evolved as part of an imitative-creative process which presupposes awareness and perception of the environment, the internalization of perceptual contents, and their individual refashioning in a freely chosen medium such as stone, horn, or bone.

The evolutionary leap forward that occurred around 40,000 years BCE may have been due to the growing population and dispersal of *Homo sapiens*, the predecessor of modern humans, who, unlike its forerunners, did possess creative imagination. The fact that these early humans did not simply imitate or adopt earlier creations but produced new objects to meet their inner and outer needs suggests an overlapping of imitation and creative invention, because if imitative learning had only evolved for the purpose of continuing and cultivating a tradition, tools would never have become more sophisticated nor would symbolic art ever have evolved. Tool-making techniques would not have resulted in industrial serial production, nor would humans working with tools have been replaced by machines, and art would not find expression in ever new creations. Today, the principle of imitation is widespread and often unintendedly one-sided: the robots that are being developed are meant to learn skills humanity has taken more than two million years to acquire, including competences that are important in psychology and social care. Scientists predict that, in future, robots will adapt to changed conditions and that they will be able to generate something they were not originally programmed to generate. Obviously, they can choose from a multitude of solutions and designs much more quickly than we ever could, and this creates the impression that machines are inventive. But so far, they have only been able to respond according to hardcoded algorithms and combine infinite variations. They are *not yet* able to bring about entirely new creations, in the way human beings are as a result of imitative or mimetic learning. For if human actions only required selecting, combining, and mere copying, there would be no innovations or inventions. The danger we are facing is not only that robots might surpass us when it comes to the variety of actions, but that we turn into imitators of programmed machines and forfeit our creativity and imagination in the process.

Imitating, learning, and taking action rely on a creative element that comes to expression as we acquire speech and develop thinking in play, movement, and activity. We can copy or imitate an observed action when we practice performing it by following a role model; similarly we can produce a piece of work by copying how someone else does it. But as we imitate we always have the possibility to change, vary, give up on, or newly invent a movement, action, or piece of work. We are not fixed on a role model but can choose to be guided by it.

Thomas Metscher referred to this original imitative way of learning and creative potential as a "productive force in conjunction with ποίησις (poiesis[1])," as a combination of creativity and human self-formation (Metscher 2004, p. 14). The example given earlier of the evolution of tools illustrates that such learning processes are not only self-educating and poietic but also socially and culturally creative. Christoph Wulf refers to this dimension of the imitative process. For him, mimesis or imitation, like performativity[2] and ritual, are prerequisite to a "genesis of the social life" (Wulf 2005) that, in the widest sense, also includes education and its practical applications.

To summarize: "Cultural learning is largely mimetic learning, which forms the center of many educational and self-educational processes, which is directed at other individuals, social communities, and cultural goods, and which guarantees their vitality" (ibid., p. 60). Mimesis as creative imitation and activity occurs in the meeting with others and the environment, and it finds its expression in symbolic and self-educational learning processes that are culturally and socially creative.

---

1 The activity of creating something that did not exist before.
2 The power of language to bring about change in the world.

4.4 Imitation as a body-forming experience—a critical look at neurobiology

Contemporary sciences and disciplines, education included, refer to the findings of neurobiological research to explain consciousness, mental phenomena such as perception, thinking, feeling, will, as well as learning and imitative processes; but also the origin of these phenomena and processes. Joachim Bauer's widely read publications (2006, 2016) on emotional and mental transmission mechanisms caused by mirror neurons have been well received, by teachers in particular. Since the discovery of mirror neurons in the 1990s, scientists have been pursuing the notion that the physiological brain, above all the activity of mirror neurons, could be responsible for imitative processes (Rizzolatti/Sinigaglia 2014). What characterizes mirror neurons is that they are not only "firing" when we carry out a particular action but also when we observe this action being carried out by someone else (ibid., p. 91). Their crucial function seems to consist in what is known as "visuomotor coupling," that is, the coordination of visual impressions and motor activity, which is also assumed to correspond to the ability to mentally simulate movements ("motor imagery") that is essential to imitative learning (ibid. p. 101ff.). Scientists have, however, so far not been able to explain how the neurons produce this "motor imagery," from what age it is part of the imitative process, whether it is innate or acquired later, and whether it is at all a precondition for imitative behavior.

There is no evidence either as to how the transition or mediation from perceptions to subsequent actions actually occurs. "We cannot establish any qualitative laws of consciousness on the basis of processes and effects that have been observed and described at a purely neuronal level" (Wagemann 2010, p. 36), nor do these observations provide any insights into the inner soul experience involved in imitative processes. In other words, the inner volitional, mental, and emotional processes that occur during imitation are not identical with the neuronal processes, they merely occur simultaneously with them, possibly as stimulators and activators of neurons. According to research conducted by Thomas Fuchs (2013, 2016), the transmission of behaviors, gestures, feelings, and thoughts that accompanies the imitative process corresponds to a permanent "resonance" between the brain and the organism. This resonance is on the one hand a "prerequisite for conscious experience" (Fuchs 2013, p. 142), but on the other hand also for body-related effectiveness. Hans Jürgen Scheurle also speaks of a resonance that verifiably exists between physical and neuronal states but that does not amount to the representation of perceived events

(Scheurle 2016). According to the current state of research imitative learning and imitative experiences undoubtedly cause resonances and imprints in the brain. What needs to be questioned, however, is that neuronal activities produce sensory, emotional, and cognitive experiences. Precisely because the structures of the brain only develop in the first three years of childhood, they cannot be used to explain mental processes, nor can they support imitation.

Critical scrutiny puts the conclusions derived from neurobiological processes and applied to the imitative process into perspective, especially if one looks at imitative learning as a perceptual and formative event. One then sees particularly that the concept of imitation adopted in neurobiology is restricted to mere copying, the repeating of actions, and the acquisition of new behavior patterns (Rizzolatti/Sinigaglia 2014, p. 144), while a more comprehensive understanding of imitation or mimesis views it as a process that is perceptual as well as creative. For an anthropological and pedagogical understanding of imitation and imitative learning, the study of neurobiology can therefore only provide useful information in so far as the phases of imitation—perception, internalization, and potential formation and action—are seen as occurring in resonance with the surrounding world and the nervous organization, and in so far as the latter is necessary for body-forming experiences. The neurobiological explanations of imitative processes cannot, however, be uncritically adopted for education, least of all for Waldorf education where compassion, empathy, and resonance are seen as capacities that support imitation and that are accessible to direct and phenomenological observation.

4.5 Imitation and behavior as expressions of the will to learn

Imitation and learning always happen naturally in childhood unless the basic needs to meet and interact with the world through perception and discovery are restricted. Newborn babies trust in their environment and live in harmony with it. They feel enveloped by their mother's warmth, respond to her smile, and enjoy the resistance they feel when they touch something with their hands and feet. This direct response, the infant's pure imitation of expression, very soon "exceeds the innate simple copying and turns to the target of other people's actions" (Fuchs 2013, p. 204). While children in the first months of life interact "dyadically" with the world—that is, by looking at another person or an object—they start, from around the ninth month, to notice how their caregivers turn their attention toward other objects or persons. They learn to share the other person's experience by looking where he or she is looking (Tomasello 2006, p. 84f.). For Michael Tomasello this "triadic" behavior constitutes the beginning of actual imitative learning (ibid.), which is generally referred to as imitation in Waldorf education. This "joint attention" (ibid., p. 84) between the child and a familiar person is an expression of the child's basic need to learn from and relate to others (Krautz/Schieren 2013, p. 11). As intentional beings, children increasingly learn to follow their own interest (Tomasello 2006, p. 83ff.) and no longer merely react to their environment, but actively engage with it. They imitate how people close to them behave and act, not only immediately but also after some time has passed.

To this day, the empirical research results published by Jean Piaget as early as 1945 constitute guidelines worth discussing when it comes to the assessment of imitative development. Piaget's observations led him to conclude that between the ages of two and seven children gradually proceed from sensory-motor imitation—the kind of immediate imitation that involves all senses and the entire movement organism—to "representative imitation" (Piaget 1945/2003, p. 96ff.). He pointed out that children, as soon as they begin imitating "representatively," learn to internalize perceptions and recall them later as memories, that is, as inner pictures of the perceived event. The mental representation inserting itself between the act of perception and the subsequent imitative act is, according to Piaget, like an "internal model" that can, usually unnoticed by the child, trigger reactions, actions, or presentations. The dual nature of imitation is characterized by the close connection between the preceding perception and the mental representation. "[...] on the one hand imitation is merely the continuation of the accommodations of sensory-motor intelligence, and on the other the first mental images are interiorized imitation" (ibid., p. 96f.).[3]

Albert Bandura and his team examined this research on imitation in relation to social learning and self-development (Bandura/Walter 1963/1970). Their Social Learning Theory delineates imitation as "learning through modeling" which Bandura explicitly does not wish to be understood as conditioning (Bandura 1976, p. 250ff.). His studies therefore focus on the learning of behaviors from (role) models, where the processes of imitation and identification together constitute the "modeling" (ibid., p. 13)—a term that extends the psychological effect of the modeling influences far beyond the simple mimicry implied [according to Bandura] in the concept of imitation (ibid.), because modeling can have three

---

3 English translation in Jean Piaget, *Play, Dreams and Imitation in Childhood*, Routledge 2000, tr. C. Gattegno and F.M. Hodgson, p. 75.

effects: firstly, the learning of behaviors through observation; secondly, the reinforcing or weakening of previously learned responses as a result of rewards or punishment; and thirdly, the disinhibiting of previously inhibited behaviors as a result of new observations. The modeling process itself unfolds in four stages, from 1. conscious attentional focus on events; 2. retention of the "modeled event" in memory; 3. motoric reproduction steered by symbolic representations of the modeled behavioral patterns; and 4. reinforcement and motivation, which both crucially influence observational learning (ibid., p. 24ff.). Bandura sees the modeling stimuli involved in these processes as sources of information for the imitative performances (ibid.) that do not have to be similar to the model but can be expressions of creative self-efficacy. The intensity of the inner symbolic representations accompanying any modeling process determines, according to Bandura, the nature of the imitative acts and the development of capacities in general (ibid., p. 108f.). In summary, Bandura's theory of "modeled learning" posits that behavioral changes or new behaviors can occur as a result of observed behaviors and their consequences.

Although there are various reasons why both Piaget's and Bandura's research should be discussed critically, certain variations of core elements of their work appear again and again in later studies. Remo Largo, for instance, who defines imitation as a "disposition" for acquiring new faculties such as walking, speaking, thinking (Largo 2010, p. 64), distinguishes between the mental level of internalization and retention and the actual processing and act of imitation: what is initially pure observation and perception develops through internal formative processes into new and individualized faculties. Like Piaget, Largo proposes that imitative processes in earlier years consist in direct mimicking while they later transition through internal encoding, mental pictures for instance, to individual direct or delayed actions, behaviors, and attributes. According to Largo children up to their tenth year learn mainly from concrete actions and experiences which they internalize, while instructions and admonitions from adults are nowhere near as effective (ibid., p. 64f.).

The anthropologist and developmental psychologist Michael Tomasello explores what happens "internally" in imitative processes that are triggered by human interaction (Tomasello 2006, p. 16f.):

> [...] imitative learning, instructed learning, and collaborative learning [...] are made possible by a single very special form of social cognition, namely, the ability of individual organisms to understand con-specifics as beings like themselves who have intentional and mental lives like their own. This understanding enables individuals

to imagine themselves 'in the mental shoes' of some other person, so that they cannot just learn from the other but through the other. This understanding of others as intentional beings like the self is crucial in human cultural learning [...][4]

The intentional perception that underlies imitative learning (ibid., p. 93) allows children to appropriate—through imitation in communicative or dialogical situations—thoughts, intentions, and moral values and perpetuate them as cultural inheritance. Imitative learning encompasses all sensory perceptions and experiences of the direct environment including the use of artifacts, symbols, and speech acts, which is why Tomasello refers to it as another form of cultural learning (ibid., p. 72f.) based on three qualities that need to be practiced in the social context: intentionally recognizing others, imitating social activities, and learning to speak (ibid., p. 143).

Based on many years of research into the origin and development of thinking, Peter Hobson—similarly to Tomasello—recognizes the child's intentional perception as a given rather than learned faculty (Hobson 2003). Like many others he has to admit that it is ultimately not possible to know everything about a young child's mental processes, because his conclusions regarding the development of thinking are derived from external behaviors and reactions observed in children. He arrives at the claim that seems instrumental to him that the child, from the moment of birth, develops the need "to grasp the mental dimension of human beings through her bodily anchored relations with others" (ibid., p. 19).[5] In Theory of Mind research it was possible to demonstrate that four-year-olds perceive and internalize the intentions, thoughts, feelings, wishes, and moral attitudes of others (Bischof-Köhler 2011). Imitating and learning are consequently not based on external behaviors only but include the emotional and mental resonances present in human co-existence. Piaget, Bandura, Largo, Tomasello, and Hobson describe imitation as an elementary faculty experienced in relationships through compassion and cooperation that can be observed in, but is not limited to, behaviors and behavioral changes.

The findings of attachment research have become more prominent recently in the context of child development and education. Attachment theory sees the ability to imitate as a fundamental precondition for healthy attachment behavior and attachment security, but also for social learning (Bischof-Köhler 2011; Grossmann/Grossmann 2017). While

---

4 Michael Tomasello, *The Cultural Origins of Human Cognition*, Harvard University Press, p. 5
5 Peter Hobson, *The Cradle of Thought*, Macmillan London 2002, p. 4

imitation is not the main focus of attachment theory, its studies illustrate clearly that early secure attachments to the individuals closest to them enable children later to meet other people and the world around them with trust and courage: an essential precondition for imitative learning. Children who grow up securely attached to their mothers are empathetic and open to new experiences, to meeting other people, social learning, and participation in everything they observe in other people's way of being. Attachment security constitutes the basis for a full participation in life, healthy imitation, intrinsic learning, and for developing independence and self-determination.

From the scientific approaches cited so far we can conclude for our further discussion that imitation in secure attachment enables learning and development to occur intentionally through modeling in the social realm of relationships. Imitation means that—through the interweaving of attentive and perceptive observation, identification and internalization, inner images and memories—children gain the ability to perform imitative and creative acts of self-expression. The basic disposition for intentional perception highlighted by Tomasello and Hobson not only explains the conditions of education but demands an educational approach that considers the sensitivity of young children, because they perceive and internalize what happens around them as well as the behaviors and the mental and moral makeup of the persons close to them.

4.6 Imitation as creative activity

The outcomes of the studies cited reveal that imitation is not just copying or reproducing but that it involves a complex process of perception, retention, and expression. By including the mimesis research conducted by Gunter Gebauer and Christoph Wulf one adds a further, anthropological dimension. In their publications of the last three decades, Gebauer and Wulf cast a light on Plato's and Aristotle's wrestling with the concepts of imitation and mimesis, on the eventual rooting of these concepts in aestheticism, and their ongoing discussion in modern philosophy and cultural studies.[6] The fifth and fourth centuries BCE, when Greek philosophy flourished, were still informed by an oral culture that only gradually transitioned to literacy with the textualization of cultural knowledge. Mimesis, which was presumably first identified as a theme in the context ˹dance and music, was consequently associated with literature, paint-˺ and sculpture, that is to say with the sensuous appearance or beauty ˹ct of these art forms. Forms of expression with a temporal dimension,

˹uer/Wulf 1992, p. 50ff.; 1998, 2003; Wulf 2005, 2014, 2017.

such as dance, music, and spoken poetry, as well as those with a spatial dimension, such as sculptures and paintings, may have their origin in mimetic expression. Imitation can best be verified when its results become visible or objective, which means that one infers from appearances to the imitative process itself. If a literary work is meant to reflect what happened to certain persons at a particular place and time, all aspects need to be perceived, then retained in mental images or preliminarily recorded before they are recreated in a new medium such as poetic language or a painting. That the reproduction can be either an imitation or a more imaginatively fashioned new creation goes without saying. Imitation and mimesis cannot be clearly defined but range from direct copying to self- or newly created reproductions.

Gebauer and Wulf point out that, in the Middle Ages, mimesis was mainly understood as imitation in the sense of copying and that the concept only expanded with the aesthetic theories of the eighteenth century (Gebauer/Wulf 1992, p. 93ff.). This weighing up and rethinking of the meaning of mimesis that started with Aristotle continues through the philosophical and aesthetic reflections of the twentieth century (Metscher 2004) and on to this day. According to Thomas Metscher, the philosophies of, among others, Walter Benjamin, Theodor Adorno, Georg Lukács, and Heinz Holz—even if their reasoning differs—recognize mimesis as a "universal faculty" and as an anticipatory and productive force supporting adaptation and assimilation to the surrounding world (ibid., p. 10). Mimesis generates a second reality next to the first one, a reality of self-creation, social creativity, and cultural formation. In philosophy and aesthetics imitation, or mimesis, is not a clearly defined concept but presents a whole range of debatable qualities or variables whose basic anthropological principle is relevant to education. The dual nature of the imitative process needs to be considered: the initial, perceptual, encounter is followed by an internalizing, or subjectifying, a kind of becoming one (in an anticipatory sense). This, in turn, is followed by an externalizing or objectifying process, in which the result of the initial process appears, or is expressed, in the most diverse ways (in a productive sense). The outcome of the imitative act merely allows us to guess at what went before, in the process of empathetic attention and absorption. The internalization through mental pictures and creative imagination is such a personal process of appropriation that knowledge of it can only be attained through and from the reflexes of a possibly artistic externalization that does, however, not necessarily occur. Imitation or mimesis proceeds from the outside in and then back out again.

From the anthropological point of view we can summarize that meeting oneself and the world through imitation appears to be an elementary need that makes possible meaningful experiences of self and world. It gives us the ability both to educate ourselves and to make our mark on the world.

4.7 Anthropological aspects of imitation in Waldorf education

Waldorf education focuses on imitation and imitative learning more than most other educational approaches. It sees the ability to imitate not only as a universal human faculty but as an elementary learning disposition that facilitates physical, mental and spiritual education. The preceding considerations add a dimension to the concept of imitation that has so far not been fully explored in the theory and practice of Waldorf education, either in the early years or in the grades (Wiehl 2015, p. 170ff.). On the basis of these interdisciplinary research results the wider dimensions of the imitative faculty that Steiner only touched upon but that are fundamental to Waldorf education can be investigated in greater depth and discussed as an independent branch of educational psychology and anthropology. Because the secondary literature on Waldorf education accepts imitation as a given and does therefore not subject it to in-depth scrutiny, it seems appropriate, and worthwhile, to categorize Steiner's primary reflections on the topic and make them available as guidelines for the practice of Waldorf education.

Steiner's mostly aphoristic characterizations of imitation do not relate to any contemporary specialist literature or empirical psychological studies. They arise from the "observation" of the object of cognition (Steiner GA 304, p. 98) and its meditative contemplation (Wiehl 2015, p. 174; Chapter 6), which means that they are accessible to phenomenological observation. In his early (1888) reflections on aesthetics Steiner starts from Aristotle's concept of imitation that, he says, knows no other artistic principle than that of "imitating nature" (Steiner GA 271, p. 17). But, Steiner says, just as art does not stop with the imitation of nature but goes further than that (ibid., p. 20), the child's imitative activity goes beyond the mere copying of what is perceived in the surrounding world. In the essay *The Education of the Child in the Light of Anthroposophy*, Steiner's most comprehensive discussion of imitation (S 10), which was first published in 1907 (Steiner GA 34, p. 309ff.), he points out that Aristotle referred to humans as "the most imitative of all animals" and that this was true for no age in life as much as for childhood, for children imitated everything that was going on in their physical environment, everything accessible to sensory perception, and all "that can work from the sur-rounding physical space upon the inner powers of the child." In the pro-cess of imitation, Steiner continues, the child's "physical organs are cast into the forms which then become permanent" (ibid., p. 324).[7] Steiner characterized this capacity of young children to perceive and imitate the world around them with body, soul, and spirit by saying that, in their way of experiencing the world, children were like "finely tuned sense organs."[8] Children have the capacity to make their own being into an image of their environment, to make their inner being resemble the outer world.[9] He uses the term "sense organ" here as a metaphor for the child's sensory constitution (chapter 3), that is not yet specialized into twelve separate sensory spheres but is, as a consonance of all sensory dispositions, open to perceiving the world in the way described for the motor-sensory phase of life. Younger children absorb all sensory impressions empathetically as if they were themselves sense organs.

Children bring this profound capacity for imitation with them from prenatal life, when they were dwelling as spirit-soul beings in oneness with their spirit-soul environment before embarking on their earthly development during pregnancy, protected by the maternal womb. Ac-cording to Steiner, this oneness can be conceived of as physical, emo-tional, and spiritual participation during which young children form their constitution through imitation. The world around, the behavior of familiar people, as well as their feelings, moods, thoughts, and moral atti-tudes directly affect the development of the child's body and inner being (Steiner GA 307, p.107). Steiner recognizes imitation as a "comprehensive perceptual process," in which children "surrender themselves wholly, with all their senses, to the surrounding world" (Wiehl 2015, p. 175; Steiner GA 297, p. 282).

In early education Steiner therefore recommends "no other method but to be a human being worth imitating" (Steiner 304a, p. 155). Rules and instructions, he states, have no effect on children, but what does have an effect is "what the grown-up people do visibly before [the child's] eyes." "Healthy role models" should live "what children can imitate" (Steiner GA 34, p. 324ff.). The most important task of parents and educators is therefore to be such role models and shape the child's environment in a way that is worth imitating and that promotes child development. As they imitate the role model and the outer conditions in general, inner forces first arise in the children, forming their organs, before imagination

---

7 English translation by George and Mary Adams, Anthroposophic Press 1981, p. 13
8 Steiner GA 84, p. 177; GA 297a, p. 142; GA 304a, p. 130; GA 307, p. 107; Selg 2015b.
9 Steiner GA 277a, p. 19; GA 300c, p. 11; GA 302, p. 129.

gradually awakens (Steiner GA 55, p. 123ff.) and comes to expression in play, speaking, and thinking. For the early age of imitation, Steiner attaches more importance to the inner forming of the organs and imagination than to the imitated outer behaviors (Steiner GA 59, p. 27ff.) from which empiric research gains its insights. These behaviors are just the bridge for a comprehensive self-educating and forming of body, soul, and spirit. The less the imitative forces are needed for the development of body and organs, the more they are available as a potential for imagination, ideation, and thinking.

Many studies into early child development confirm the detailed observations that Steiner wove into his lectures on education. By around the first year, the early childhood reflexes have largely been integrated to give way to controlled movements. The unfolding movement organization, which has, partly thanks to Emmi Pikler's work (Pikler 2001), become the subject of many educational concepts, is a precondition for healthy child development. Children develop their ability to move in accordance with their own individual rhythm, and this ability then serves as a basis for the development of speech, imagination, and thinking. Diversity of movement manifests physically in secure upright walking and limb activity, and mentally in melodious, rhythmic, and imaginative speech and imaginative thinking that then comes to expression in symbolic playing.

As the movement organism gradually matures children acquire, through imitation, the ability to walk upright, speak, and think (Steiner GA 124, p. 115ff.) while the brain develops under the influence of their physical and mental experiences (Steiner GA 306, p. 44ff.). Like Tomasello (2013) and Scheurle (2016), Steiner sees the brain as an imprint of the soul life rather than its generator. As children form their movement organism through imitation, forces arise that metamorphose into speech and thinking (Steiner GA 81, p. 80f.). Steiner describes speech as "applied movement" and "applied balance" (Steiner GA 224, p. 115). The forming of mental images is promoted by forces that have become free from the environment and from external impressions (Steiner GA 81, p. 80f.). The transformed, inward-turning formative forces support the imaginative thinking (Steiner GA 301, p. 57) that develops best in a creative and imaginative environment where children can play with toys that are not perfect and complete but allow their imagination to unfold (Steiner GA 55, p. 125f.). As a result, the memories, which are initially tied to certain situations and physical faculties, can then, at around the age of five, become inner pictures. This allows children to "understand the spiritual" (Steiner GA 307, p. 103ff.) but also forms the foundation for later intellectual thinking when memory pictures are processed through thinking and cognition (Steiner GA 308, 78f.). School education often neglects this imaginative thinking and focuses on intellectual development although there is evidence that children are inwardly disposed toward imagination and spirituality. According to Lisa Miller's studies, this disposition is eliminated in children by the modern lifestyles of grown-ups who can no longer relate to spirituality (Miller/Barker 2016). It is precisely in children's capacity for imagination and play that the creative will, which is inspired by spiritual formative forces, comes to expression.

Motor skills, speech, and thinking are consequently not inherited, nor are they based on purely external imitation but, according to Steiner, on a "prepondering will" that continues to be effective into the ninth year. (Steiner GA 297, p. 64). Children learn movements, speech, and thinking through imitation, putting all their efforts into learning human faculties from role models. Children's behaviors directly mirror the way the adults around them move and speak. The life stories of "feral children" (Bruland 2008), such as the famous wolf boy of Aveyron (Lane 1985), illustrate how closely children model themselves on the beings—in this case animals—around them. Some of these feral children survived in nature for years, behaving instinctively like animals. They were, however, unable to develop morality, culture, and a religious awareness, because that would have required a human environment. Deprived of human contact, "wild children" can only become "nature beings" who, if they subsequently experience human community, are mostly incapable of acquiring human behaviors and faculties, a fact that also proves that, while physical dispositions are inherited, human faculties are not.

Steiner describes how children absorb moral ideas through language, actions, and through their experience of gratitude (Steiner GA 303, p. 303ff.), and how they imitate the moral, or immoral, content of such actions deep down in their inner organization (Steiner GA 307, p. 103ff.). If children perceive meaningful gestures, he says, a feeling of gratitude arises in them, forming the foundation for religious devotion and love. According to Steiner, imitation is a "physical religion" because children strive in their entire behavior to be permeated with religious feelings, and this religious devotion will later turn into love (Steiner GA 306, p. 116ff.). Individually, through imitation, children acquire the ability to walk upright, speak, and think along with an inner sense of morality and capacity for reverence which is essential for them to realize their humanity.

By bringing Steiner's observations on imitation together with the various research results presented above we learn several things: Psychology tends to examine behaviors and draw conclusions from comparing the initial action with the resulting imitation. Anthropology and aesthetics phenomenologically observe processes of perception, internalization, and externalization that manifest as mental and creative potentials in art and culture. Steiner deepens the anthropological view aesthetically in that he recognizes imitation as a transformative process that can lead to creative actions as well as self-educational processes. According to his observations, the formative forces that come to expression in the faculties of imagination and thinking are related to the forces that form the body and the organs. Young children need all their formative forces for their physical development. Once they learn to speak, a part of these forces emancipates itself as imagination and will later be available to the intellect as thinking forces. Steiner sees imitation as fundamental to the formation of body, soul, and spirit that occurs when forces of spirit and soul metamorphose into body-forming processes. He refers to the energy effective in these formative processes as ether or life forces. These life forces manifest in artistic and creative acts but they are also responsible for maintaining and building up the entire human organization. Imitation in the sense of mimesis is like a playing with the formative life forces that originate in the spiritual world before birth, build up the body, differentiate in the first year of life into forces effective in body, soul, and spirit, and continue to exist in imagination and thinking. By imitating meaningful life actions children prepare themselves for a thoughtful and autonomous human existence.

4.8 Imitation, play, and artistic learning in Waldorf education

Inspired by Rudolf Steiner, Waldorf education strives to offer an environment that facilitates imitative learning. Its practice in Waldorf kindergartens and schools has generated a multitude of educational applications that are well documented in numerous publications, complemented with practical examples. Many of these publications point out that early childhood learning requires special protection. Up until the Rubicon, the crisis point around the ninth or tenth year when children begin to experience themselves consciously as separate from the world (Chapter 1), children gradually attune themselves to life and learning through imitation, that is to say, mostly perceptually. Kindergartens and schools therefore have to create an environment worth imitating, in which children can move, play, work, and learn in accordance with their developmental needs. What characterizes playful learning in childhood and the transition from kindergarten to the grades will be outlined below in relation to imitative learning.

Child play evolves from free, creative, and imaginative experimentation with imitation and reenactments of behaviors, activities, and events. Children slip into other roles and identify with tasks. Every action or object, however inconspicuous, assumes a meaning and comes to life in a child's imagination. A wooden block with a hole becomes a camera; the knife rests discovered in grandma's cutlery drawer are lined up to form a train. Watching how the flow of water in a brook is arrested by a stone inspires children to build a dam. All child play is an attempt at creative self-realization through the imitation of life. The child's actions touch on the meaningfulness of life, of people, their behaviors, their activities, but also their object world, and through their imitative activities children make this world their own. Even four- or five-year-olds copy complex grown-up activities in their play: a table and chairs turn into a fire engine in which the children race to a burning house and extinguish the flames with hosepipes that consist of felted strips of fabric. Pieces of furniture covered with blankets represent an elephant one can ride on. Children continue to copy adults in their play right into the school years. Up until their eleventh or twelfth year they set up shop on the beach and sell sand pizza, or they act out how their teacher behaves in certain situations. The imitating of life and work situations awakens in them the capacity for meaningful self-development. Children try out and practice possible behaviors, educating themselves in the process (Patzlaff 2014, p. 19). They set themselves new tasks that they then try to resolve either by themselves or with their friends. It seems that there is no age when we learn as freely and intensely as in childhood and that modern culture, rather than digital and virtual games, urgently needs natural spaces that facilitate free and imaginative play (Kutik 2012, 2013; Vinzens 2013; id. et. al. 2011).

Since children start formal schooling at an ever earlier age, it is important for school education to accommodate the naturally imitative and playfully explorative way in which children learn, and gradually guides them toward a life-filled, memory-forming learning by the time the Rubicon phase starts. When it comes to imitation, three aspects are absolutely essential in Waldorf education: 1. the pedagogical relationship between teachers and pupils, 2. the need for movement and rhythm, 3. artistic imaginative learning. Each of these aspects shall be briefly explained:

At the transition from kindergarten to the grade school children face the challenge of having to enter into new relationships and make new friends. Much depends on how these children experience the class community and whether they can build a trustful, authority-based relationship with their teacher. In the first years of school children don't learn for themselves or in order to get good grades; they learn for the people they love, for "their" teachers and parents. At the beginning of grade school they still look for role models and imitate everything they perceive, down to external aspects such as the colors teachers wear, the way they move in singing games, the melody and rhythm of their speech, their handwriting, and so on. Some children like to reenact the whole school experience at home, memorizing many things through repetition. This is how children can increasingly appropriate what lived in the lessons, and in doing so reinforce and increase their memory. The healthy teacher-student relationship is a foundation for this.

Among the other elements that facilitate learning in the lower grades are movement and rhythm, which is why, in the 1990s, Wolfgang-M. Auer developed the concept of the *Moving Classroom* (Auer 2017; Chapter 3.5). The moving classroom no longer has desks and chairs lined up in rows, facing a writing board, but instead a variety of furniture that can be arranged by the children themselves depending on a given activity or task: children can get together to learn socially, in varying groups, in games and movement exercises, or in quiet listening and reflection—in rhythmic alternation between movement and stillness. With diversity and variety many discipline problems can be avoided because the children are not restricted but inspired in their need for movement and learning, while the initially purely imitative learning is expanded to accommodate teacher-guided learning. The repeated rhythmic participation in communal exercises encourages children to gradually develop self-determined learning. Attachment figures, role models, and good habits play an important part in the first years of school and for the further learning development. When the children reach school age, the immediate imitating of actions and attitudes gives way first to the recognition of an accepted authority, and then, from puberty, to self-determination and insight as to who is to be recognized as a role model worth imitating when it comes to particular tasks.

One of the hallmarks of Waldorf education is the pictorial, imaginative method of teaching recommended by Steiner, above all for the lower grades (Steiner GA 307, p. 121ff.; Wiehl 2015 p. 197ff.). Unlike Pestalozzi's "art of observation" (Pestalozzi 2009, p. 178) where elements of reading, writing, and arithmetic are taught through sensory experience, or the "ABC of observation," and then learned by rote, pictorial teaching aims to stimulate imagination and thinking in ways that allow children to absorb and internalize learning contents and activities in their own individual way. As the child's memory continues to form in the school years, its development is enhanced by feeling-based and action-oriented experiences that are imaginatively reenacted and remembered. By listening to stories, folktales, descriptions of plants and animals, or vividly related events—all always orally presented—children acquire the ability to actively pursue a train of imaginative thoughts, live themselves into the contents, and become creative out of the experience of these images. The letters of the alphabet are also introduced according to this method: every letter is derived from a story and from pictures that the children experience inwardly and then paint as pictures (Dühnfort/Kranich 1996; Wiehl 2015, p. 203ff.). Letters are not learned as abstract signs but the children go through an experience of how each letter could have emerged from an original image. The teacher may tell the story of a queen, for instance, and in drawing a picture of this story conceal the letter Q in it, which is then discovered by the children. This will be the "Queen letter" until the children have learned to isolate it and recognize it in diverse words. According to Steiner, the basic principle of pictorial teaching consists in letting all contents arise from images since this instills mobile thinking and living concepts in the children. Pictorial and imitative learning are related because, in both processes, the inner images are at the same time a reproduction and anticipatory creative potential. When children are inspired by varied and pictorial teaching, their playful imitative capacity can gradually transition into a learning capacity that becomes increasingly conscious and memory-forming.

The various research results presented here and the positions derived from them, above all the view of mimesis in anthropology and aesthetics, can form the foundation for an understanding of imitative learning and for concepts in child education that allow space for free and imaginative play in kindergarten and for artistic teaching and learning in grade school. If, in the light of Waldorf anthropology, one studies the inner processes involved in imitation and includes more recent research results, it becomes apparent that the child's inner formative forces and symbolizing imagination are instrumental to child development, to the organic and mental constitution, to learning, and to the capacity to participate in the social and cultural life. The forces of imitation are active throughout life, first in forming the organs and in moral development, then, from the time when children acquire speech, as awakeners of imagination and thinking. They can fully unfold when children have the possibility to play freely and they are practiced through artistic learning; as the children grow older, these forces manifest increasingly as living thinking and creativity. Waldorf kindergartens and schools were conceived as institutions where educators and teachers undergo training that gives particular consideration to imitative learning, both in the early years and in the grades. Artistic practice, sensory development, nature education, aesthetic appreciation, imaginative learning and teaching methods, child-appropriate story material and learning contents, the art of creating a suitable environment in kindergarten and school, and biographical-educational support are part of teacher development and make it possible to create conditions for children to develop and learn that are appropriate for our time. Learning—imitative learning in particular—takes place from person to person, in the human encounter.

5 Source Texts

Rudolf Steiner on the anthropology and education of childhood

INTRODUCED AND WITH A COMMENTARY BY

ANGELIKA WIEHL AND WOLFGANG-M. AUER

5.1 Introduction

Many statements and some longer passages on child development can be found scattered across Steiner's writings and lectures. Often, he takes up earlier statements and expands on them, looking at them from new angles and in different contexts. Certain basic motifs and processes are repeated or briefly touched on in order to underline what is essential and typical in child development. These specific aspects are also apparent in the selected source texts.

The topics addressed in the selected sources relate to the foundations and key aspects of anthroposophical childhood education. Our text study takes us from the anthroposophical image of the human being and understanding of human development (S1 to 6) to imitation, sense perception, and imagination as the three soul faculties that are essential influences in childhood (S 7 to 15), to the educational effect of folktale images, play, rhythm, and the temperaments (S 16 to 26), and finally to education as self-education, educational intuition, and meditative exercises (S 27 to 35). Steiner's statements are aphoristic: he outlines or hints at the topics briefly and explains or describes them, but they ultimately remain fragmentary, providing inspiration for the teaching practice in only an indirect way. Steiner's concern was that educators should, by studying spiritual science and anthroposophy, acquire a wider understanding of child development, the ability to observe the individual child, and a good educational attitude. His aphoristic presentations therefore serve as an orientation and inspiration for independent deepening.

Our selection of source texts does not cover all childhood-related aspects addressed in Steiner's work, nor does it claim to be a systematic synthesis. Rather, in addition to providing material for reading, the text passages aim to motivate readers to find creative ways of working in their individual studies, in groups of teachers working together, and in training seminars (see Chapter 6 for some ideas on teaching methods).

Steiner's idiosyncratic style, his enlivened concepts, and his specific anthroposophical terminology are only commented on in the brief introductions to the source text sections if that enhances comprehension. General as well as specific questions can nowadays be looked up online. It should just be mentioned here that, up until 1910 or 1911, Steiner referred to his anthroposophy, or anthroposophical spiritual science, as theosophy.

The source texts (= S) appearing at the end of each of the following subsections are taken from Steiner's collected works (GA, or *Gesamtwerk* in German), in other words from his numerous writings and lectures, irrespective of the audience he addressed in each individual case: whether he spoke publicly or in a theosophical or anthroposophical context. Figures 1 to 3 are taken from the sources indicated.

Translator's note to the English edition: This chapter contains many extracts from Steiner's writings and lecture cycles. A number of them were newly translated for this book, but some have also been taken from existing translations. Where this was the case, changes have occasionally been necessary, either in order to adapt the terminology to that of this book so as to avoid confusion or in order to update linguistic style or grammar to conform to today's requirements. I would like to express my sincere appreciation to my fellow translators for the immense amount of thought and effort that has gone into their work.

5.2 The image of the human being in Waldorf education

S 1 Body, soul, spirit (1904)

S 2 The evolving human being (1907)

Steiner presented his basic treatise on *Theosophy* in 1904 as a first contemplation of human beings as beings of body, soul, and spirit. Over the following twenty years he would add to and elaborate on these basic concepts, above all in his lectures on education. Body, soul, and spirit are the basic forms of human existence. With our physical body we are part of the physical world, just like minerals, plants, and animals. With our soul we absorb perceptions and experiences, furnishing with them our inner world. With our spirit we can rise above individual experiences and phenomena and learn about the essence of things and how they hang together. It is due to our "I," which is spiritual in nature, that we are evolving beings. The "I" lives in the soul and inspires the constituent members of our being to develop: our physical body, our ether or life body, our sentient or astral body, which is often also called the soul body. The physical body is inherited. The "I" as the bearer of our life intentions can reincarnate again and again on earth. These "repeated" lives are not to be understood as an eternal sameness, but they mean that, in each consecutive life, the "I" meets new situations and tasks that contribute to its development and growth (Chapter 2).

In the first source text (S 1) Steiner describes the human constitution of body, soul, and spirit before going on to differentiate each of these aspects further. The body consists of a physical organization, an etheric organization that generates life forces, and a soul or astral organization. Thinking, feeling, and will are soul forces. The contents of our thinking, such as rules or laws, ideas, thoughts, and mental images, are spiritual in nature. Steiner also differentiates three soul aspects: the sentient soul, which experiences and retains impressions as sensations; the mind soul, which comprehends the world in coherence; and the consciousness or spiritual soul, which he also calls the "soul within the soul," in which truth lives (Steiner GA 9, p. 31ff.).

Based on these anthropological considerations, Steiner spoke in 1906 and 1907 in various places about educational questions and went on to publish these talks himself in a small book called *The Education of the Child in the Light of Anthroposophy* (Steiner 1907). In the extracts from this book presented here (S 2) he speaks more concretely about the three constituent parts of the human organization that receive the "I" as their spiritual essence: the sentient or soul body, the life body, and the physical body, specifying the conditions they need for their development. Starting from birth, one of these constituents prevails for around six to seven years. Directly after birth, the physical body continues to develop; once school readiness is attained at the age of six or seven, the life body informs the child's development; in adolescence it is the soul body that dominates up until the birth of the "I" around the twentieth or twenty-first year, when young adults take hold of their own biography. Waldorf education allows the relevant constituent to develop in each of the seven-year phases of life so that the next "birth," or the unfolding of the next constituent, can take place in the right way.

These anthroposophical key aspects can be studied further in Bernard Lievegoed's book *Phases of Childhood: Growing in Body, Soul, and Spirit* (2005), as well as in Ernst-Michael Kranich's book on the anthropological foundations of Waldorf education (1999) and in Johannes W. Rohen's work on a functional and spiritual anthropology (2009), of which the latter two are only available in German.

S 1 Body, soul, spirit (1904)

By body is meant the means by which the things in our environment [...] reveal themselves to us. The word soul designates the means by which we link these things to our own personal existence, by which we experience likes and dislikes, pleasure and displeasure, joy and sorrow. By spirit is meant what becomes apparent in us when, as "quasi-divine beings," to use Goethe's expression, we look at the things of the world. In this sense, each person consists of body, soul and spirit. [...]

I. The Bodily Nature of the Human Being

We learn about the human body by means of our bodily senses, and our mode of observation can be no different than if we were learning about other sense-perceptible things. We can observe the human being in the same way that we observe minerals, plants and animals, and as human beings, we are related to these three other forms of existence. Like the minerals, we build up our bodies out of natural substances; like the plants, we grow and reproduce; like the animals, we perceive the objects around us and develop inner experiences based on the impressions they make on us. Therefore, we may attribute a mineral, a plant and an animal existence to the human being. The structural differences between minerals, plants and animals correspond to their three modes of existence.

Their structure or *Gestalt* (form) is what we can perceive with our senses, and this alone is what may be called "the body." The human body, however, is different from the animal body. We all recognize this difference, no matter what we may think about how humans are related to animals. [...]

Just as we attribute mineral, plant and animal modes of existence to the human body, we must also attribute to it a fourth and distinctively *human* mode. Through the mineral mode of existence we are related to everything visible, through the plant-like mode to everything that grows and reproduces, and through the animal mode to all creatures that perceive their environment and have inner experiences based on outer impressions. But through the human mode, even with regard to the physical body, we make up a kingdom that is ours alone.

II. The Soul Nature of the Human Being

As an *individual private* inner world, soul nature is different from bodily nature. Its intrinsic privateness becomes apparent as soon as we turn our attention to the simplest act of sensing. We cannot know whether or not others experience this simple sensation in exactly the same way. We know that some people are color-blind and experience things only in different shades of gray, while others are partially color-blind and cannot perceive certain gradations of color. The image of the world that their eyes provide is different from that of a so-called normal person. The same applies to the other senses, too, more or less. This is already enough to demonstrate that even a simple sensation belongs to the private inner world. With my bodily senses, I can perceive the same red table that someone else perceives, but I cannot perceive that person's sensation of red. Therefore, we must describe this sensation as *belonging to the soul*. Once we are quite clear about this, we will stop looking at inner experiences as mere brain processes or something of that sort.

Feeling follows closely on sensation, with one sensation arousing pleasure in us and another displeasure. These are the stirrings of our inner soul life. We each create an inner world of feelings in addition to the world that works in on us from outside. Then there is a third factor, our *will*, through which we work back upon the outside world, leaving the imprint of our own inner being on it. In will activity, the soul flows outward, in a sense. The fact that our actions bear the stamp of our inner life distinguishes them from natural events taking place in the outer world. In this way the soul sets itself up as something personal and private in contrast to the world outside. It receives stimuli from the outer world, but constructs an inner private world in accordance with them. Bodily existence becomes the basis for soul existence.

III. The Spirit Nature of the Human Being

The soul element in a human being is not determined exclusively by the body. We do not wander aimlessly and without direction from one sense impression to another, nor do we respond to every random stimulus that acts on us from outside or through our bodily processes. Instead, we think about our sensations and our actions. By thinking about our sensations, we come to an understanding of things; by thinking about our actions, we create a rational coherence in our lives. And we know that we are only worthily fulfilling our tasks as human beings when we let ourselves be guided by the *right thoughts*, both in knowing and in acting. Therefore, the human soul faces a dual necessity. Out of natural necessity, it is governed by the laws of the body, but because it freely recognizes their necessity it also allows itself to be governed by the laws that lead to correct thinking. Nature subjects us to the laws of metabolism, but as human beings we subject ourselves to the laws of thought.

Through this process, we make ourselves members of a higher order than the one we belong to through the body. This is the spiritual order. Soul is different from spirit, as different as it is from the body. As long as we simply speak of the particles of carbon, hydrogen, oxygen and nitrogen moving around in our body, we do not have the soul in view. The life of the soul begins only at the point where sensation arises within such movement, where we taste something sweet or feel pleasure. In the same way, we do not have the spirit in view as long as we consider only the inner experiences that pass through us when we give ourselves completely to the outer world and to the life of the body. Rather, this soul existence is the basis for the spiritual, just as bodily existence is the basis for soul existence. The natural scientist (biologist) deals with the body, the soul scientist (psychologist) with the soul, and the spiritual scientist with the spirit. Anyone trying to understand the essential nature of the human being by means of thinking is first required to come, through self-reflection, to a clear understanding of the difference between body, soul and spirit.

In: Rudolf Steiner (GA 9) (1994): *Theosophy. An Introduction to the Spiritual Processes in Human Life and in the Cosmos.* Hudson NY 1994, tr. Catherine E. Creeger. Chapter 1: The Essential Nature of the Human Being, p. 24 ff.

S 2 The evolving human being (1907)

If we look at life more deeply, we cannot help but feel that people today are often not adequately equipped to deal with the demands of modern life. Many try to reform life without truly understanding its foundations. Anyone wishing to submit proposals for the future must not be content with knowing life superficially. Life wants to be explored in all its deeper aspects.

As a whole, life is like a plant that contains more than what we see with our eyes. Like a plant, it holds its future potential hidden inside. When we see a plant that has only just developed leaves we know that, in due time, it will also produce blossoms and fruit. No one, unless they have gained insight into the plant's nature, can tell from its present appearance what these future organs will look like.

Human life also conceals its future potential within it, and in order to say anything about this future, one must explore its hidden nature. People today have little inclination to do this. Instead they are content to investigate what appears on the surface, fearing to step on uncertain ground when they are asked to penetrate to life's hidden depths. This is of course much easier in the case of plants. We know that a certain plant species has borne flowers and fruit before, while each human life is unique: the flowers it will bear were not there before, and yet they lie dormant in us just like the flowers do in a plant that has, so far, only developed stem and leaves.

And yet, we have the possibility to say something about this future human development if we look more deeply at human nature and penetrate to its very essence. The various reform ideas people have today can only become fruitful and practical if they grow out of such a deeper understanding of human nature.

It must be the task of spiritual science, which is well equipped for this, to provide a practical concept of the world that encompasses the essence of the human being. [...] Spiritual science does not invent programs but reads its program from reality, a program that includes the nature of evolution.

This is why a deepened spiritual-scientific investigation of human nature will provide the most fertile and practical means for resolving today's most urgent questions of life.

The example presented here relates to the question of education, and rather than express demands and establish programs, we shall simply describe the nature of the child. The essence of human evolution itself will provide the aspects that need to be considered in education.

In order to understand the growing child we must first explore the hidden aspects of human nature. What we learn about human nature when we observe it with our senses is all that counts in materialism, but for spiritual science it is only a part of human nature; it is merely the human physical body, which is subject to the laws of physical life and composed of the same substances and forces as everything else in the lifeless world. Spiritual science therefore holds that we have a physical body in common with the mineral world and that this physical body causes the same substances to intermingle, combine, arrange themselves, and dissolve that are at work in the mineral world in accordance with the same physical laws.

Beyond the physical body, spiritual science recognizes a second constituent principle, or mode of existence, which it refers to as life or ether body. Physicists should not be taken aback by the designation "ether body." Ether in this context is not the same as the hypothetical ether in physics. It should just be seen as a name for what is described below. [...]

Humans have this ether body or life body in common with plants and animals. The life body inhabits the physical body and is its architect and shaper, causing it to grow and reproduce and keeping all essential body fluids in movement. The physical body could therefore be seen as an image or impression of the life body. In humans, both bodies are similar but not entirely identical in form and size, while in animals, and even more so in plants, the life body differs considerably in shape and extension from the physical body.

The third constituent principle in human beings is the soul or astral body, the vehicle of pain and pleasure, of drives, desires, and passions. Beings that only consist of physical and life body do not have this dimension that we could call sentience. Plants are not sentient. Scholars today only reveal that they know nothing about sensation when they conclude that certain plants have sentience because they move or respond in some other way to external stimulation. Sentience is not a response to external stimuli but an inner reflection of such stimuli as pleasure or pain, drive, desire, and so on. If one does not consider this, one can just as well say that blue litmus paper has sensation because it turns red when it comes into contact with certain substances.

The sentient body—the bearer of sentience—we therefore only share with the animals.

It would be wrong to assume, as some theosophists do, that the life body and the sentient body merely consist of more subtle substances than the physical body. That would be quite a materialistic view of human nature. The life body is a force; it consists of active forces, not of substance. And the sentient or soul body consists of mobile, colorful, radiant images.

The soul body differs in form and size from the physical body. In humans, it is of a rounded oblong shape into which the physical body and the life body are embedded. Like a luminous figure it extends beyond both of them in all directions.

Human beings have a fourth constituent that no other earthly creature possesses and this constituent is the bearer of the "I". This little word "I" is a name that is different from any other name. Reflecting on this in the right way can help us to come to a deeper understanding of human nature. Any other name can be applied by everyone else to the object in question. Everyone can call a table "table" and a chair "chair." This is not the case with the name "I". No one can call another person "I"; we can only refer to ourselves as "I". I will never hear the word "I" applied to myself by someone else. By referring to myself as "I", I must inwardly name myself. A being that can say "I" to itself is a world in itself. The religions that are based on spiritual science have always sensed this and have therefore said that with the "I", the God who, to lower creatures, only reveals himself outwardly, in the phenomena of the world, begins to speak internally. The vehicle of the faculty described here is the I-body, the fourth constituent principle of the human organization.

This I-body is the vehicle of the higher human soul and makes humans the crown of earthly creation. But the "I" is not a uniform entity today. We understand its nature better when we compare various evolutionary stages, for instance so-called "primitive," uneducated people with those who strive for higher ideals. All of them are able to say "I" to themselves but while the "I" of the more primitive person will be guided by passions, drives, and desires, the more developed individual will decide to follow some impulses and drives whilst checking or suppressing others. Idealists will have developed higher inclinations and passions in addition to the original ones. They were able to do this because their "I" has worked on the other members of the human organization. The "I" has the task to ennoble and purify these other members of its own accord.

In those who have grown beyond the condition they originally found themselves in, the lower constituents have been transformed to a greater or lesser degree under the influence of the "I". In humans who have just begun to rise above animals, whose "I" is only just lighting up, the lower constituents are still animal-like. Their life body mainly carries the forces of life, growth, and reproduction, while their sentient body primarily expresses drives, desires, and passions that are stimulated by external nature.

By rising from this primitive to higher evolutionary stages through successive lives or incarnations, the "I" transforms the other human constituents. The sentient body becomes the vehicle for purified feelings of pleasure and displeasure, of refined wishes and desires. The life body also changes and become the vehicle of habits, lasting inclinations, temperament and memory. Someone whose "I" has not yet worked on their life body cannot remember former experiences but simply lives out what outer nature has implanted in them.

The whole of cultural evolution is expressed in this working of the "I" on the constituents subordinated to it, down to the physical body. Under the influence of the "I" the physiognomy changes, gestures and movements change, as does the appearance of the physical body.

One can even distinguish how the different cultural and educational measures work on the individual human constituents. Ordinary cultural factors have an effect on the sentient body, teaching it other kinds of pleasure and displeasure, drives, and so on than it originally experienced. Contemplating works of art has an effect on the life body. Because works of art awaken in us an inkling of something that is higher and nobler than what the sensory world has to offer; devoting ourselves to them transforms the life body. Religious impulses also have an important mission in human evolution because religion is another powerful tool for purifying and ennobling the life body.

What we call conscience is nothing other than the result of the "I" working on the life body through many incarnations. Conscience arises when we realize that we shouldn't do this or that and when this insight leaves an impression in us strong enough to imprint itself on the life body.

The work of the "I" on the subordinate constituents can either be of the kind that concerns humanity as a whole or it can be the "I" working on the individual self. In the first case the whole of humanity is involved in bringing about this transformation, in the latter it is the individual "I". When the "I" grows so powerful that it can, by itself, transform the sentient body, we call the result of this transformation of the sentient body "spirit self" (the oriental name is *Manas*). This transformation is essentially a learning process in which the inner being is enriched by higher ideas and visions.

The "I" can achieve something even higher when it works on our own self. This happens when it not only enriches the sentient (or soul) body but the life body, too. We learn much in the course of a lifetime. When we look back on our life at any point, we can say that we have learned a lot, but we will less often be able to speak of having managed to transform our temperament or character, or of having been able to strengthen or weaken our memory during life. Learning relates to the soul body, while the latter transformations relate to the ether or life body. It is therefore not a bad picture to compare the changes of the soul body to the progress of a clock's minute hand and the transformation of the life body to that of the hour hand.

When we embark on higher (or esoteric) development it is therefore essential that we achieve the latter transformation out of the power of our own "I". We must work on transforming our habits, temperament, character, memory and so forth entirely consciously and individually. The more we work into the life body in this way the closer we will come to transforming this life body into "life spirit," as this higher constituent is called in spiritual science (the oriental term is *Buddhi*).

At the next higher level we can then acquire powers that are able to transform the physical body (blood circulation or pulse, for instance). The transformed physical body then becomes the Spirit Human (*Atma* in oriental terminology). The transformations of the lower constituents that we achieve on behalf of humanity as a whole, or on behalf of a part of humanity such as an ethnicity, tribe, or family, have the following names in spiritual science: the sentient or soul body once it has been transformed by the "I" becomes the sentient soul; the transformed life body becomes the mind soul, and the transformed physical body becomes the consciousness (or spiritual) soul. This transformation of the three subordinate constituents does not occur consecutively but it happens simultaneously as soon as the spark of the "I" lights up. We only perceive this work of the "I" once a part of the consciousness soul has been developed.

From what has been said one can see that we can speak of four constituent members of the human being: physical body, ether or life body, astral or sentient body, and "I". Sentient soul, mind soul, consciousness or spiritual soul, and even the even higher modes of human existence—spirit self, life spirit, spirit human—arise as a result of the transformation of the first four constituents. It is also in these four that we find human characteristics and qualities.

As educators we address these four modes of being and in order to work on them in the right way we must examine them in depth. It would be wrong to assume that they are equally developed at any time in life, at birth for instance. They develop differently in the various stages of life. Knowing these developmental laws in human nature is the necessary foundation for teaching and education.

Before physical birth the developing child is surrounded by another physical body and does not yet have direct contact with the outside physical world. The mother's physical body is the child's natural surrounding and only this body can have an effect on the evolving human being. Physical birth means that the physical maternal womb releases the child who is from then on exposed to the influences of the surrounding physical world. The senses open toward this outside world. The outside world now takes on what the maternal womb did before.

From the point of view represented by spiritual science this moment means that the physical body has been born but the life body hasn't yet. Just as we are enveloped by the maternal womb up until the moment of birth, we are enveloped by ether and astral layers up until the change of teeth at around the age of seven. With this second dentition the astral layer releases the life body. The astral "womb" remains in place until puberty when the astral body (or soul body) is also set free, just as the life body was at the time of the change of teeth and the physical body in the moment of physical birth.

In spiritual science we therefore have to speak of three moments of birth. Up until the change of teeth, impressions that are meant to reach the life body can reach it as little as the light and air of the physical world can reach the physical body whilst it is still rests within the maternal womb.

In: Rudolf Steiner (1907): *Die Erziehung des Kindes vom Gesichtspunkte der Geisteswissenschaft*. In: id. (GA 34) (1987): *Lucifer – Gnosis. Grundlegende Aufsätze zur Anthroposophie und Berichte aus Zeitschriften «Luzifer» und «Lucifer – Gnosis» 1903 – 1908*. Second, revised edition. Dornach: Rudolf Steiner Verlag, p. 309ff. (First publication: *Lucifer-Gnosis* 33/1907).

5.3 Child development

The following source texts on child development focus on the first three years of life. The first (S 3) is taken from the beginning of the book *The Spiritual Guidance of Humanity and of the Individual* (Steiner GA 15), a series of lectures Steiner gave in 1911. It is about human beings as I-beings who are not determined by inheritance alone, but allow the fruits and tasks of previous incarnations to become effective from birth, as their own individual destiny. In the first years of life in particular, a child's "aura" can be perceived as a special radiance. This radiance is an expression of spiritual forces and, above all, of the child's higher self. It makes it possible for young children to learn to stand up, walk, speak, think and develop their brain. Out of spiritual forces, they achieve something unconsciously that we would not be able to achieve consciously. Only once these forces withdraw to the inside in the third year do children begin to feel as I-beings and develop memory (S 3). What is noteworthy in the second source text (S 4) is Steiner's reference to the differentiation of arms and legs that is expressed in the melody and rhythm of speech. For their development, particularly for their growth and organ formation, young children initially need their whole potential of formative forces in spirit and soul. Only once these generative processes have come to a conclusion with the second dentition will some of the formative forces become available for memory, imagination, and the love for things and people (S 5 and S 6). The formative (or etheric) forces are spiritual or soul-like in nature; they are at work in all life and growth processes, but they also form the foundation of our mental and spiritual faculties.

Jochen Bockemühl's *Toward a Phenomenology of the Etheric World* (Bockemühl et. al. 1985) or Ernst-Michael Kranich's anthropological foundations of Waldorf education (*Anthropologische Grundlagen der Waldorfpädagogik*, 1999) can give inspiration for further deepening. As an introduction we also recommend Karl König's *The First Three Years of Childhood*, which has been re-edited again and again since 1957 (König 2004).

S 3 Spiritual forces in child development (1911)

If we reflect upon ourselves, we soon come to realize that, in addition to the self we encompass with our thoughts, feelings, and fully conscious impulses of will, we bear in ourselves a second, more powerful self. We become aware that we subordinate ourselves to this second self as to a higher power. At first, this second self seems to us a lower being when compared to the one we encompass with our clear, fully conscious soul and its natural inclination toward the good and the true. And so, initially, we may strive to overcome this seemingly lower self.

Closer self-examination, however, can teach us something else about this second self. If periodically we look back on what we have experienced or done in life, we make a strange discovery, one that becomes more meaningful for us the older we become. Whenever we think about what we did or said at some time in the past, it turns out that we did a great many things we actually understood only at a later date. When we think of things we did seven or eight years ago—or perhaps even twenty years ago—we realize that only now, after a long time, our mind is sufficiently developed to understand what we did or said then. There are people who do not make such self-discoveries because they do not try to. Nevertheless, this sort of soul-searching is extraordinarily fruitful. For in such moments, as we become aware that we are only now beginning to understand something we did in our earlier years—that in the past our minds were not mature enough to understand what we did or said then—a new feeling emerges in our soul. We feel ourselves as if sheltered by a benevolent power presiding in the depths of our own being. We begin to trust more and more that, in the highest sense of the word, we are not alone in the world and that whatever we can understand or do consciously is fundamentally only a small part of what we accomplish in the world.

After we have gone through this process of discovery a number of times, an insight that is theoretically easy to understand can become part of our practical lives. We know, in theory at any rate, that we would not get very far in life if we had to do everything in full consciousness, rationally understanding all the circumstances and ramifications in every case. To see that this is so we need only consider how and when we accomplish those acts that are the wisest and most important for our existence. A moment's thought will reveal that we act most wisely in the time between birth and the moment at which memory, that first moment we can remember when in later years we try to recall our early life, begins.

This is to say that, as we think back to what we did three, four, or five and more years ago, we reach a certain point in childhood beyond which our memory does not extend. Our memory does not go back any further. Parents or other people can tell us what happened before that time, but our own memory does not go back beyond a certain point. This is the point in our lives when we first began to perceive ourselves as an "I". People whose memory is intact can usually remember back to, but not earlier than, this moment. Our souls, however, have already performed their wisest deeds *before* this time. Never again in later life, after we have attained full consciousness, will we be able to accomplish such splendid and tremendous deeds as those we accomplished out of the unconscious depths of our souls in the first years of childhood. As we know, we bring the fruits of earlier lives on earth with us into the physical world at birth. For example, at birth our physical brain is still an incomplete and unfinished instrument. The soul must then work on it, adding the finer, detailed structures that make it the medium of all the soul's faculties. In fact, before the soul is fully conscious, it works on the brain to transform it into an instrument to express all the capacities, aptitudes, characteristics, and so on, that it has as a consequence of earlier lives. This work on our own body is guided from a perspective that is wiser than anything we can achieve later with our full consciousness. Moreover, during this time when the brain is being transformed, we must also acquire the three most important capacities for life on earth.

The first capacity we must learn is to orient our body in space. People today do not realize what this means and that it touches on the most essential differences between human beings and animals. Animals are destined from the beginning to achieve their equilibrium in a certain way: one is destined to be a climber, another a swimmer, and so on. Animals are so constituted that from the outset they can orient themselves in space correctly. This is true even of primates. If zoologists were aware of this, they would put less emphasis on the number of similar bones, muscles, and so forth that human beings and animals have. After all, this is not nearly as important as the fact that human beings are not given an innate way to achieve equilibrium in space but must develop it out of their total being. It is significant that we must work on ourselves to develop from beings that cannot walk into ones that walk upright. We achieve our vertical position, our position of equilibrium in space, by ourselves. In other words, we establish our own relationship to gravity. Those who do not wish to consider the question deeply will, of course, easily dispute our explanation on apparently good grounds. They may claim, for example, that we are just as well constituted for walking upright as climbing animals are for climbing. Upon closer examination, however, we find that animals' orientation in space is determined by their physical organization. In human beings, it is the soul that establishes the relationship to space and shapes the organization.

The second capacity we learn out of ourselves from our essential being—which remains the same through successive incarnations—is *language*. This allows us to relate to our fellow human beings and makes us bearers of the spiritual life that permeates the physical world primarily by means of human beings. It has often been emphasized, and with good reason, that someone stranded on a desert island who had had no contact with other human beings before learning to speak would never acquire speech. What we receive through heredity, on the other hand, what is implanted in us for development in later years, does not depend on our interactions with other human beings. For example, we are predisposed by heredity to change teeth in our seventh year. Even on a desert island our second set of teeth would grow if we reached that age. But if our soul being, the part of us that continues from one life to the next, is not stimulated we will not learn to speak. In a sense, we must sow the seed for the development of the larynx in the time before our earliest memory—before we attain full I-consciousness—so that the larynx can then become an organ of speech.

There is still a third capacity, of which it is even less well known that we learn it on our own through what we bear within us through successive incarnations. I am referring here to our ability to live within the world of thoughts. Our brain is formed and worked on because it is the tool of *thinking*. At the beginning of life, the brain is still malleable because we must shape it ourselves to make it an instrument for the thinking appropriate to our essential being. The brain at birth is the result of the work of forces inherited from our parents, grandparents, and so on. It is in our thinking that we bring to expression what we are as individuals in conformity with our former earthly lives. Therefore, after birth, when we have become physically independent of our parents and ancestors, we must transform the brain we have inherited.

Clearly, then, we accomplish significant steps in the early years of life. We work on ourselves in accordance with the highest wisdom. In fact, if we had to rely on our own intelligence, we could not achieve what we must accomplish *without* our intelligence in the first few years of our lives. Why is this so? Why must all these things be accomplished from soul depths that lie *outside* our consciousness? Because, in the first years of our lives, our souls, as well as our whole being, are much more closely connected with the spiritual worlds of the higher hierarchies than is the case later. Clairvoyants, who can trace the spiritual processes involved because they have undergone spiritual training, discover that something tremendously significant happens at the moment when we achieve I-consciousness, that is, at the moment of our earliest memory. They can see that, during the early years of childhood, an aura hovers about us like a wonderful human-superhuman power. This aura, which is actually our higher part, extends everywhere into the spiritual world. But at the earliest moment we can remember, this aura penetrates more deeply into our inner being. We can experience ourselves as a coherent "I" from this point on because what had previously been connected to the higher worlds then entered the "I". Thereafter, our consciousness establishes its own relationship to the outer world. This conscious relationship to the outer world does not yet exist in early childhood. In childhood, a dream world still seems to hover about us. We work on ourselves with a wisdom that is *not* in us, a wisdom that is more powerful and comprehensive than all the conscious wisdom we acquire later. This higher wisdom works from the spiritual world deep into the body; it enables us to form the brain out of the spirit. We can rightly say, then, that even the wisest person can learn from a child. For the wisdom at work in children does not become part of our consciousness in later life. It is obscured and exchanged for consciousness. In the first years of life, however, this higher wisdom functions like a "telephone connection" to the spiritual beings in whose world we find ourselves between death and rebirth. Something from this world still flows into our aura during childhood. As individuals we are then directly subject to the guidance of the *entire* spiritual world to which we belong. When we are children—up to the moment of our earliest memory—the spiritual forces from this world flow into us, enabling us to develop our particular relationship to gravity. At the same time, the same forces also form our larynx and shape our brain into living organs for the expression of thought, feeling, and will.

During childhood, then, we work out of a self that is still in direct contact with the higher worlds. Indeed, to a certain degree, we can still do this even in later life, although conditions change. Whenever we feel that we did or said something in earlier years that we are only now coming to understand, we have an indication that we were guided by a higher wisdom at that earlier time. Only years later do we manage to gain insight into the motives of our past conduct. All this indicates that at birth we did not entirely leave behind the world we lived in before entering into our new, physical existence. In fact, we never leave it behind completely. What we have as our part of higher spirituality enters our physical life and remains with us. Thus, what we bear within us is not only a higher self that has to be developed gradually, but one that already exists and that often leads us to rise above ourselves.

All that we can produce in the way of ideals and artistic creativity—as also the natural healing forces in our body, which continuously compensate for the injuries life inflicts—originates not in our ordinary, rational minds but in the deeper forces that work in our early years on our orientation in space, on the formation of the larynx, and on the development of the brain. These same forces are still present in us later. People often say of the damages and injuries we sustain in life that external forces will not be of any help and that our organism must develop its own inherent healing powers. What they are talking about is a wise, benevolent influence working upon us.

In: Rudolf Steiner (GA 15), *The Spiritual Guidance of the Individual and Humanity*, Hudson NY 1992, beginning of Lecture 1, p. 3ff., tr. Samuel Desch.

S 4 Walking, speaking, thinking (1923)

Let's look now at young children as they grow into earthly life. Let our observations be straightforward and simple, and we shall find that there are three things with which they have to come to terms, three activities that become a decisive factor for the entire life to come. These are what are simply called walking, speaking, and thinking. [...]

The capacity to walk comprises far more than is generally realized. It is by no means simply a case of the young child—after the stage of crawling—managing to stand up and take the first steps in order to develop what will eventually become an individual and characteristic way of *walking*. An inner adjustment underlies learning to walk; there is an inner orientation of the young child. The equilibrium of the organism, with all its possibilities for movement, becomes related to the equilibrium and all the possibilities for movement of the whole universe, because the child stands within it. While learning to walk, children are seeking to relate their own equilibrium to that of the entire cosmos. They are also seeking the specifically human relationship between the activities of arms and hands and those of the other limbs. The movements of arms and hands have a special affinity to the life of the soul, while those of the legs lag behind, serving more the physical body. This is of immense importance for the whole of later life. The differentiation between the activities of legs and feet and those of arms and hands represents the human quest for balance of soul that is lifelong. When raising themselves up, young children are first of all seeking physical balance. But when freely moving arms and hands, they are also seeking balance of soul. There is infinitely more than meets the eye hidden behind what is commonly called "learning to walk," as everyone can find out. The expression "learning to walk" signifies only the most obvious and outwardly important aspect perceptible to our senses. A deeper look at this phenomenon would make one wish to characterize it in the following way. To learn to walk is to learn to experience the principles of statics and dynamics in one's own inner being and to relate these to the entire universe. [...] Better still, to learn to walk is to meet the forces of statics and dynamics both in body and soul and to relate these experiences to the whole cosmos. This is what learning to walk is all about. But through the fact that the movements of arms and hands have become emancipated from those of the legs and feet, something else has happened. A basis has been created for attaining a purely human development. Children who are learning to walk adapt themselves outwardly to the external, visible world with their own rhythms and beat, as well as inwardly with their entire inner being.

So you see that something very noteworthy is woven into the development of the human being. The activities of the legs, in a certain way, have the effect of producing in the physical and soul life a stronger connection with what is of the nature of beat, of what cuts into life. In the characteristic attunement of the movements of right and left leg, we learn to relate ourselves to what lies below our feet. And then, through the emancipation of the movements of our arms from those of our legs, a new musical and melodious element is introduced into the beat and rhythm provided by the activities of our legs. The contents of our lives—or one might say, the themes of our lives—come to the fore in the movements of our arms. Their activity, in turn, forms the basis for what is being developed when the child is learning to speak. Outwardly, this is already shown through the fact that with most people, the stronger activity of the right arm corresponds to the formation of the left speech organ. From the relationship between the activities of legs and arms, as you can observe them in a freely moving human being, yet another relationship comes into being. It is the relationship that the child gains to the surrounding world through learning to speak.

When you look at how all this is interconnected and belongs together, when you see how in the process of sentence formation the legs are working upwards into speech, and how the content, the meaning of words, enters into the process of sound production—that is, into the inner experience of the structure of the sentences— you have an impression of how the beat-like, rhythmical element of the moving legs works upon the more musical-thematic and inward element of the moving arms and hands. Consequently, if children walk with firm and even steps, if their walk does not tend to be slovenly, you have the physical basis—which, naturally, is a manifestation of the spirit, as we shall see later—for a good feeling for the structure of both spoken and written sentences. Through the movement of the legs, children learn to form correct sentences. You will also find that if children have a slouching gait, they will have difficulties finding the right intervals between sentences, and that the contours of their sentences become blurred. Likewise, if children do not learn to move their arms harmoniously, their speech will become rasping and unmelodious. In addition, if you cannot help children to become sensitive in their fingertips, they will not develop the right sense for modulation in speech. [...]

The third faculty children must learn on the basis of walking and speaking is thinking, which should gradually become more and more conscious. But this faculty must develop last, for it lies in the child's nature to learn to think only through speaking. In its early stages, speaking is an imitation of the sounds that the children hear. Because of their deeply rooted characteristic relationship between the movements of legs and arms, children absorb the sounds they hear and imitate them, initially without linking any thoughts to them. At first, they only connect feelings with the sounds. The thinking that then emerges can develop only out of speech. Therefore, the correct sequence we need to encourage in the growing child is learning to walk, learning to speak, and finally, learning to think.

In: Rudolf Steiner (GA 306) (1996): *The Child's Changing Consciousness as the Basis of Pedagogical Practice,* Hudson NY: Anthroposophic Press, Lecture 2, April 16, 1923, tr. R. Everett. Translation adapted

S 5 The first seven years (1924)

A newborn baby is truly the greatest wonder to be found in all earthly life. Anyone who is open-minded is certain to experience this. Children enter the world with a still unformed physiognomy, an almost "neutral" physiognomy, and with jerky and uncoordinated movements. We may feel, possibly with a sense of superiority, that babies are not yet suited to live in this world, that they are not yet fit for earthly experience. Children lack the primitive skill of grasping objects properly; they cannot yet focus their eyes properly, cannot express the dictates of the will through limb movement. One of the most sublime experiences is to see gradually evolve, out of the central core of human nature, out of inner forces, what gives the physiognomy its godlike features, what coordinates the limb movements to suit outer conditions and so on. And yet, if one observes children from a supersensible perspective, one cannot say that they have a physical body, an etheric or life body, and astral or soul body plus an "I", just as one cannot say that water in its natural state is composed of hydrogen and oxygen. Water does consist of hydrogen and oxygen, but these two elements are most intimately fused together. Similarly, in the child's organism until the change of teeth, the four human members are so intimately merged together that for the time being it is impossible to differentiate between them. Only with the change of teeth, around the seventh year, when children enter primary education, does the life body come into its own as the basis of growth, nutrition, and so on; it is also the basis for imagination, for the forces of mind and soul, and for the forces of love. If one observes children of seven with supersensible vision, it is as if a supersensible etheric cloud were emerging, containing forces that were as yet little in control because, prior to the change of teeth, they were still deeply embedded in the physical organism and accustomed to working homogeneously within the physical body. With the coming of the second teeth these forces become freer to work more independently and only some of them descend into the physical body. The rest then works in the processes of growth, nutrition, and so on, but also has free rein in supporting the child's life of imagination. These life forces do not yet work in the intellectual sphere, in thinking or ideas, but they want to appear on a higher level in a love for things and in a love for human beings. The soul has become free in the child's life body. Having gone through the change of teeth the child, basically, has become a different being.

Now another life period begins, from the change of teeth until puberty. When children reach sexual maturity, the soul body, which so far could be differentiated only very little, emerges. Children noticeably gain a different relationship to the outer world. The more of the soul body is born, the greater the change in the children. Previously it was as if the soul body were embedded in the physical and etheric organization.

To summarize: First, physical birth occurs when the embryo leaves the maternal body. Second, the etheric or life body is born when the child's own life body wrests itself free. Due to the emergence of the life body we can begin to teach children. Third, the astral or soul body emerges with the coming of puberty, which enables the adolescent to develop a loving interest in the outside world and to experience the differences between human beings, because sexual maturity is linked not only with an awakening of sexual knowledge, but also with a knowledge gained through the adolescent's immersion in all aspects of life. Fourth, I-consciousness is born only in the twenty-first or twenty-second year. Only then do we become independent I-beings.

In: Rudolf Steiner (GA 304a) (1996): *Waldorf Education and Anthroposophy 2*, Hudson NY: Anthroposophic Press, p. 205 ff., lecture of August 30, 1924. Tr. Roland Everett. Translation adapted

S 6 Developmental stages in the first seven years (1921)

Younger children are least accessible to the outside world. In the very first years, in particular, the gates to their soul life are closed off to any outside influences and to the will and intentions of the adults around them. To put it simply: they do what they want. And if we are honest with ourselves we have to admit that we are powerless as adults, especially with regard to what will become of the children in their later, and sometimes even latest stages in life. [...]

I have pointed out that suprasensory observation of human nature lets us distinguish a more refined body aside from the physical body. We have called this body "life body": the body of formative life forces. The life body, which provides the forces for growing, nutrition, and memory, is only really born when the change of teeth occurs. It is born out of the whole human being just as the physical body is born from the mother. This means that, up until the change of teeth, we will find its forces mainly at work in the child's organic growth processes. Later, they withdraw from this to a certain extent and we find them active in thinking, memory, and other mental activities that children begin to develop with the change of teeth.

Children only change their teeth once. The forces in the organism that drive out the second teeth are already active before these teeth appear; after that they are no longer needed in the organism and they are set free. What comes to a conclusion when the second teeth appear is, however, only an expression of the forces that are generally at work in the lower organism. A whole range of these forces becomes free for mental development at the end of this first stage of life. We can divide the whole course of human life into such stages, with the first of them lasting approximately until the seventh year. Each of these stages can be subdivided again into three distinct parts. When we look at this gradual liberation of certain forces of the life body from birth until around the seventh year, we see how in the first two and a half years after birth, this life body frees itself from the head, in the second two and half years from the chest, and then, up until the change of teeth, from the organism of metabolism and limbs. This explains why the life body, as long as it is still active in the head region, rejects the external will of the educator.

This is the phase in life when we learn the most important things, and we learn them by working inwardly on everything we have brought with us from our former existence. Just think how children learn to speak and walk at this time, faculties that are most intimately connected with personal and social self-assertion. These crucial faculties are acquired whilst the forces of the life body are still working on the brain, radiating out into the entire organism. [...] The work that is going on in there makes the young children inaccessible to any intentional outer influences: it closes the gates to the outside world. The children want to work on themselves inwardly.

In these first two and a half years it is particularly important that children are not susceptible to the will of others. They have a very fine, instinctive perceptiveness for everything that is going on around them, especially within the people, the educators, with whom they have an inner connection. This is not to say that they have sharpened their senses. That is not the case. They don't observe with their eyes but perceive in a subtle way with their whole being everything that happens in their environment, with the exception of any influences one tries to exert on them from the outside. In the first two and a half years, children instinctively reject anything that is aimed at influencing them. For us adults this means, however, that we need to take this susceptibility into account that keeps the child's consciousness submerged in feeling. [...]

Children in the first two and a half years have a similar inner connection with their educators—if these educators behave in the right way—and become their imitators in the most profound sense. We must therefore not try to impose our will on the children as a means of educating them. Our task is a slightly less comfortable one: we must make sure that our behaviors and attitudes are at all time worth imitating, because children are susceptible to everything we do, how we move and so on. Later they will imitate all of this, but now they develop inner imitative tendencies which they imprint into their bodily development with the help of the organic soul forces. Children are equally susceptible to our feelings and thoughts. In these first two and a half years, education can therefore only consist in our educating ourselves so that we are, in our thinking, feeling, and will, worthy of being imitated by the children. This continues for a few years, because the age of imitation continues until around the change of teeth. [...]

In the first two and a half years, children will be influenced by how we are around them. As they learn to speak, we must refrain from imposing anything on them through our will that we want them to say. All we need to do is speak naturally in their presence so that they can listen to us; and we need to have certain moral standards. Children take in what they hear and educate themselves accordingly.

Children don't learn to walk by our demonstrating to them how to stand. That can be done later in the gym lessons. Trying to make them stand and walk can have lasting detrimental effects on their nerve processes. It is best to leave the children to observe the uprightness of adults. They are imitators and will, when the time has come, stand up by themselves. When children have just entered life, we must look at them as imitating beings and arrange our education accordingly.

Once the children are around two and a half years old, the development of their head organization has advanced far enough for the life forces that have been working on it to be set free. In the next two and a half years, up until the age of around five, these forces will also be gradually released from the chest region. Breathing and circulation become free from these forces to a certain extent. The forces that are released from the head once the children have learned to speak and walk are then joined by those gradually released from their activity upon the chest organism. All these forces are now available for mental development and we see this in the vivid memory and imagination children unfold between the ages of two and half and five. As educators we have to pay particular attention to this twofold activity: the forming of memory on the one hand and the development of imagination on the other. The children continue to be imitators. In this respect, too, we must make sure that we don't intervene and impose our will on the children by drawing prematurely on their memory forces. At that age children must be left free to memorize what they want to memorize, what they want to remember. Memory exercises are most unsuitable at this age! [...]

As children approach the age of five, the part of the life body that has so far been working on breathing and blood circulation is set free. Up until the change of teeth, the life forces that are no longer needed for building up the systems of limbs and metabolism will also gradually wrest themselves free. We already sense the impact of these forces. They will only be fully released after the age of seven [...] but they are already shining through during this final part of the first main stage of child development. The formative forces released from the chest region are particularly susceptible to authoritative education. Unlike before, when they were purely imitators, children can now listen to instructions and see meaning in what they are told to do.

To summarize: During this first developmental stage, up until the change of teeth, children are imitators. They gradually develop memory and imagination, and only toward the end of this stage will a feeling for authority arise in them toward adults and educators in particular, with whom they have a close relationship. Knowing this will inspire the right attitude in educators, as well as the insight that, before the change of teeth, children can be educated but not taught. It therefore pains me to see that children have to start school at the age of six. Formal education should not start before seven.

In: Rudolf Steiner (GA 303) (1985): *Die gesunde Entwickelung des Menschenwesens. Eine Einführung in die anthroposophische Pädagogik und Didaktik.* 1921-1922, fourth edition. Dornach, p. 120ff. (Lecture 7: Children before the age of seven)

5.4 Imitation

S 7 Children learn from their environment (1923)

S 8 The child as sense organ (1922)

S 9 Imitation and development (1924)

S 10 Imitation and role models (1907)

In many of the lectures in which Steiner focuses on the second and third seven-year periods he refers to specific aspects of the first seven years, too, in order to convey an overall impression of child development from birth to adolescence. For Steiner, the child's imitative faculty is the most important foundation for a healthy development of body, soul, and mind. What characterizes imitation in childhood is that it goes beyond the mere copying of the children's surroundings or of the behaviors and attributes of people close to them; it has an artistic quality in that it holds the potential for creating and shaping something new (Steiner GA 271, p. 20; Chapter 4). When Steiner uses the word "imitate" he refers to the children's ability to perceive the world around them as "wholly sensory beings," with body, soul and spirit. Children take in everything that goes on around them, including attitudes and moods, to such an extent that it forms their physical organization, even if the children are not copying anything outwardly. Because children do not only imitate physical aspects but also the inner attitudes and moral orientation of those around them, it falls to educators to create an environment that has a beneficial effect on children, and to be role-models worth imitating by carrying out meaningful activities around the children and cultivating a positive inner attitude. The following four source texts describe the conditions for imitation in relation to aspects such as "religious devotion to the world" (S 7), "the child as sense organ" (S 8), "imitation forms the organism and the organs"

(S 9 and 10), and "duties and responsibilities of educators as role-models" (S 10). The first three extracts are taken from lectures on education that Steiner gave in various places between 1922 and 1924, speaking on the further development of Waldorf education from an anthropological point of view. The fourth text—his most in-depth description of imitation—is taken from the 1907 essay *The Education of the Child in the Light of Anthroposophy* (Steiner GA 34).

S 7 Children learn from their environment (1923)

You must always bear in mind that, pre-eminently during the first stage of childhood, but also up to the change of teeth, the child is one big sense organ. This is what makes children receptive to everything that comes from their surroundings. But it also causes them to recreate inwardly everything that is going on in their environment. One could say—to choose just one particular sense organ—that a young child is all eye. Just as the eye receives stimuli from the external world and, in keeping with its organization, reproduces what is happening there, so human beings during the first period of life inwardly reproduce everything that happens around them. But children take in what is coming from the environment with a specific, characteristic form of inner experience. For example, when seeing their father or mother moving a hand or an arm, children will immediately feel an impulse to make a similar movement. And so, by imitating the movements of others in the immediate environment, the usual irregular and fidgety movements of the baby gradually become more purposeful. In this way children also learn to walk. But we must not overemphasize the aspect of heredity in the acquisition of this faculty, because this constant reference to heredity is merely a fashion in contemporary natural-scientific circles. Whether a child first puts down the heel or the toes when walking is also due to imitating the father, mother, or anyone else who is close. Whether a child is more inclined to imitate one parent or the other depends on how close the connection is with the particular person, the affinity "in between the lines" of life, if I may put it this way. A subtle psychological-physiological process is happening here that cannot be recognized by the blunt tools of today's theories of heredity. To express it more pictorially: Just as the finer particles fall through the meshes of a sieve while the coarser ones are retained, so does the sieve of the modern world-view allow the finer elements of what is actually happening to slip through. In this way only the coarser similarities between child and father, or child and mother, only the "rough and ready" side of life is reckoned with, disregarding life's finer and more subtle points. The teacher and educator, however, needs a trained eye for what is specifically human.

Now it would be natural to assume that it must surely be love that motivates a child to imitate one particular person. But if one looks at how love is revealed in later life, even in a very loving person, one will come to realize that if one maintains that the child chooses on the basis of love, then what is actually happening has not been fully appreciated. For in reality, the child chooses to imitate out of an even higher motive than that of love. The child is prompted by what one might, in later life, call religious or pious devotion. Although this may sound paradoxical, it is nevertheless true. The child's entire sentient-physical behavior in imitation flows from a physical yearning to become imbued with feelings found in later life only in deeply religious devotion or during participation in a religious ritual. This soul attitude is strongest during the child's earliest years, and it continues, gradually declining, until the change of teeth. The physical body of a newborn baby is totally permeated by an inner need for deeply religious devotion. What we call love in later life is just a weakened form of this pious and devotional reverence. It could be said that until the change of teeth the child is fundamentally an imitative being. But the kind of inner experience that pulses through the child's imitation as its very life blood—and here I must ask you not to misunderstand what I am going to say, for sometimes one has to resort to unfamiliar modes of expression to characterize something that has become alien to our culture—this is religion in a physical, bodily guise. Until the change of teeth, the child lives in a kind of "bodily religion." We must never underestimate the delicate influences (one could also call them imponderable influences) that, only through a child's powers of perception, emanate from the environment, summoning an urge to imitate. We must in no way underestimate this most fundamental and important aspect of early childhood.

In: Rudolf Steiner (GA 306) (1996): *The Child's Changing Consciousness and Waldorf Education as the Basis of Pedagogical Practice*. Hudson NY: Anthroposophic Press. Lecture 3, April 17, 1923, p. 44f. Tr. R. Everett

S 8 The child as sense organ (1922)

In the first phase of life, up until the change of teeth, [...] the child is all sense organ. The child, one could say, is all head and all development arises from the neurosensory system as the source of the entire organism's formative forces. The neurosensory system permeates the whole organism and all outer impressions work through the whole organism. Later on they only work physically on the periphery of the sensory system, while their effect on the inside of the body is of a soul nature.

One could say that in adults the physical effects of light cease in the eye and the eye sends only the feeling-infused idea of the light into the organism. In children, every blood cell is physically stimulated by the light. However, these are not effects that can be verified with coarse physical methods. Children are still wholly devoted to the effects of the etheric essences that will later only be active on the body surface, in the sense organs, so that we can inwardly develop something entirely different. Up until the change of teeth, children are sense organs through and through, while adults are sense beings on the periphery and soul within. We can see this when we look at concrete examples. Adults who are looking after infants or babies will become their educators with their whole being. Imagine you are someone who tends to worry, and you have reason to worry. The physical consequences of your anxiety only subtly manifest in your constitution, facial expression and movements. When we worry, our mouth tends to be a little dry. And when worrying becomes a habit, when it persists, we walk around with a dry mouth, a dry tongue, and a bitter taste in the mouth, we even become slightly breathless. In adults, these physical states are merely dim undertones of life.

Children who grow up with adults imitate even their most subtle physical expressions. Because children are wholly sense organ, they absorb what they perceive in the adult's appearance, the anxiety expressed in the adult's voice and way of being. There is an imponderable interaction between children and adults. When adults worry, this is a state of soul but it will manifest physically. Children, being imitators, perceive these physical effects and their inner development will be affected by them just as the eye permeates itself with the effect of light. Children absorb the inner gesture manifest in the dry tongue and the bitter taste in the mouth. The adult's physical state imprints itself on the child's entire organism.

Children absorb the paleness they see in the anxious adult's face but not the inner content of their anxiety. They merely imitate the physical consequences of that anxiety. As a result, the child's physical constitution is permeated by the spiritual formative forces that reside in the neurosensory system. The adult's physically expressed anxiety affects the development of the child's inner physical and more refined organs and this child will later be disposed to worrying in a way other children are not.

Children can be educated by their physical organism to become worriers. It is essential that we know about such subtle effects if we want to educate children in the right way. This knowledge is as essential for educators and teachers as the ability to observe the effect of colors is for painters.

In: Rudolf Steiner (GA 305) (1991): *Die geistig-seelischen Grundkräfte der Erziehungskunst. Spirituelle Werte in Erziehung und sozialem Leben*. 1922. 3rd edition. Dornach: Rudolf Steiner Verlag, p. 58ff. (Lecture 4: Educating young children and the basic mood of the educator. August 19, 1922).

S 9 Imitation and development (1924)

I pointed out yesterday that, with the change of teeth, a radical change occurs in the child's development. What we call heredity or inherited characteristics only has a direct effect in the first phase of life. In addition, a second life organism is gradually built up physically during these first seven years. It is modeled on the inherited organism and will be complete once the change of teeth occurs. If the individuality descending from the spiritual, pre-earthly is weak, the second life organism will be similar to the inherited one. If the individuality is strong, we see how it gradually, between the change of teeth at around seven and puberty at around fourteen, gains a victory over the inherited characteristics. These children become quite different, even in their outer bodily form.

It is particularly interesting to look at the soul qualities that emerge in this second phase of life. In the first phase, before the second dentition, the child is—quite literally—wholly sense organ.

Take for example the human eye or ear. What is characteristic of such a sense-organ is its acute sensitivity to the impressions of the outer world. When we look at the eye in more detail we can see the kind of process that unfolds in it. In the first seven years the child is "all eye" so to speak. Now consider that of every object out there a picture is formed in the eye, an inverted picture. This is what we learn in physics today. The objects in the outside world occur as pictures in the eye. Physics leaves it there. But this picture-forming process is really only the beginning of what we should know about the eye. It is only the most external physical fact. [...]

But the child in the first seven years is really wholly eye. If something striking happens around a child, say an adult has a fit of anger, the whole child will have an inner picture of this outburst. The ether body takes in a picture of it. Something of this outburst permeates the child's entire circulation and metabolism.

This happens in the first seven years and the organism develops accordingly. These are very subtle processes, of course. The vascular system, the blood vessels, of children who grow up around an angry father or educator will adjust to this anger and the effect of this will last for life.

It is essential to know this about children. It is not what you say to the children and what you teach them that leaves an impression, even though they may copy what you say to them; what matters is what you are: whether you are good and this goodness manifests in your gestures, or whether you are bad or bad-tempered and this appears in your gestures—in short, everything you do is transmitted to and permeates the child. This is important to know. Children are wholly sense-organ and they react to all the impressions we evoke in them. It is essential that we realize that children don't learn what is good or bad, but that what we do around them is transformed into spirit, soul, and body within the child's organism. Children's health, throughout life, depends on the way we behave around them. The inclinations children develop depend on how we behave around them.

All the things one is advised to do in kindergartens are quite useless, however sophisticated they are made out to be. We are expected to be delighted with the clever ideas that have been developed for kindergartens in the course of the nineteenth century. Children learn so much. They almost learn to read. They are given letters of the alphabet and asked to fit them into cut-out shapes, and things like that. It all looks awfully clever and one is tempted to think that it actually benefits the children. But it doesn't. Not in the least. The work they do in kindergartens is soul-destroying. It affects the children's body and health adversely, because it weakens them in body and soul.

If, on the other hand, we receive the children in kindergarten and behave in a way that is worth imitating, if we do things children can imitate of their own accord, in the way they were accustomed to in their pre-earthly existence, then this may have the effect that they become like us and it is therefore our task to become worthy of this imitation.

In: Rudolf Steiner (GA 311) (1989): *Die Kunst des Erziehens aus dem Erfassen der Menschenwesenheit.* 1924. 5th edition. Dornach: Rudolf Steiner Verlag, p. 24ff. (Lecture 2 of August 13, 1924)

S 10 Imitation and role models (1907)

Before the change of teeth the life body is not yet free to work within the human being. Just as the physical body of the unborn child receives forces that are not its own while it gradually develops its own forces in the protected environment of the maternal womb, the life body continues to develop, up until the change of teeth, its own forces in conjunction with the inherited, foreign ones. During this first stage, as the life body is coming free, the physical body is already independent. The life body, as it liberates itself, is developing what it has to give to the physical body. When this work comes to an end the child's own teeth will have replaced the inherited ones. These new teeth are the densest substance embedded in the physical body and therefore only appear at the end of this developmental stage.

From then on, the life body alone is responsible for growth, although it is still under the influence of the as yet unborn astral or soul body. As soon as this soul body comes free, the life body reaches the end of a developmental phase and this conclusion manifests in the onset of puberty. The reproductive organs become independent because the soul body, which is free now, no longer works inwardly but meets the outside world directly.

Just as we can't expose the unborn child to the physical influences of the outside world, we should not, before the change of teeth, expose the life body to forces that have the same effect on it as impressions of the physical world have on the physical body. And the corresponding influences should not be allowed to affect the soul body until the beginning of puberty. [...]

With physical birth our physical body, which was until then protected by the maternal womb, is exposed to the physical environment of the outside world. It is now up to the forces and elements of the external world to take on the tasks that were previously carried out by the forces and fluids of the maternal organism. Up until the change of teeth around the child's seventh year, the physical body needs to work on itself in ways that differ essentially from what needs to happen in any other stages of life. The physical organs need to be formed in a particular way so that certain tendencies and directions can be imprinted in their structure. Any growth that will occur later will rely on the forms that emerge at this stage, up until the change of teeth. If the right forms evolve now, the right forms will grow later; abnormalities at this stage will result in wrong forms developing later. We will not be able to make up later for anything that was neglected by educators during this first developmental stage before the age of seven. Just as nature provides the right environment for our physical body before birth, educators have to provide the right physical environment after birth. This is essential so that the child's organs can form themselves in the right way.

There are two magic words to describe how children relate to the world around them: imitation and example. The Greek philosopher Aristotle referred to humans as the most imitative of all animals. At no time is this statement truer than in the first stage of childhood up until the change of teeth. Children imitate everything that is going on in their physical environment and as they imitate, their physical organs develop the forms that will then become permanent. The term "physical environment" needs to be understood in the widest possible sense, however. It is not restricted to material aspects but includes everything that happens around children, everything they perceive with their senses, everything that might work on their spiritual powers from the physical space around them, including any moral or immoral behaviors, clever or foolish actions they experience.

It is not our moralizing and admonishing that will have an effect on the children, but what we do visibly as adults in front of their eyes. Admonitions don't form the physical body, they form the life body. But until the age of seven the life body, or ether body, is enveloped by a protective etheric womb, just as the physical body is protected by a physical womb until physical birth occurs. All the ideas, habits, and memories that need to be formed in the life body before the seventh year, must form "by themselves," just as the eyes and ears are formed in the womb without the influence of external light. [...] What

Jean Paul wrote in his excellent educational book *Levana or Science of Education* is undoubtedly true: a traveler will learn more from his nurse in early childhood than he will on all his later journeys around the world. But children do not learn through instruction, they learn through imitation. Their physical organs form themselves under the influence of their physical environment.

Children develop good eyesight if we make sure that they are surrounded by the right color and light conditions; and the right physical foundations for a healthy sense of morality will be created in the brain and blood circulation if children experience moral behavior around them. If children only perceive foolish actions around them before the age of seven, their brain will be formed in such a way that they themselves are only capable of foolish actions in later life.

Just as the muscles in our hands only grow strong if they are allowed to carry out the appropriate movements, the brain and the other organs of the physical body will only develop in the right way if they can absorb the right impressions from their environment. I give you an example: you can make a doll for a child by tying an old napkin in the middle, turning two ends into legs and the other two into arms, making a knot for a head, and indicating eyes, nose, and mouth with blots of ink. Or you can give the child a "pretty" doll with real hair and painted cheeks that you have bought in a shop. This is not even about the fact that this doll is horrible and will spoil the child's aesthetic sense for life. The main point that interests us as educators is that children who play with rag dolls need to use their imagination to fill in what makes the doll look human. This use of the imagination forms the brain and makes it grow stronger just as the muscles of the hand grow stronger when they perform activities suited to them. If we give children "pretty" dolls, their brain has nothing to do and it will dry out rather than grow stronger. If people could look into the developing brain in the way spiritual scientists can, they would only give their children toys that stimulate formative brain activity. Toys that are based on dead mathematical forms have a dulling, deadening effect on the children's formative forces, while everything that inspires living ideas works on them in a desirable way. Good toys are rare in our materialistic times. A healthy toy is, for example, one that consists in two movable wooden figures representing blacksmiths who face each other and are hammering an anvil. You can still find such toys in more rural areas. Or picture books with moveable parts that can be set in motion by pulling threads, so that the children can transform the still images into representations of living actions. This keeps the inner organs mobile and allows them to form in the right way. [...]

I would like to mention a few more examples. Nervous and excited children require a different environment from children who are quiet and lethargic. This applies as much to the colors of the room and other objects that are usually around children as to the colors of the clothes one gives them to wear. It is easy to go wrong in this respect if one is not guided by spiritual science because materialistic minds will often do the exact opposite of what is healthy. Excitable children need to be surrounded by red and reddish-yellow colors and they should also wear clothes in these colors, while one should choose blue or bluish green shades for lethargic children. The important thing to know is that the children inwardly create the complementary color to the one they perceive externally. The complementary color to red is green and that to blue is orangey-yellow. You can try this out by looking for a while at a red or blue surface and then at a white one. The complementary color is produced by the child's physical organs and then brings about the corresponding organic structures that the child needs. If excitable children are surrounded by red, they will produce the complementary color, green, within and this inner creating of green has a calming effect on them. The organs absorb the calming tendency.

With this age group it is essential to realize that the physical body creates its own benchmarks for what it can tolerate. It does this by adjusting its level of desire. Generally speaking one can say that the healthy physical body desires what is good for it. And as long as the growing child's physical development is our main concern, we need to look closely at what the body desires, enjoys, and needs. Joy and pleasure are the forces that most promote the forming of the physical organs. We can make serious mistakes in this respect if we don't help the children adjust physically to their environment in the right way, especially when it comes to their food instincts. If we give them too much of something they might lose their healthy eating instincts, while the right nutrition can help them retain these instincts, so that they will always ask for what is good for them, down to a glass of water, and reject what could harm them. [...]

Joy in their surroundings is therefore among the forces that form children's physical organs; the cheerful faces of educators and above all their honest and unaffected love: a love that streams warmly through the child's physical environment "breeds" the forms of the physical organs.

Children are in their element when they can imitate healthy role-models in such a loving atmosphere, and this is why we must make sure that nothing happens around the children that they must not imitate. You should do nothing of which you have to say to the children that they must not do it. How keen children are on imitation is apparent from the way they happily draw or paint letters long before they can understand their meaning. And it is good that they draw them by imitation first and only later understand what they are, because imitation belongs to the period when the physical body develops, while meaning speaks to the life body, and the life body should not be worked on until after the change of teeth, when the outer etheric layers have fallen away. At this stage it is essential that the children learn to speak by imitation. Children best learn to speak when they listen. Rules and artificial instruction will be of no use.

Children's songs are an important educational tool in early childhood because of the rhythmic impression they make on the senses. The beauty of the sound is what counts, not the meaning of the words. The more refreshing their effect is on eyes and ears the better. Don't underestimate how powerfully dancing to musical rhythms impacts on the building up of physical organs.

In: Rudolf Steiner (1907): *Die Erziehung des Kindes vom Gesichtspunkte der Geisteswissenschaft.* In: id.. (GA 34) (1987): *Lucifer – Gnosis. Grundlegende Aufsätze zur Anthroposophie und Berichte aus Zeitschriften «Luzifer» und «Lucifer – Gnosis» 1903-1908.* 2nd, newly revised edition. Dornach: Rudolf Steiner Verlag, p. 309ff. (First published in *Lucifer Gnosis* No 33, May 1907).

5.5 The sensory organization

S 11 The twelve senses (1916)

S 12 Twelve senses and seven life processes (1916)

"The child is all sense organ" is how Rudolf Steiner characterizes children's imitative relationship with the world. When children imitate, their whole organism resonates with their environment, responding like one whole sense organ to external impressions, absorbing them and being shaped by them. Of course, this doesn't mean that children only need one sense. Right from the beginning, all the senses are active as children perceive others and learn from them, through imitation, how to move, walk upright, speak, and think. All the senses are available from birth, but before children can use them they first have to develop their sensory organization, which happens as the children absorb the perceptions *we*, particularly in the first six to seven years, enable them to have. The following texts contain Steiner's descriptions of the twelve senses, which encompass the whole spectrum of our perceptive capacity. He uses varying categories in his presentation of the senses, attributing them, for instance, to the zodiac or dividing them into lower, middle, and higher senses, or into will senses, feeling senses, and thinking senses. In the first text (S 11) he separates the senses into two groups: day senses and night senses. When we use the "night senses," our perceptions remain more or less unconscious and are difficult to remember, while they are relatively conscious, as in bright daylight, when we use the "day senses." It needs to be pointed out that the passage about the organ and the development of the sense of balance does not entirely correspond to modern research (Chapter 3). In the second text (S 12) Steiner discusses how we relate to the world through the different senses: when are we more inside our body, when more outside in the world, and when we even penetrate the external world. This is followed by a discussion of the seven life processes that permeate everything that lives, including our senses. Although these processes are not so well known they play an important role in any kind of learning.

More information on the seven life processes, particularly in relation to early childhood, can be found in Gelitz and Strehlow's (2016) introduction to the theme. Auer has published an in-depth study of the senses with extensive bibliographical notes (Auer 2007; Soesman 2017; Chapter 3).

S 11 The twelve senses (1916)

Everything we have in us, everything we experience in our soul, is related to the outer world through the twelve senses. These are the senses of touch, life, movement, balance, smell, taste, sight, warmth, hearing, speech, thinking, and the sense of "I". Our inner life moves through this circle of the twelve senses just as the sun moves through the circle of the twelve signs of the zodiac. But we can take this external analogy even further. In the course of a year, the sun has to move through all the signs of the zodiac from Aries to Libra; it moves through the upper signs during the day and through the lower ones at night. The sun's passage through these lower signs is hidden from outer light. It is the same with the life of our soul and the twelve senses. Half of the twelve are day senses, just as half of the signs of the zodiac are day signs; the others are night senses.

You see, our sense of touch pushes us into the night life of our soul, so to speak, for with the sense of touch, one of our coarser senses, we bump into the world around us. The sense of touch is barely connected with the day life of our soul, that is, with the really conscious life of the soul. You can see for yourself that this is true when you consider how easily we can store the impressions of our other senses in our memory and how difficult it is to remember the impressions of the sense of touch. Just try it and you'll see how difficult it is to remember, for example, the feel of a piece of fabric you touched a few years ago. Indeed you'll find you have little need or desire to remember it. The impression sinks down in the same way as the light fades into twilight when the sun descends into the sign of Libra at night, into the region of the night signs. And the other senses are then completely hidden from our waking, conscious soul life.

As for the sense of life, conventional psychological studies hardly mention it at all. They usually list only five senses, the day senses or senses of waking consciousness. But that need not concern us further. The sense of life enables us to feel our life in us, but only when that life has been disturbed, when it is sick, when something causes us pain or hurts us. Then the sense of life tells us we are hurting here or there. When we are healthy, we are not aware of the life in us; it sinks into the depths, just as there is no light when the sun is in the sign of Scorpio or in any other night sign.

The same applies to the sense of movement. It allows us to perceive what is happening in us when we have set some part of our body in motion. Conventional science is only now beginning to pay attention to this sense of movement. It is only just beginning to find out that the way joints impact on one another—for example, when I bend my finger, this joint impacts on that one—tells us about the movements our body is carrying out. We walk, but we walk unconsciously. The sense underlying our ability to walk, namely, the perception of our mobility, is cast into the night of consciousness.

Let us now look at the sense of balance. We acquire this sense only gradually in life; we just don't think about it because it also remains in the night of consciousness. Infants have not yet acquired this sense, and therefore they can only crawl. It was only in the last decade that science discovered the organ for the sense of balance. I have mentioned the three canals in our ears before; they are shaped like semicircles and are vertical to each other in the three dimensions of space. If these canals are damaged, we get dizzy; we lose our balance. We have the outer ears for our sense of hearing, the eyes for the sense of sight, and for the sense of balance we have these three semicircular canals. Their connection with the ears and the sense of hearing is a vestige of the kinship between sound and balance. The canals, located in the cavity in the petrosal bone, consist of three semicircles of tiny, very minute, bones. If they are the least bit injured, we can no longer keep our balance. We acquire our receptivity for the sense of balance in early childhood, but it remains submerged in the night of consciousness; we are not conscious of this sense. Then comes the dawn and casts its rays into consciousness.

But just think how little the other hidden senses, those of smell and taste, actually have to do with our inner life in a higher sense. We have to delve deeply into the life of our body to be able to get a sense for smell. The sense of taste already brings us a growing half-light; day begins to dawn in our consciousness. But you can still make the same experiment I mentioned before concerning the sense of touch, and you will find it very difficult to remember the perceptions of the senses of smell and of taste. Only when we enter more deeply into our unconscious with our soul does the latter consciously perceive the sense of smell. As you may know, certain composers were especially inspired when surrounded by a pleasant fragrance they had smelled previously while creating music. It is not the fragrance that rises up out of memory, but the soul processes connected with the sense of smell emerge into consciousness. The sense of taste, however, is for most people almost in the light of consciousness, though not quite; it is still partly in the night of consciousness for most of us. After all, very few people will be satisfied with the soul impression of taste alone. Otherwise we should be just as pleased with remembering something that tasted good as we are when we eat it again. As you know, this is not the case. People want to eat again what tasted good to them and are not satisfied with just remembering it.

The sense of sight, on the other hand, is the sense where the sun of consciousness rises, and we reach full waking consciousness. The sun rises higher and higher. It rises to the sense of warmth, to the sense of hearing, and from there to the sense of speech and then reaches its zenith. The zenith of our inner life lies between the senses of hearing and speech. Then we have the sense of thinking, and the sense of "I", which is not the sense for perceiving our own "I" but that of others. [...] What is important here is not so much knowing about our own "I", but meeting other people who reveal their "I" to us. Perception of the other person's "I", not of our own, that is the function of the "I" sense.

Our soul has the same relationship to these twelve senses as the sun does to the twelve signs of the zodiac.

In: Rudolf Steiner (GA 169) (1990): *Toward Imagination. Culture and the Individual.* Hudson NY: Anthroposophic Press. Tr. Sabine H. Seiler. Lecture 3, June 20, 1916: "The Twelve Human Senses".

S 12 The twelve senses and seven life processes (1916)

An understanding of how human beings relate to the world requires us to distinguish twelve senses. Today I would like, once again, to describe these twelve senses.

The sense of touch is the sense that relates us to the most material aspect of the external world. With our sense of touch we, so to speak, bump into the external world; through touch we are continually involved in a coarse kind of exchange with the external world. Nevertheless, the process of touching takes place within the boundaries of our skin. Our skin collides with an object. What then happens to give us a perception of the object must, as a matter of course, take place within the boundaries of our skin, within our body. What happens in touching, in the process of touch, therefore happens inside us.

The sense that we shall call the sense of life involves processes that lie still more deeply embedded in the human organism. This sense exists within us, but we tend to ignore it, for the life sense manifests indistinctly from within the human organism. Nevertheless, throughout all our daily waking hours, the harmonious collaboration of all the bodily organs expresses itself through the life sense, through the state of life in us. We usually pay no attention to it because we expect it as our natural right. We expect to be filled with a certain feeling of wellbeing, with the feeling of being alive. If our feeling of alive-ness is diminished, we try to recover a little so that it is refreshed again. This vital enlivening or damping down is something we are aware of, but generally we are too accustomed to the feeling of being alive to be constantly aware of it. The sense of life, however, is a distinct sense in its own right. Through it we feel the life in us, precisely as we see what is around us with our eyes. We sense ourselves through the life sense just as we see with our eyes. Without this internal sense of life we would know nothing about our own vital state.

What can be called the sense of movement is still more inward, more physically inward, more bodily inward. Through feelings of wellbeing or of discontent the life sense makes us conscious of the state of the whole organism. Having a sense of movement, on the other hand, means being able to be aware of the way parts of the body move with respect to each other. I do not refer here to movements of the whole person—that is something else. I am referring to movements such as the bending of an arm or leg, or the movements of the larynx when you speak. The sense of movement makes you aware of all these inner movements that entail changes in the position of separate parts of the organism.

A further sense that must be distinguished is the sense we will call balance. We do not normally pay any attention to it. If we get dizzy and fall, or if we feel faint, it is because the sense of balance has been interrupted. This is exactly analogous to the way the sense of sight is interrupted when we close our eyes. When we relate ourselves to the world, orienting ourselves with respect to above and below and to right and left so that we feel upright, we are employing our sense of balance, just as we employ the sense of movement when we are aware of internal changes of position. Our sense of balance [...] is a proper sense in its own right.

[...] The first sense to take you outside yourself is the sense of smell. With smell you already come into contact with the external world. But you will have the feeling that smell does not take you very far outside yourself. You do not experience much about the external world through the sense of smell. Furthermore, people—unlike dogs—are not interested in the intimate connection with the world that a developed sense of smell can give. They are willing to use the sense of smell to perceive the world, but they do not want the world to come very close. It is not a sense through which people want to get very much involved with the outer world.

With the sense of taste we get more deeply involved with the world. When we taste sugar or salt, the experience of its qualities is already very inward. What is external is taken inward—more so than with smell. So there is already more of a connection established between inner world and outer world.

The sense of sight involves us even more with the external world. In seeing, we take into ourselves more of the properties of the external world than we do with the sense of smell. And we take yet more into ourselves with the sense of warmth. What we see, what we perceive through the sense of sight, remains more foreign to us than what we perceive through the sense of warmth. The relationship to the outer world perceived through the sense of warmth is already a very intimate one. When we are aware of the warmth or the coldness of an object we also experience this warmth or coldness—we experience it along with the object. On the other hand, in experiencing the sweetness of sugar, for example, one is not so involved with the object. In the case of sugar we are interested in what it becomes as we taste it, not in what it is out there in the world. Such a distinction ceases to be possible with the sense of warmth. With warmth we are already participating in what is within the object perceived.

When we turn to the sense of hearing, the relation to the external world acquires a further degree of intimacy. A sound tells us very much indeed about the inner structure of an object—more than what the sense of warmth can tell, and very much more than what sight reveals. Sight only gives us pictures, so to speak, pictures of the outer surface. But when a metal resonates it tells us what is going on within it. The sense of warmth also reaches into the object. When I take hold of something, a piece of ice, say, I am sure that the ice is cold through and through, not just on its outer surface. When I look at something, I can see only the colors at its outer limits, on its surface; but when I make an object resonate, the sounds bring me into a particular relationship with what is within it.

And the intimacy is greater still if the sounds contain meaning. Thus we arrive at the sense of tone: perhaps it would be better to call it the sense of speech or the sense of word. It is simply nonsense to think that perception of words is the same as perception of sounds. The two are as distinct and different from one another as are taste and sight. To be sure, sounds open the inner world of objects to our perception, but these sounds must become much more inward before they can become meaningful words. Therefore it is a step into a deeper intimacy with the world when we proceed from perceiving sounds through the sense of hearing to perceiving meaning through the sense of the word. And yet, when I perceive a mere word I am still not so intimately connected with the object, with the external thing, as I am connected with it when I perceive the thoughts behind the words. At this stage, most people cease to make any distinctions. But there is a distinction between merely perceiving words and actually perceiving the thoughts behind the words. After all, you still can perceive words when a phonograph—or writing, for that matter—has separated them from their thinker. But a sense that goes deeper than the usual word sense must come into play before I can come into a living relationship with the being that is forming the words, before I can enter through the words and transpose myself directly into the being that is doing the thinking and forming the concepts. That further step calls for the sense I would like to call the sense of thought. And there is another sense that gives an even more intimate sense of the outer world than the sense of thought. It is the sense that enables you to feel another being as yourself and that makes it possible to be aware of yourself while at one with another being. That is what happens if one turns one's thinking, one's living thinking, towards the being of another. Through living thinking one can behold the "I" of this being: the sense of "I". [...] When we speak of the sense of "I", we are referring to the ability of one person to be aware of the "I" of another. [...] In truth, when we meet someone and perceive their "I" we perceive it just as directly as we perceive a color. It really is sheer ignorance to believe that the presence of another "I" is deduced from bodily perceptions, for this obscures the truth that humans have a special, higher sense for perceiving the "I" of another. The "I" of another is perceived directly by the sense of "I", just as brightness and darkness and colors are perceived through the eyes. It is a particular sense that relates us to another "I". This is something that has to be experienced. Just as a color affects me directly through my eyes, so another person's "I" affects me directly through my sense of "I". The time will come when we will speak about the sense organ for this sense of "I" in the same way we speak about the sense organs of seeing, of sight. With sight it is simply easier to refer to material manifestations than it is in the case of the sense of "I", but each sense has its own particular organ.

If you view your senses from a certain perspective you can say: each sense particularizes and differentiates my organism. There is a real differentiation, for seeing is not the same as perception of tone, perception of tone is different from hearing, hearing is not the same as perception of thought, perception of thought is not touching. Each of these senses demarcates a separate and particular region of the human being. It is this separation of each into its special sphere to which I want you to pay close attention, for it is this separation that makes it possible to picture the senses as a circle divided into twelve distinct regions. (Fig. 1)

The situation of these powers of perception is different from the situation of forces that could be said to reside more deeply embedded within us. Seeing is bound up with the eyes and these constitute a particular region in the human organism. Hearing is bound up with the organs of hearing, at least principally so, but it needs more besides—hearing involves much more of the organism than just the ear, which is what is normally thought of as the region of hearing. Life flows equally through each of these regions of the senses. The eye is alive, the ear is alive, and the foundation of all these senses is alive; the basis of touch is alive—all of it is alive. Life resides in all the senses; it flows through all the regions of the senses.

Fig. 1

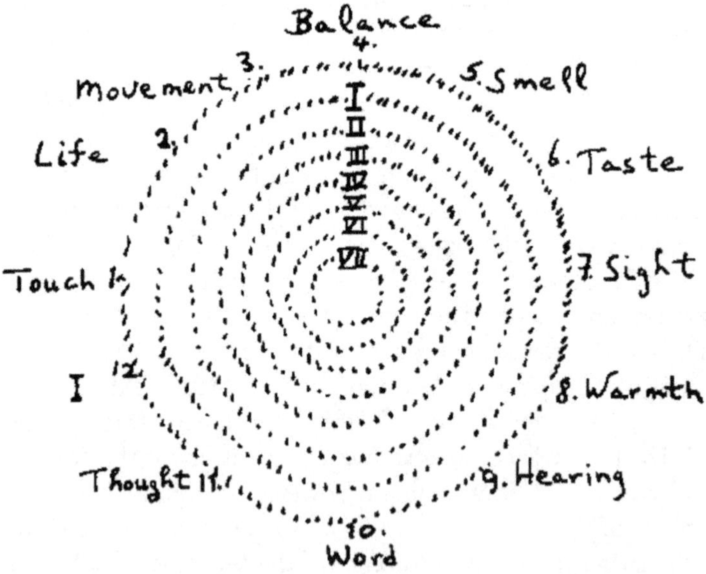

If we look more closely at this life, it also proves to be differentiated. There is not just one life process. And you must also distinguish what we have been calling the sense of life, through which we perceive our own vital state, from the subject of our present discussion. What I am talking about now is the very life that flows through us. That life also differentiates itself within us. It does so in the following manner (Fig. 2). The twelve regions of the twelve senses are to be pictured as being static, at rest within the organism. But life pulsates through the whole organism, and this life is manifested in various ways. First of all there is breathing, a manifestation of life necessary to all living things. Every living organism must enter into a breathing relationship with the external world. Today I cannot go into the details of how this differs for animals, plants and human beings, but will only point out that every living thing must have its way of breathing. Human breathing is perpetually renewed by what we take in from the outer world, and this benefits all the regions associated with the senses. The sense of smell could not manifest itself—nor sight or the sense of tone—if the benefits of breathing did not enliven it. Thus, I must assign "breathing" to every sense. We breathe—that is one process— but the benefits of that process of breathing flow to all the senses.

Fig. 2

The second process we can distinguish is warming. This occurs along with breathing, but it is a separate process. Warming, the inner process of warming something through, is the second of the life-sustaining processes. The third process that sustains life is nourishment. So here we have three ways in which life comes to us from without: breathing, warming, nourishing. The outer world is part of each of these. Something must be there to be breathed—in the case of humans, and also animals, that substance is air. Warming requires a certain amount of warmth in the surroundings; we interact with it. Just think how impossible it would be for you to maintain proper inner warmth if the temperature of your surroundings were much hotter or much colder. If it were one hundred degrees lower your warmth processes would cease, they would not be possible; at one hundred degrees hotter you would do more than just sweat! Similarly, we need food to nourish us as long as we are considering the life processes in their earthly aspects.

At this stage, the life processes take us deeper into the internal world. We now find processes that re-form what has been taken in from outside—processes that transform and internalize it. To characterize this re-forming, I would like to use the same expressions that we have used on previous occasions. Our scientists are not yet aware of these things and therefore have no names for them, so we must formulate our own. The purely inner process that is the basis of the re-forming of what we take in from outside us can be seen to be fourfold. Following the process of nourishing, the first internal process is the process of secretion, of elimination. When the nourishment we have taken in is distributed to our body, this is already the process of secretion; through the process of secretion it becomes part of our organism. The process of elimination does not just work outward, it also separates out that part of our nourishment that is to be absorbed into us. Excretion and absorption are two sides of the processes by which organs of secretion deal with our nourishment. One part of the secretion performed by organs of digestion separates out nutriments by sending them into the organism. Whatever is thus secreted into the organism must remain connected with the life processes, and this involves a further process which we will call maintaining. But for there to be life, it is not enough for what is taken in to be maintained, there also must be growth. Every living thing depends on a process of inner growth: a process of growth, taken in the widest sense. Growth processes are part of life; both nourishment and growth are part of life.

And, finally, life on earth includes reproducing the whole being; the process of growth only requires that one part produce another part. Reproduction produces the whole individual being and is a higher process than mere growth.

There are no further inner life processes beyond these seven. Life divides into seven definite processes. But, since they serve all twelve

of the sensory regions, we cannot assign definite regions to these—
the seven life processes enliven all the sensory regions. Therefore,
when we look at the way the seven relate to the twelve we see
that we have (1) breathing, (2) warming, (3) nourishing, (4) secreting,
(5) maintaining, (6) growing, (7) reproducing. These are distinct
processes, but all of them relate to and flow through each of the
senses: their relationship with the senses is mobile. The living human
being must be pictured as having twelve separate sensory regions
through which the sevenfold life is pulsing: mobile, sevenfold life.

In: Rudolf Steiner (GA 170) (1990): *The Riddle of Humanity. The Spiritual
Background of Human History.* Forest Row: Rudolf Steiner Press. Tr. John
Logan. Lecture 7, August 12, 1916. (Translation adapted)

5.6 Imagination

S 13 Artistic imagination (1918)

S 14 Hidden imagination (1923)

S 15 The development of imagination (1924)

Imagination enriches our inner life. Through imagination a word over-
heard incidentally, a leaf on the ground, an occurrence that surprises us
may become a poem, a painting, a collage, maybe a new fairy tale. Imagination can transform the most inconspicuous event into something new
and even special. It seizes hold of something, transforms it, lets it grow,
and integrates details into a living whole. Young children don't yet have
this kind of imagination. Their forces of imagination are busily active in
all their perceptual processes, internalizing impressions that then form
and structure the body and its organs. In young children, imagination
is still a formative, growth-enhancing force that serves to build up the
organs (S 14). Once these forces are no longer needed by the body from
the age of four or five, and more so after the change of teeth, the emancipated formative forces will appear as imagination, as a "symbolizing gift"
in child play (S 15). Steiner therefore refers to imagination as a "metamorphosed growth force" (S 14) that in the first phase of life supports
mostly the formation of the organs and then gradually emancipates itself
as a soul force. From then on we can and should work on the children's
imagination by not presenting them with ready-made, perfect toys, but
the kind of toys they can add to or shape themselves. An example Steiner
mentions repeatedly is that of the simple doll made from a piece of cloth
or a napkin (S 20 and S 21)

S 13 Artistic imagination (1918)

When we are creative out of artistic imagination, we do not—as we would usually when we perceive with our senses and reflect on what we have perceived—absorb the external sense world and represent it inwardly. We change it; we idealize it, or whatever you wish to call it. The orientation does not matter. Whether you absorb it in a realistic or idealistic way, whether you are an impressionist or an expressionist, does not matter. What matters is that artistic creativity always transforms what we would otherwise merely represent inwardly of the reality. In artistic creation the artist's perceptions of the external world stay alive. Artists adhere to their perception of the outside world. In artistic creation the mental images that are derived from outer perception are preserved and merge with memories that are connected with these images. Everything artists take in throughout their life continues to resonate in their subconscious; and the more or the better the experiences that have been stored in the soul can reverberate, the more will the artistic output be—as an expression of the artist's attention to the external sense impressions, mental images and memories—be infused with artistic imagination.

In: Rudolf Steiner (GA 271) (1985): *Kunst und Kunsterkenntnis. Grundlagen einer neuen Ästhetik. 1888 – 1921.* Third edition, with four added essays from 1890 and 1898. Dornach: Rudolf Steiner Verlag, p. 145f. Lecture 2, May 6, 1918: The Sources of Artistic Imagination and the Sources of Suprasensible Knowledge.

S 14 Hidden imagination (1923)

Let us look at childhood in order to gain a better understanding of imagination. Children don't yet have imagination as such. At best they have dreams. Freely creative imagination does not yet live in children, not obviously. And yet, it is not something that suddenly appears in us at a certain age, out of nothing. There is imagination in children, but it is hidden. It may not manifest itself but children are full of imagination. So what is this imagination doing in children? The unbiased spiritual observer of human evolution can see how incompletely, compared to their later form, the brain, but also the rest of the organism, are developed in early infancy. No sculptor could create such wonderful worldly forms out of the cosmos as children do when they form their brain and their whole organism between birth and the change of teeth. Children are wonderful sculptors; it is just that the sculpting they do occurs in the organs, as an inner formative force of growth. In addition, children are musicians because they tune their nerve strands in quite a musical way. Again, the imagination acts as a force of growth, a force that harmonizes the organism.

As children grow older and approach the second dentition around the seventh year, and as they grow on toward puberty, they no longer need as many sculptural and musical forces as before for growing and forming their organism. These excess forces are set free and become imagination. The power of imagination is nothing other than the natural forces of growth metamorphosed into soul forces. If you really want to understand imagination, you need to study the living forces in the plant forms; study the living force in the configurations of the internal organism that are brought about by the "I". Study everything that is formative force in the entire universe, everything that brings about form, shape, and growth in the unconscious regions of the cosmos. Then you will also have an idea of what remains when children have advanced far enough with building up their organism that they no longer need all the formative growth forces available to them. The excessive forces then rise up to the soul and become imagination. And what is then left right at the end—I can't call it the final sediment because sediment settles below whereas this rises up—is the intellect, the power of reason. That is what remains at the very end when the last of the imagination has been sifted through: the intellect.

The intellect is sifted-through imagination. People don't know this and therefore assign greater reality to the intellect than to imagination. But imagination is the first child of the natural forces of growth and configuration. This is why imagination does not express reality directly, because as long as the growth forces are working on reality they cannot become imagination. Only when reality has received all it needs there will be something left for the soul as imagination. But in itself, qualitatively and essentially, imagination is exactly the same as the forces of growth. What makes our arm grow from small to big is the same force that is at work in poetic or generally artistic activity, only that it has been transformed into a soul force. This cannot be understood intellectually, you need to grasp it with your feeling and will, because then you will also develop the right respect for the working of the imagination, and possibly also the sense of humor that is required for understanding how imagination works. In short, you are encouraged to feel that imagination is a divine force that is active in the world.

In: Rudolf Steiner (GA 276) (2002): *Das Künstlerische in seiner Weltmission. Der Genius der Sprache. Die Welt des sich offenbarenden strahlenden Scheines. Anthroposophie und Kunst Anthroposophie und Dichtung.* 1923. Fourth edition. Dornach: Rudolf Steiner Verlag, p. 141ff. Lecture of May 20, 1923.

S 15 The development of imagination (1924)

When you observe and experience the transition that takes place with the change of teeth, you will find that children draw above all the gift of symbolism, the gift of imagination, from having been wholly sense organ before. This fact needs to be recognized, even in their playing. Many sins are committed in this respect in our materialistic times. Think of the "pretty" dolls you can buy for children everywhere, with their perfectly formed faces, painted cheeks, genuine hair, and goodness knows what. They even close their eyes when you lay them down! But this kills the child's imagination. There is nothing left for children to apply their imagination to. Nor do children really enjoy such dolls. If you make a doll yourself, on the other hand, out of a napkin or piece of cloth, with two ink dots as eyes and a dab of ink for a mouth, and then fashion a pair of arms somehow, then there is so much left that children can add in their imagination. It is good for children if they can add as much as possible, if they can unfold their imagination and symbolizing activity. This is what you have to bear in mind: give children as few perfectly formed, pretty toys as possible. For the beauty of the doll I have just described, with real hair and so on, is only a conventional beauty. In truth, the doll is horrid because it is so inartistic.

It is important for teachers to know that around the time of the second dentition children move on to a life that is informed by imagination, not by the intellect; and as teachers and educators you can do this too. You will be able to develop a life of imagination if you really and truly, in your soul, understand human nature. Knowing human nature lets your inner soul life "thaw" and brings a smile to your face. Ignorance breeds grumpiness. Of course, you might have an inner illness that is reflected in your face, but that wouldn't matter, because children take no notice of such things. What rises up from a soul imbued with the living knowledge of human nature and expresses itself in the face—that is what makes you a real educator.

This means that, between the change of teeth and puberty, we must teach out of imagination, for the forces that were present in children in the first years, when they were wholly sense organ, now turn inward and become soul forces. Sense organs don't think. They perceive pictures, or rather they form pictures of external objects. And even though children, when they are still wholly sense organ, produce something that is initially soul-like, that will not turn into thought. It turns into an image, albeit a soul image, an imaginative picture. This is why, as teachers, we need to work with images.

In: Rudolf Steiner (GA 311) (1989): *Die Kunst des Erziehens aus dem Erfassen der Menschenwesenheit.* 1924. Fifth edition. Dornach: Rudolf Steiner Verlag, p. 29f. (Lecture 2, August 13, 1924).

5.7 The images of folktales

S 16 The sources of folktales (1913)

S 17 The uplifting power of folktale images (1914)

S 18 Folktale images and their effect on life (1911)

The most important source of imaginative education is folktales and their images. They will have a direct effect on children through their feeling life up until their ninth or tenth year. Steiner wrote folktales himself, for instance the *Tale of the Rock-Spring Wonder* (Steiner GA 14, p. 53ff.) or *The Child of Light* (Ibid., p. 84f.; Steiner 1996, p. 119ff.), and he studied the sources of traditional folktales and described them as expressions of unconscious soul experiences. The following three source texts are not taken from an educational context but reflect the findings of Steiner's research into consciousness that he characterized as a state of clairvoyance (S 16). They cast light on diverse qualities at work in the images of folktales: these images nurture the child soul as long as the child's own forces of imagination are still focused on physical growth (S 16); as described earlier, they stimulate the formative forces both of the bodily organism and of the spirit-soul; they kindle imaginative forces, enliven the soul, and provide meaning (S 17) because they reveal truths and wisdoms of life (S 18); and they do all that by expressing the most profound aspects of spiritual life in the simplest possible way (S 16). Folktales experienced in childhood have a rejuvenating effect (S 17).

Chapter 6 and 7 have recommendations on telling folktales to younger children and on understanding "invisible friends" (S 16); further inspiration can be found in Steiner (2006) and Almut Bockemühl (2010), not currently available in English.

S 16 The sources of folktales (1913)

> We little suspect how deeply hidden lie the springs that have given rise through centuries of human history to all the enchantment of genuine fairy tale poetry. [...]

> In ancient times human beings could more fully perceive their union with the spiritual world outside themselves. They saw how everything going on in their soul, the happenings deep in their soul, were related to certain spiritual realities alive in the universe. They saw these realities moving through the soul, felt closely related to the spirit-soul beings and realities of the universe. This was a characteristic of humankind's primeval clairvoyance. In ancient times, not only artists but quite primitive people frequently had a feeling that I am going to describe, which today we arrive at only in quite special moods.

> It can really happen that, living gently in the depths of the soul, as gently as anything can be, there is an experience of the spiritual realities mentioned above, one that does not come to consciousness. Nothing of it is perceived in the wide-awake life of the day. But something is there in the soul, just as hunger often is there in the physical organism, and just as we have a need for something to satisfy our hunger, we have also a need for something to satisfy this delicate need in our soul. It is at this moment that one feels urged either to come to a fairy tale or a legend that one knows, or else, perhaps, if one has an artistic nature, to create something of the kind oneself, even though one senses that all the words one could theoretically use would only reach a kind of stammering about such experiences. This is how the fairy tale images arise. The nourishment that satisfies the hunger we spoke of is just this conscious filling of the soul with fairy tale pictures.

> In the earlier times of humanity's evolution, the human soul was closer to a clairvoyant perception of its inner spiritual experiences; often, therefore, the simple country folk felt this hunger more distinctly than we do today, and this led them to search for nourishing pictures arising out of their creative soul life; we find these today in the fairy tales coming down to us as folk traditions in various parts of the world. In those earlier times the human soul felt its connection to spiritual existence and felt more or less consciously the

inner battles it had to undergo, even without understanding them. The soul formed these into pictures and images which had only a distant resemblance to what was happening in its depths. But still one can feel that there is a connection between the happenings of a fairy tale and the unfathomable, profound experiences of the soul.

It is evident—many can confirm this—that some children are able to create within themselves a "friend" who is present only for them, and who always stays by their side whatever they do. Probably everyone knows children with such invisible spirit-friends. These unseen playmates you have to imagine as being with the children wherever they are, sharing all their joys and sorrows. And then you see someone "sensible" coming along, who hears about this invisible playmate and tries to talk the child out of it, even believes it's a healthy thing he's doing—but it has a bad effect on the child's feeling-life. Children will grieve for their soul-comrade and if they are susceptible to inner spiritual moods, the grief will be weighty and can develop into a pining away or sickliness. This is actual experience, related to deep, inward happenings of the human soul.

We can take to heart, without dispelling the fragrance of such a tale, the Grimms' story of the child and the paddock (a small frog). A little girl lets the paddock eat with her out of her bowl of bread and milk; the paddock only drinks the milk. The child talks to the little creature as to another human being, saying one day, "Eat the bread crumbs as well, little thing." The mother hears this, comes out to the yard, and kills the paddock. And now the child loses her rosy cheeks, wastes away and dies.

In this tale we can feel an echo of certain moods that really and truly are present in the depths of our soul. They are there not only at certain periods of our life, but whether we are children or adults we recognize such moods because we are human. Every one of us can feel reverberating in us how this something we experience but don't understand, something we don't even bring to consciousness, is connected with the effect of the fairy tale on our soul like the taste of food on our tongue. And then the fairy tale becomes for the soul very much like nutritious food when it is put to use by the whole organism. It is tempting to search in these deep-lying soul experiences for what reverberates in each different tale. Of course it would be a tremendous task over a long time, given the great collections of fairy tales from everywhere in the world, to probe into them just for this. However, what can be looked at in a few tales can be used in a general way for all of them, if the few are genuine fairy tales.

Take one of the stories that the brothers Grimm collected, *Rumpelstiltskin*. When a miller claims that his daughter can spin straw into gold, the king has him bring her to the castle in order to test her art. She comes to the king, is locked in a room with a bundle of straw and "there sat the poor miller's daughter and for the life of her could not tell what to do." As she begins to weep, there appears a little man who says, "What will you give me if I spin the straw into gold for you?" The girl gives him her necklace and the little man spins the straw into gold. The king next morning is astonished and delighted but wants more; she should spin straw into gold again. She is locked in another room with even more straw, and when the little man appears again and asks, "What will you give me if I spin the straw into gold for you?" she gives him her ring. By morning all the straw is spun into glittering gold. But the king is still not satisfied. The manikin comes again, but now the girl has nothing more to give him. "Then promise me, if you should become queen, to give me your first child," says the little man, and so she promises. And when, after a year, the child is there and the manikin comes and reminds the queen of her promise, she begs him to wait. "I will give you three days' time," he replies. "If you know my name by that time, you shall keep your child." The miller's daughter sends messengers far and wide. She must find every name and also the particular name of the little man. Finally, after several wrong guesses, she succeeds in naming the little man by his right name: Rumpelstiltskin.

No other work of art gives us the feeling of utmost inner joy as the fairy tale with its unsophisticated pictures, yet we can also know the deep soul experience from which such a tale arises. [...]

The soul would certainly come to grief if she did not surmise that within her own conscious being a still deeper being is present, something she can trust, something she might be able to describe like this: You, Soul, are still at such an imperfect stage—but there is something in you, another entity, who is far more clever than you, who can help you to accomplish the most difficult tasks and give you wings to rise up and look over wide perspectives into an infinite future. Someday you will be able to do what is still impossible, for there is something within you that is far, far greater than the part of you now that "knows;" it will be a loyal helper if you can enter into an alliance with it. But you must truly be able to form a concept of this being who lives within you and is so much wiser, cleverer, more skillful than you are yourself.

When you try to imagine this conversation of the soul with itself, an unconscious conversation with the more capable part of the soul, you can then try to catch this nuance in the Rumpelstiltskin fairy tale: what the miller's daughter had to experience in not being able to spin straw into gold and then finding a loyal helper in the little manikin. [...]

Because fairy tales belong to our innermost feeling and emotional life and to everything connected with it, they are of all forms of literature the most appropriate for children's hearts and minds. It is evident that they are able to combine the richest spiritual wisdom with the simplest manner of expression. One has the feeling that in the magnificent world of art there is no greater art than this one, which traces the path from the unknown, unknowable depths of the soul to the charming and often playful fairy tale pictures.

When what is most difficult to understand can be put in the most clearly perceptible form, the result will be great art, intrinsic art, art that belongs at a fundamental level to the human being. Human nature in the child is linked to the life of the whole world in such a primary way that children must have fairy tales as soul-nourishment. The expression of spiritual force can move much more freely when it comes toward a child. It should not be entangled in abstract, theoretical ideas if the child's soul is not to become dry and disturbed, instead of remaining linked to the deep roots of human life.

Therefore there is nothing of greater blessing for children than to nourish them with everything that brings the roots of human life together with the roots of existence. Children still have to work creatively, forming themselves, bringing about the growth of their body, unfolding their inner tendencies; they need the wonderful soul-nourishment they find in fairy tale pictures, for in them the child's roots are united with the life of the world. Even we adults, given to reason and intelligence, can never be torn away from these roots of existence; we are most connected with them just when we have to be fully involved with the life of the time. Therefore at various parts of our life, if we have a healthy, open-hearted mind, we will happily turn back to fairy tales. Certainly there is not a single age or stage of human life that can take us away from what flows out of a fairy tale, for otherwise we would be giving up the deepest and most important part of our nature; we would be giving up what is incomprehensible for the intellect: a sensing within ourselves, a sense for what is pictured in a simple fairy tale and in the simple, artless, primordial fairy tale mood.

In: Rudolf Steiner (GA 62) (1989): *The Poetry and Meaning of Fairy Tales.* Spring Valley: Mercury Press. Tr. Ruth Pusch. Lecture of February 6, 1913. Translation adapted

S 17 The uplifting power of folktale images (1914)

In ancient times, religious ideas, myths, and fairy tales gave souls light for the spiritual world. It is easy to say that myths and fairy tales developed in the childhood stages of the human race. Of course, people did not physically meet the angels that myths and fairy tales speak about. But thinking based on philosophy will be of little use in the spiritual world where such knowledge has no meaning. It is easy to say fairy tales are not based on truth. Spiritual researchers are not so naive, and know that fiery dragons do not really fly through the air. However, they always knew it was necessary to form the imagination of the fiery dragon, for when it lives in the soul, it casts light on the spiritual world. These are powerful imaginations. That is the principle behind all myths; they are not intended to reflect external reality accurately, but to enable us to live in the spiritual world. Materialists say myths and fairy tales originate in the childhood stage of the human race. But in its childhood, humanity was taught by the gods. In the process of our evolution, myths and fairy tales are gradually lost, but children should not grow up without them. It makes a tremendous difference whether or not children are allowed to grow up with fairy tales. The power of the fairy tale images, which give wings to the soul, becomes apparent only at a later age. Growing up without fairy tales leads later to boredom, to world-weariness. Indeed, it can even cause physical symptoms—fairy tales can help to prevent illnesses. The qualities that seep into our soul from fairy tales later emerge as a zest for life, enthusiasm for being alive, and an ability to cope with life, all of which can be seen even in old age. Children have to experience the power of the content of fairy tales while they are young and can still do so.

In: Rudolf Steiner (GA 154) (1990): *The Presence of the Dead on the Spiritual Path.* Hudson: Anthroposophic Press. Tr. Christian von Arnim. Lecture of May 26, 1914.

S 18 Folktale images and their effect on life (1911)

Imagine a young person meets an older one and feels a shy sense of reverence that he may not even be able to explain. People who possess this inner broadmindedness are often, we find, also people who remain young for a long time; they generally stay young, a young heart beats within them even when their hair has gone all gray. They retain a certain mobility in life, and in particular they preserve throughout their whole life an ability to quickly adapt to situations and to respond aptly in any circumstances. People who are open to life in their youth will find that life will open up to them more and more as they grow older. Their capacity of seeing into the things increases and they much more easily acquire the ability to sense the spiritual behind the worldly phenomena. They will themselves become ever more spiritual. It is different with people who develop mainly their intellect in youth. They tend toward early senility. This is not their fault but it's the karma of the community they live in. People who are more intellectual become increasingly isolated from the world and the world becomes increasingly incomprehensible to them. As a result they tend to be critical of their environment. "When I was young," they will say, "everything was good, now everything's rotten." This grumpiness and discontentedness with everything, this withdrawing and living in childhood memories alone is the result of a one-sidedly intellectual focus in younger years. We can't therefore do enough in order to provide children with a broad education of heart and mind, an education based on imagination.

The world seems to go in the opposite direction today. One no longer tells children "lies" about the stork delivering the babies. But that is just a picture, and it has more truth in it than what children are usually told today, which is that they are the product of their father and mother. The image of the stork—or whatever image it is—is an expression of our heavenly origin. It opens up a world to children that goes beyond trivialities and allows them to build the foundations for an understanding of the truth that will only later be formed.

Describing the image of the stork as untrue reveals a lack of imagination, an inability to clothe into a suitable picture a process that cannot be explained to children as reincarnation. But—people will object—children no longer believe in such images! The reason for the disbelief lies in the fact that the adults themselves who tell children such stories don't believe in them. As soon as we don't ourselves believe in what is expressed in these images, the children will not believe it either. If, on the other hand, these images are for us an expression of the truth that is hidden behind them, if we have enough imagination to clothe the truth into a picture, then the children will believe it. It is fine to say to children that a part of them comes from the mother and another from the father, and that there is a third part that is carried down from heaven toward the mother and father on the wings of other beings. This is an appropriate picture and it is also true. In conveying rich and imaginative ideas to children we enhance their soul development, and we give them the gift of youthfulness which they will be able to preserve to a ripe old age. This kind of imaginative education that particularly also underlies the child's playing is immensely important.

In: Rudolf Steiner (GA 127) (1989): *Die Mission der neuen Geistesoffenbarung. Das Christus-Ereignis als Mittelpunktsgeschehen der Erdenevolution*. 1911. Dornach: Rudolf Steiner Verlag, p. 40f. (Lecture of January 7, 1911: The effect of moral qualities on karma)

5.8 Child play

S 19 Playing as a free activity (1912)

S 20 Imitation, imagination, and play (1923)

S 21 Playing and the inner formative forces (1923)

"For to say it straight out, we only play when we are fully human and we are only fully human when we play," Friedrich Schiller wrote in 1795 in his *Letters on the Aesthetic Education of Humanity* (Schiller 1795/2004, p. 93). Steiner's appreciation of these letters (Steiner GA 53, p. 403f.) and of this particular motto speak clearly out of his aphoristic references to playing. Like imitation, playing is a faculty of the higher self. These faculties arise from our own forces and our inner need for self-activity and for putting our own will to the test (S 19). Children never need instructions for imitating and playing, on the contrary: instruction inhibits their inner urge for activity and, like sitting in front of a monitor, it makes them passive participators in world events. Children are natural creators and inventors. They imitate the activities and movements of adults and, on the basis of this, they create their own imaginative life world. According to Steiner, we enhance rather than stifle children's creativity if we give them simple, imperfect toys, such as a doll made from a napkin, that enable them to apply and unfold their imagination (S 20 and 21). For completing everything that is not given to them ready-made stimulates the inner forces in them that also form and differentiate the brain (S 21). Playing gives young children the greatest possible freedom and allows them to unfold the highest degree of inner formative activity, which explains Steiner's resolute criticism of ready-made and outwardly perfect toys and artificially contrived kindergarten activities. Books on Waldorf kindergarten education such as Vinzens' *Lasst die Kinder spielen* (Let the children play) (Vinzens et. al. 2011) argue convincingly against early intellectual intervention and in favor of free play for preschool children and opportunities to imitate, of their own accord, meaningful activities in family and kindergarten settings.

S 19 Playing as a free activity (1912)

Knowing our own extended self that enables us to intimately know other beings, we can say of children, too, that [...] they have a higher being outside their ordinary self that is working on them. So, we find that there is some kind of education already taking place in children while we, with our ordinary education, can only address the child's personal self. Where do we find this active higher being in children that belongs to them but does not enter consciousness? It might seem strange but is nevertheless true that it is active in children in rational, well-guided play. When children play we can only create the conditions for education. But what the playing achieves happens through their own activity, through everything that we cannot confine in strict rules. The essence and educational value of playing lies precisely in the fact that we need to hold back with our rules and our educational theories and entrust the children to their own forces. Because what do children do when we leave them to their own forces? They playfully try out the effect of their self-activity on external objects. They apply their own will in activity and movement and learn from the way the external objects respond to their will activity. This is how children educate themselves, even though they are "only" playing, and they do it in quite a different way than they would under the influence of teachers and their educational principles. This is why it is so important that we introduce as little intellectuality as possible into child play. Child play is the more fruitful the more it is based not on intellectual comprehension but on the observation of vibrant life. When we therefore give children toys that are moving, where one can pull threads or otherwise cause animals or persons or other objects to move, we educate them better through play than when we give them the most perfect building bricks. Because these require too much intellectual activity and that belongs to a more personal principle than the playing around and trying out of something living and mobile that is not understood rationally but observed in its full activity. The less prescriptive and thought-out playing is the better, because then something higher can come in, something that cannot be forced into consciousness, because children's approach to life is experimental rather than intellectual. Children are educated by something higher than personal influences.

In: Rudolf Steiner (GA 61) (1983): *Menschengeschichte im Lichte der Geistesforschung*. 1911 – 1912. Second edition. Dornach: Rudolf Steiner Verlag, p. 428f. Lecture 14, March 14, 1912: Self-education in the light of spiritual science.

S 20 Imitation, imagination, and play (1923)

We must not lose sight of the fact that up to the second dentition the child lives by imitation. The serious side of life, with all its demands in daily work, is re-enacted in deep earnestness by children in their play, as I mentioned yesterday. The difference between a child's play and an adult's work is that an adult's contribution to society is governed by a sense of purpose and has to fit into outer demands, whereas the child wants to be active simply out of an inborn and natural impulse. Play activity streams outward from within. Adult work takes the opposite direction, namely inwards from the periphery. The significant and most important task for grade school consists in just this gradual progression from play to work. And if one is able to answer in practical terms the great question of how a child's play can gradually be transformed into work, one has solved the fundamental problem during those middle years from seven to fourteen.

In their play, children mirror what happens around them; they want to imitate. But because the key to childhood has been lost through inadequate knowledge of the human being, all kinds of artificial play activities for children of kindergarten age have been intellectually contrived by adults. Since children want to imitate the work of the adults, special games have been invented for their benefit, such as *Lay the Little Sticks*, or whatever else these things are called. These artificial activities actually deflect the child's inner forces from flowing out of the organism as a living stream that finds a natural outlet in the child's desire to imitate those who are older. Through all kinds of mechanical manipulations children are encouraged to do things not at all suitable to their age. Particularly during the nineteenth century, programs for preschool education were determined that entailed activities a child should not really do; for the entire life of a preschool class revolves around the children adapting to the few people in charge, who should behave naturally so that the children feel stimulated to imitate whatever their teachers do. It is unnecessary for preschool staff to go from one child to another and show each one what to do. Children do not yet want to follow given instructions. All they want is to copy what the adult does, so the task of a kindergarten teacher is to adjust the work taken from daily life so that it becomes suitable for the children's play activities. There is no need to devise occupations like those adults meet in life—except under special circumstances—such as work that requires specialized skills. For example, children of preschool age are told to make parallel cuts in strips of paper and then to push multi-colored paper strips through the slits so that a woven colored pattern finally emerges. This kind of mechanical process in a kindergarten actually prevents children from engaging in normal or congenial activities. It would be better to give them some very simple sewing or embroidery to do. Whatever a young child is told to do should not be artificially contrived by adults who are comfortable in our intellectual culture, but should arise from the tasks of ordinary life. The whole point of a preschool is to give young children the opportunity to imitate life in a simple and wholesome way. [...]

Give a child a handkerchief or a piece of cloth, knot it so that a head appears above and two legs below, and you have made a doll or a kind of clown. With a few ink stains you can give it eyes, nose, and mouth, or even better, allow the child to do it, and with such a doll, you will see a healthy child have great joy. Now the child can add many other features belonging to a doll, through imagination and imitation within the soul. It is far better if you make a doll out of a linen rag than if you give the child one of those perfect dolls, possibly with highly colored cheeks and smartly dressed, a doll that even closes its eyes when put down horizontally, and so on. What are you doing if you give the child such a doll? You are preventing the unfolding of the child's own soul activity. Every time a completely finished object catches their eye, children have to suppress an innate desire for soul activity, the unfolding of a wonderfully delicate, awakening imagination. You thus separate children from life, because you hold them back from their own inner activity. So much for the child until the change of teeth.

In: Rudolf Steiner (GA 306) (1996): *The Child's Changing Consciousness as the Basis of Pedagogical Practice*. Hudson NY: Anthroposophic Press, tr. Roland Everett. Lecture 4, April 18, 1923.

S 21 Playing and the inner formative forces (1923)

Parents often think it desirable to give their little girl a beautiful doll as a plaything. This "beautiful" doll is a fearful production because for one thing it is so utterly inartistic, in spite of its "real" hair, painted cheeks and eyes which close when it is laid down or open when it is lifted up! We often give our children toys that are dreadfully inartistic copies of life. The doll is merely one example. All modern toys are of the same type and they constitute a form of cruel punishment to the child's inner nature. Children often behave well in the presence of others merely from a fear of conventional punishments; equally they do not always express aversion from toys like the "beautiful doll," although this dislike is deeply rooted in their souls. However strongly we may suggest to children that they ought to love such toys, the forces of their unconscious and subconscious life are stronger, and the children have an intense antipathy to anything resembling the beautiful doll. For, as I will now show you, such toys really amount to an inner punishment.

Suppose that in the making of our toys we were to take into consideration what children have actually experienced in their infant thoughts up to the age of six or seven in the processes of learning to walk after learning to stand upright and then we were to make a doll out of a handkerchief, for instance, showing a head at the top with two ink-spots for eyes. The child can understand and, moreover, really love such a doll. Primitively this doll possesses all the qualities of the human form, in so far at any rate as the child is capable of observing them at this early age. A child knows no more about human beings than that they stand upright, that there is an "upper" and a "lower" part of their being, that they have a head and a pair of eyes. As for the mouth, you will often find it on the forehead in a child's drawings! There is as yet no clear consciousness of the exact position of the mouth. What a child actually experiences is all contained in a doll made from a handkerchief with ink-spots for eyes.

An inner, plastic force is at work in children. All that comes to them from their environment passes over into their being and becomes there an inner formative power, a power that also builds up the organs of the body.

If the child has a father who is constantly ill-tempered and irritable, and the child as a result of this lives in an environment of perpetual shocks and unreasonableness, all this turmoil expresses itself in his breathing and the circulation of the blood. The lungs, heart and the whole venal system are affected by such a condition. Throughout the whole of his life the child bears within him the inner effects upon the organs of his father's ill-temper.

This is merely an example to show you that children possess a wonderful plastic power and are perpetually at work as kind of inner sculptors upon their own being. If we give the child the kind of doll made from a handkerchief, these plastic, creative forces that arise in the human organism from the rhythmic system of the breathing and blood circulation and build up the brain, flow gently upwards. They mould the brain like a sculptor who works upon his material with a fine and supple hand, a hand permeated with the forces of the soul and spirit. In the child's perception of the handkerchief-doll these plastically creative elements are called upon and healthy forces are generated which then flow upwards from the rhythmic system and work upon the structure of the brain.

If, on the contrary, we give the child one of the so-called "beautiful" dolls, with moving eyes and painted cheeks, real hair and so on—a hideous, ghostly production from the artistic point of view—then the plastic, brain-building forces that are generated in the rhythmic system have the effect of the constant lashing of a whip. All that the child cannot as yet understand works upon the brain like the lashings of a whip. The whole brain is lashed to its very foundations in a terrible way. Such is the secret of the "beautiful" doll, and it can be applied to many of the playthings given to the child today.

In: Rudolf Steiner (GA 307) (2004): *A Modern Art of Education*. Great Barrington: Anthroposophic Press, tr. R. Lathe, N. Whittaker. Lecture 6, August 10, 1923.

5.9 Rhythmic life

S 22 Learning to breathe–healthy sleeping and waking (1919)

S 23 Human breathing in relation to the rhythms of the cosmos (1917)

Establishing healthy rhythms in the kindergarten day or in a school lesson not only creates a mood that is conducive to playing and learning and makes the everyday activities easier, it can also be seen as a response to our natural connection with the rhythms of the cosmos (S 23). Newborn children have to develop their own individual breathing rhythm and their rhythm of waking and sleeping; they gradually have to adjust to the rhythms and habits of their family and find their own personal rhythm. As they alternate between waking and sleeping, children learn to internalize the experiences they had during the day and take them into the night, into the "spiritual world," in order to then draw on their night experiences on the following day (S 22). Helping children to establish their circadian rhythm is an important task of education. Steiner begins his main work on education and anthropology with this question: the series of lectures he gave in 1919 as a first teachers' course, just before the opening of the first Waldorf school (Steiner GA 293). The source text (S 22) is taken from the first of these lectures and deals with the two basic aspects of educational method: respiration and the rhythm of sleeping and waking. Just as we need to inhale and exhale in order to live bodily, we need, for a healthy soul life, the alternation between calm, attentive perception and free movement, between concentration and activity. We help children to learn this way of "breathing" if we structure the school day so that concentration, listening, and participating—guided activities in other words—alternate with periods of free play, activity, and movement. Every school lesson or training session needs this alternation. And if, as Steiner explains (S 22), children have problems taking the experiences and contents of the day into their sleep, we can help by conveying to them experiences and contents that are close to the dreaming consciousness, as we find them in folktales, for instance. It is interesting that, in this context, Steiner calls attention to the fact that we can only become effective teachers if we study these questions of human development.

The second source is about breathing in its threefold relationship with the cosmos: the pulmonary breathing that connects us with the elements of the earth, the alternation between waking and sleeping as two states of consciousness that can be compared to sunrise and sunset, and finally, the cycle of life and death that the soul goes through just as the Sun progresses through the zodiac (S 23). Steiner uses these examples to explain how the rhythm of breathing forms the foundation of our body, soul, and spirit existence.

Chronobiology is the modern scientific discipline exploring further phenomena and laws of rhythm that are also of interest for the teaching practice (Rosslenbroich 1994).

S 22 Learning to breathe–healthy sleeping and waking (1919)

We need to know, however, that children's breathing, as they enter physical existence, is not yet in tune with their neurosensory system. They have not learned yet to breathe in a way that would adequately support the neurosensory processes. This is a subtle indication as to what we have to do with the children. We first need to acquire an anthropological-anthroposophical understanding of the human being; the most important step in education will then be to observe everything that helps to integrate the child's breathing into the neurosensory process. In a higher sense, children need to learn to receive the gift they were endowed with by having been born to breathe. This side of education is preoccupied with the spirit-soul: in harmonizing breathing and neurosensory activity, we draw the spirit-soul into the child's physical life. Roughly speaking we can say that children are not yet able to breathe properly inwardly and that education means teaching them to do that.

There is something else that children aren't so good at yet and which we need to facilitate in order to harmonize the relationship between the enlivened physical body and the spirit-soul. At the beginning of their earthly existence—you will notice that the spiritual and physical principles generally seem to contradict each other—children don't find the right rhythm of sleeping and waking. One would think from the outside that they are rather good at sleeping, seeing that they sleep more than they will ever again in later life. They essentially sleep their way into life.

What they cannot achieve yet has to do with the deeper foundations of sleeping and waking. Children have many experiences in the physical world: they move, eat, drink, and breathe; but although they alternately sleep and are awake, they are not yet able to carry their impressions—what they see with their eyes, hear with their ears, do with their hands, or how they kick their little legs—into the spiritual world for them to be processed there so that the result of this processing can be taken back to their physical life. Their sleep is very different from the sleep of adults. When adults sleep, they process the experiences garnered between waking up and going to sleep. Infants cannot do this yet and they consequently enter, when they sleep, into the universal world order without taking their outer physical experiences with them. The right kind of education will help them to bear their physical world impressions into the activities that the spirit-soul carries out between falling asleep and waking up. We cannot teach the children anything of the higher world, because what streams into them from the higher world streams in between falling asleep and waking up. All we can do is use the time the children spend on the physical plane in ways that enable them to carry what we do with them here into the spiritual world, so that they can bring back with them into their physical existence the spiritual strength that they gain in the spiritual world and that will help them to unfold their humanity.

The teaching aims we pursue are very high, as you see: we aim to teach the right breathing and the right rhythm between sleeping and waking. The educational methods we will get to know will not involve training the children in breathing or sleeping and waking. All that will merely be in the background. We will learn about concrete teaching methods. But we must be profoundly aware of what we are doing. We must be aware in teaching a particular subject whether what we are doing draws the spirit-soul into the physical body or whether it draws the physical body into the spirit-soul.

Don't underestimate the importance of what has just been said. You cannot be good educators and teachers if you only look at what you are doing, and not at what you are. Anthroposophical spiritual science teaches us that. It is not irrelevant which teacher enters the classroom to meet the children. There is a big difference, not only because one teacher might be more competent than the other. What makes the difference is the way teachers think, the attitude to life they carry into the classroom. Teachers who reflect on the evolving human being have a different effect on their students than those who know nothing about it and are not interested. What happens when you think such thoughts, when you begin to understand the importance of the breathing process and its transformation through education, or the cosmic significance of the rhythm between sleeping and waking? As soon as you think such thoughts, something in you begins to overcome your self-centeredness. Something of what lives in you because you are physical beings is eliminated and as a result, forces arise in you as you enter the classroom that help you to establish a relationship with your pupils.

In: Rudolf Steiner (GA 293) (1992): *Allgemeine Menschenkunde als Grundlage der Pädagogik*. 1919. Ninth edition, newly revised and extended. Dornach: Rudolf Steiner Verlag, p. 25ff. (Lecture 1, August 21, 1919). English translation from a new edition of Rudolf Steiner's First Teachers' Course (GAs 293, 294, 295), publication due in spring 2020, tr. Margot M. Saar

S 23 Human breathing in relation to cosmic rhythms (1917)

Through our lungs we are related to the entire universe, and the entire universe works on our life body. When we pass through the portal of death, we lay aside the life body but enter what is active in our lung system—and this is connected with the entire universe. This accounts for the surprising consonance to be found in the rhythm of human life and the rhythm of breathing. I have already explained that when we calculate the number of breaths we draw in one day, we obtain 25,920 breaths per day on the basis of eighteen breaths a minute (hence 18 x 60 x 24). We breathe in and breathe out; which constitutes our smallest rhythm to start with. Then there is another rhythm in life, as I have already explained before. Every morning when we awake we breathe into our physical system, as it were, our soul nature (the astral or soul body and the "I") and we breathe them out again when we fall asleep. We do this during our whole life. Let us take an average length of life of seventy-one years. Then we can make the following calculation: We breathe in and breathe out our own being 365 times a year. If we take seventy-one years as the average length of human life, we obtain 25,915 (365 x 71). You see: it is more or less the same number (of course, the length of life differs for each of us). We find that in the life between birth and death we breathe in and out what we call our actual self 25,920 times. We can therefore say: we have the same relationship to the world as the breath we draw in has to the elements around us. In the course of our whole life we have the same rhythm in relation to the cosmos that we have in our breathing during one day. Again, if we take our life of approximately seventy-one years and call it a cosmic day, we obtain a cosmic year by multiplying this by 365. The result is 25,915 (again, approximately one year). In 25,920 years, the Sun returns to the same constellation of the zodiac. If the Sun is in Aries in a certain year, it will rise again in Aries after 25,920 years; in the course of 25,920 years the Sun moves through the entire zodiac. Thus, an entire human life breathed out into the cosmos is a cosmic breath that relates to the cosmic course of the Sun through the zodiac in exactly the same way as one human breath relates to one day in a human life. These are profound inner laws! Everything is built up on rhythm. We breathe in a threefold way, or at least we are placed into the breathing process in a threefold way. First, we breathe through our lungs in the world of the elements; this rhythm is contained in the number 25,920. Then we breathe within the entire solar system, by taking sunrise and sunset as parallel to our falling asleep and awaking. Throughout our life we breathe in a rhythm that is again contained in the number 25,920. Finally, the cosmos breathes us in and out, again in a rhythm determined by the number 25,920—the Sun's course through the zodiac.

This is how we relate to the whole visible universe. At its foundation lies the invisible universe. When we pass through the portal of death, we enter this invisible cosmos. Rhythmical life lies at the foundation of our feeling life. We enter the rhythmical life of the cosmos in the time between death and a new birth. This rhythmical life lies behind the carpet woven by our senses and determines our etheric life. If we had clairvoyant consciousness, we would see this cosmic rhythm that is, as it were, a rhythmical, surging cosmic ocean—now of an astral nature.

In: Rudolf Steiner (GA 179) (2007): *The Influence of the Dead on Destiny.* Great Barrington: SteinerBooks, Anthroposophic Press. Translator unknown. Lecture 4, December 11, 1917. Translation adapted

5.10 The four temperaments

S 24 The four basic types of temperament (1909)

S 25 Dealing with the temperaments (1919)

S 26 Educating the temperaments (1909)

The model of the four temperaments, which goes back to antiquity, is also known as humorism in medicine. Steiner developed and differentiated it further for the purposes of education. According to his research, the four temperaments—choleric, sanguine, phlegmatic, and melancholic—are based on the forces of the life body and are expressed by the soul body as different soul dispositions (Steiner GA 95, p. 64), depending on which of the four constituents of the human organization predominates. An individual's disposition usually arises from one dominant temperament interacting with two others. In children, temperaments express themselves as unconscious behaviors and characteristic traits, in adolescents and adults also as inner soul dispositions.

In education, knowledge of the four temperaments can be an important diagnostic and pedagogical tool. Conspicuous behaviors in children can be due to one-sided temperamental dispositions that can on the one hand be addressed by creating harmonizing social and play situations with other children, and on the other hand by an educational approach that turns one-sided temperaments into strengths. Steiner does not favor the counteracting of temperaments but recommends to "guide them in the right direction" (Steiner GA 57, p. 291) and encourages educators to ask themselves how children's temperament can "help them attain their life's goals" (Steiner GA 295, p. 28). The following source texts present the four temperaments as expressions of a predominance of one particular constituent of the human organization (S 24), provide insight into pedagogical possibilities (S 25), and explore the effect the educator's attitude and interest have on the child's temperament (S 26). The diversity of recommendations on how to deal with the temperaments illustrates that there is no one approach that helps but that educational creativity and an individual approach are required in each particular case. The same applies when we transfer the recommendations Steiner gave for school age children to the first seven years.

In the context of Waldorf education there are a number of publications that describe the temperaments and how to approach them pedagogically (Eller 2018; Scheer-Krüger 1996); Wolfgang Leonhardt's *Temperament und Lebenswirklichkeit* (temperament and the reality of life) (Leonhardt 2016; not available in English) is recommended. There is still no scientific research on the topic (Rittelmeyer 2010).

S 24 The four basic types of temperament (1909)

In choleric people, the "I" and the blood system predominate. Cholerics therefore come across as people who must always have their way. Their aggressiveness, everything connected with their forcefulness of will, derives from their blood circulation. In the nervous system and soul body, sensations and feelings constantly fluctuate. Any harmony or order results solely from the "I"'s restraining influence. People who do not exercise that influence appear to have no control over their thoughts and sensations. They are totally absorbed by the sensations, pictures, and ideas that ebb and flow within them.

Something like this occurs whenever the soul body predominates, as it does in sanguines, for example. Sanguines surrender themselves in a certain sense to the constant and varied flow of images, sensations, and ideas since in them the soul body and nervous system predominate. The nervous system's activity is restrained only by the circulation of the blood. That this is so becomes clear when we consider what happens when a person lacks blood or is anaemic, in other words, when the blood's restraining influence is absent. Mental images fluctuate wildly, often leading to illusions and hallucinations. A touch of this is present in sanguines. Sanguines are incapable of lingering over an impression. They cannot fix their attention on a particular image nor sustain their interest in an impression. Instead, they rush from experience to experience, from percept to percept. This is especially noticeable in sanguine children, where it can be a source of concern. The sanguine child's interest is easily kindled, a picture will easily impress, but the impression quickly vanishes.

We proceed now to the phlegmatic temperament. We observed that this temperament develops when the etheric or life body, as we call it, which regulates growth and metabolism, is predominant. The result is an inner comfortableness. The more we live in our life body, the more preoccupied we are with our internal processes. We let external events run their course while our attention is directed inward.

In melancholics we have seen that the physical body, the coarsest member of the human organization, becomes master over the others. As a result, melancholics feel that they are not master over their body, that they cannot bend it to their will. Their physical body, which is intended as an instrument of the higher members, is itself in control, and frustrates the others. Melancholics experience this as pain, as a feeling of despondency. Pain continually wells up within them. This is because their physical body resists the life body's inner sense of wellbeing, the soul body's liveliness, and the purposeful striving of the "I".

The varying combinations of the four members also manifest quite clearly in external appearance. People in whom the "I" predominates seek to triumph over all obstacles, to make their presence known.

Accordingly their "I" stunts the growth of the other members; it withholds from the soul and life bodies their due portion. This reveals itself outwardly in a very clear fashion. Johann Gottlieb Fichte, that famous German choleric, was recognizable as such purely externally. His build revealed clearly that the lower essential members had been held back in their growth. Napoleon, another classic example of the choleric, was so short because his "I" had held the other members back. Of course, one cannot generalize that all cholerics are short and all sanguines tall. It is a question of proportion. What matters is the relation of size to overall form. In sanguines the nervous system and soul body predominate. The soul body's inner liveliness animates the other members, and makes the external form as mobile as possible. Whereas cholerics have sharply chiseled facial features, the sanguines' features are mobile, expressive, changeable. We see the soul body's inner liveliness manifested in every outer detail, for example, in a slender form, a delicate bone structure, or lean muscles. The same can be observed in details of behavior. You don't need to be clairvoyant to tell from behind whether someone is a choleric or a sanguine; you don't need to be a spiritual scientist for that. If you observe how cholerics walk, you will notice that they plant each foot so solidly that it looks as if they wanted to bore down into the ground. By contrast, sanguines have a light, springy step. Even subtler external traits can be found. The inwardness of the "I", the cholerics' self-contained inwardness, is expressed in eyes that are dark and smoldering. Sanguines by contrast, whose "I" has not taken such deep root, who are filled with the liveliness of their soul body, tend to have blue eyes. Many more such distinctive traits of these temperaments could be cited.

The phlegmatic temperament manifests in a static, indifferent physiognomy, as well as in plumpness, for that is due largely to the activity of the life body. In all this the phlegmatics' inner sense of comfort is expressed. Their gait is loose-jointed and shambling, and their manner timid. They seem somehow to be not entirely in touch with their surroundings. Melancholics are distinguished by a hanging head, as if they lacked the strength necessary to straighten the neck. Their eyes are dull, not shining like the cholerics'. Their gait is firm, but in a leaden rather than a resolute way.

In: Rudolf Steiner (from GA 57) (2008): *The Four Temperaments*. Forest Row: Rudolf Steiner Press. Tr. Brian Kelly. Translation adapted.

S 25 Dealing with the temperaments (1919)

You will know from the lecture I gave years ago that the worst possible way of dealing with temperaments is to try and foster the opposite qualities in children. With sanguine children, for instance, it would be a bad idea to try and drive their sanguineness out of them through teaching. Instead, we bring as much as possible to the sanguine child's attention. By occupying them as much as possible we support their natural disposition. As a result, their disposition will gradually be mitigated and brought into harmony with the other temperaments.

With children who are prone to choleric tempers we should equally not try to avoid such outbursts but support these children in the right way from the outside. It is of course difficult to always let them have their tantrums.

There is a clear difference between phlegmatic and choleric children. Phlegmatic children are more apathetic and not very busy inwardly. As a teacher you must awaken within yourself as much sympathy as possible for these children and find interest in everything that lives in them. There will always be opportunities. When you find access to their listlessness, phlegmatic children can become very interesting. But don't show your interest! Try to appear disinterested. You need to be very interested inside and at the same time, outwardly, mirror back to them their own way of being. This will have an educational effect.

With choleric children you try to become disinterested inwardly and watch their tempers in cold blood. When they hurl down an ink jar, try to be as phlegmatic and unperturbed as possible outwardly and not let their behavior touch you inwardly either. Try to discuss the incident with them sympathetically, albeit not immediately after it has happened! Stay calm and say calmly, "Now you have broken the ink jar." On the next day when the child is calm, too, speak about the incident sympathetically. State what the child has done and show the greatest sympathy. By doing this you make the child live through the whole scene again inwardly. You can also express your dissatisfaction with what they did, with their throwing the ink jar on the floor. You will achieve much with this approach with choleric children. Other approaches will not help them to fight their own temper. [...]

You can differentiate from the way children express or present themselves, whether they observe things with much or little interest; whether they feel strongly about outer things or more strongly about their own inner states.

You also need to understand the way children change: depending on their temperament, they are either strongly engaged and rarely change, or they are less strongly engaged and change frequently. It all depends on the temperament.

Fig. 3

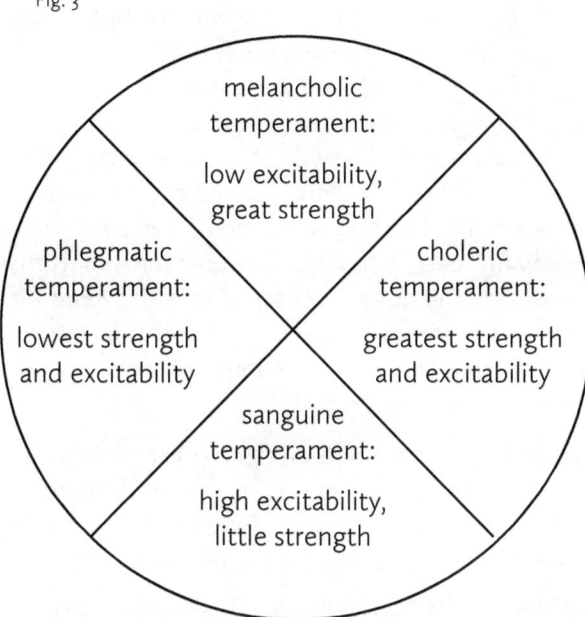

As in this diagram (Fig. 3), the sanguine and phlegmatic temperaments are often close together, while the phlegmatic temperament won't easily transition into a choleric temperament. They are as dissimilar as the North and South Poles. The same applies to the melancholic and the sanguine temperament. They are also polar opposites. Adjacent temperaments can merge into one another and become blurred. For your seating order you best keep the phlegmatic and choleric groups apart and seat the other two, the melancholic and the sanguine, in between them.

All these things relate to what I said this morning. The children's inner life, their soul life, is immensely important. Children are taught and educated from soul to soul. There is so much that is transmitted via the invisible threads that connect one soul with another. This is why so much happens inside the choleric children when you remain unperturbed, and inside the phlegmatic children when you sympathize with them inwardly. You teach suprasensibly through your own inner mood of soul. Education happens through what you are, in this case through what you make of yourself among the group of children entrusted to you. Never lose sight of this.

The children also have an effect on each other. It is remarkable how, when you divide them into four groups depending on temperament and let children with the same temperament sit together, these dispositions don't augment each other but balance each other out. In a group of sanguine children, the sanguine disposition will not be reinforced but mitigated. When you address the choleric children in your lesson, the sanguines will absorb something of that and vice versa. As teachers you let the mood of your soul work on the children, while the similar temperaments and soul moods in the children balance each other out. The children's chatting with each other, in lessons and during recess, reflects this need for balance. Choleric children are less prone to chatter amongst themselves than they would be with others. One cannot observe and judge such things in a superficial way only.

One important point to mention right at the beginning is that we will set great store by teaching in as concentrated a manner as possible. Without such concentration you cannot take all the things I have spoken about into consideration, the temperaments in particular.

In: Rudolf Steiner (GA 295) (1984): *Erziehungskunst. Seminarbesprechungen und Lehrplanvorträge*. 1919. Fourth edition. Dornach, Rudolf Steiner Verlag, p. 12ff. (Discussion of August 21, 1919). English translation from a new edition of Rudolf Steiner's First Teachers' Course (GAs 293, 294, 295), publication due in spring 2020, tr. Margot M. Saar.

S 26 Educating the temperaments (1909)

In light of all this it is clear that to guide and direct the temperaments is one of life's significant tasks. If this task is to be properly carried out, however, one basic principle must be observed, which is always to reckon with what is present, and not with what is not there. Sanguine children, for instance, will not be helped by adults trying to beat interest into them. Their temperament simply will not allow it. Instead of asking what such children lack so that we can beat it into them, we must focus on what they bring with them and base our actions on that. In principle, there is always one kind of interest we can stimulate in sanguine children, however flighty, and that is interest in a particular person. If we ourselves are that person, or if we bring the children together with someone who is, they cannot but develop an interest. Only through the medium of love for another's personality can the interest of the sanguine child be awakened. More than children of any other temperament, sanguines need someone to look up to with loving admiration. Love is the magic word here, and we must do everything we can to awaken it. We must reckon with what we have. We should see to it that sanguine children are exposed to a variety of things they have shown a deeper interest in. These things should be allowed to speak to and have an effect on them. Then they should be withdrawn so that the children's interest will be rekindled, before they are restored again. We must let them have the same effect on the children that the objects of the ordinary world have on the sanguine temperament.

Choleric children are also susceptible to being led in an indirect way. The key to their education is respect and appreciation of authority. Instead of winning affection by means of personal qualities, as we do with sanguine children, we should make sure that the choleric children's belief in their teachers' sound knowledge remains unshaken. Teachers must demonstrate their pedagogical knowledge and never show any weakness. Choleric children must be able to believe in their teachers' competence or all authority will be lost. While love for the teacher's personality is the magic key for sanguine children, respect and esteem is the key for the cholerics. Choleric children must be confronted with challenges. They must encounter resistance and difficulties so that life is not too easy for them.

Melancholic children are not easily led. But for them, there is also a magic key. What love for the personality is to the sanguine, and respect and esteem for the choleric, is for melancholics the feeling that their teachers have been tried by life, as it were, that they act and speak on the basis of past trials. Melancholic children must feel that their teacher has known real pain. Let your treatment of all of life's little details be an occasion for the children to appreciate that you have suffered. Sympathy with the fates of those around them has an educational effect on melancholic children. With melancholics too, we have to work with what the children bring with them. Melancholics have a capacity for suffering, for discomfort, that is firmly rooted in their being; it cannot be disciplined out of them, but it can be redirected. We should expose melancholic children to experiences of pain and suffering in the world around them so that they realize that such painful experiences exist. This is important. Don't distract them because that will intensify their despondency and inner suffering. Instead, let them see that objective occasions for suffering exist in life. While we must not carry it too far, it is good to redirect the melancholic child's suffering to outside objects.

Phlegmatic children should not be allowed to grow up alone. Although naturally all children should have playmates, for phlegmatics it is especially important that they do. Their playmates should have the most varied interests. Phlegmatic children learn by sharing in the interests of others, the more numerous the better. Their playmates' enthusiasm will overcome their native indifference towards the world. Whereas the important thing for melancholics is to experience another person's fate, for phlegmatic children it is to experience the whole range of their playmates' interests. Phlegmatics are not moved by events as such, but when these events are reflected in others, then their interests are reflected in the phlegmatic child's soul. We should let phlegmatic children experience objects and events to which the phlegmatic temperament is suited.

In: Rudolf Steiner (from GA 57) (2008): *The Four Temperaments*. Forest Row: Rudolf Steiner Press. Lecture 10: The Mystery of the Human Temperaments, March 4, 1909. Translation adapted.

5.11 Education and self-education

S 27 Education is self-education (1923)

S 28 Children and adults (1915)

"Education is self-education" does not only sound like a pedagogical principle but it is—and Steiner says this clearly—the very foundation of the pedagogical relationship and of practical teaching, an "education in which one is educator and student at the same time" (Steiner 2012, p. 42). According to Steiner, the educational principles of the first three seven-year stages are first "the drive to imitate," then in the second stage the "authority principle" based on trust and belief, and finally, in adolescence, "looking up to an impersonal ideal that the soul has taken hold of" (Steiner 2012, p. 42f.) and independent judgment (S 28). Based on these principles, we as adults can provide examples and inspiration so that children and adolescents can educate and develop themselves, but this requires us to work on our own self-education. Steiner devised numerous exercises to help us with this (S 31–35). The abundance of classes for meditation and self-development techniques on offer today reveals how deeply people long to rid themselves of outside influences and become self-determined. Educators and teachers who practice self-development will acquire an inner sense for the developmental needs of the individual child. According to Steiner, we have a different effect on the children we educate when we "reflect on the evolving human being" (Steiner GA 293, p. 27; S 22) and free ourselves, at least temporarily, from our "self-centeredness." Our self-education creates the possibility for the children's self-education. In a wider sense, by being role-models that are worthwhile for the children to imitate and follow, we create an environment in which the children can educate themselves (S 27). The following two source texts go in this direction. Steiner mentions three conditions for education: self-education, repeated earthly lives, favorable surroundings (S 27). Education is not aimed at the outer visible but at the invisible part of the human being (S 28). When we turn our attention to this invisible, higher being in us, our spirit-soul (Chapter 2), we understand the deeper meaning of education: teachers educate through the invisible outcome of their I-development; this gives children the impulse to develop the talents that lie dormant in their own invisible "I." In other words, education happens in the resonance of spirit and soul.

For deepening we recommend Steiner's lectures on the topic (Steiner 2012[1]) and Jörgen Smit's widely used collection of meditative exercises (1996).

S 27 Education is self-education (1923)

Essentially, there is no education other than self-education, at whatever level. This is recognized in its full depth within anthroposophy, which has conscious knowledge through spiritual investigation of repeated earthly lives. All education is self-education, and as teachers we can only provide the environment for children to educate themselves. We have to provide the most favorable conditions where, through our agency, children can educate themselves according to their own destinies.

In: Rudolf Steiner (GA 306) (1996): *The Child's Changing Consciousness and Waldorf Education as the Basis of Pedagogical Practice*. Hudson NY: Anthroposophic Press. Lecture 6, April 20, 1923.Tr. Roland Everett

---

1 Translator's note: this is a compilation of Steiner lectures on the theme of self-education that is not available in English at present, but contains, for instance, the lectures of March 14, 1912 (in GA 61) and of November 2, 1908 (in GA 107)

S 28 Children and adults (1915)

I'll give you an example of a realm where spiritual-scientific concepts can come to life: education. Let's start with the education of children through grown-ups. From a materialistic point of view one will only have a materialistic image, that of an older person educating a younger one. But that is not what happens. Outwardly, both the older and the younger person are just an illusion. But there is something in both of them that is not an illusion: the invisible self that goes from incarnation to incarnation.

We will speak about this again. Today I will mention a few things that will over time—through meditative deepening—reveal what else there is in spiritual science. I will start by pointing out that the adults we meet in the external world cannot educate, and the children as we meet them in the outside world cannot be educated. What really happens is that something invisible in the educator educates something invisible in the children. We will only understand this rightly when, in the growing children we have to educate, we focus on the gradually manifesting implications of their previous incarnations. But when everything that comes from previous incarnations has fully unfolded, there is nothing left to educate: the children will withdraw from us, especially in our time. What we are actually educating is the invisible result of earlier incarnations. We cannot educate nor have an effect on the visible child. What we work on is the invisible result of previous incarnations. This is the situation as far as the child is concerned.

Let us now look at the educator. In the child's first seven years we can only educate through that in us that can be imitated; in the second seven years through the influence we can have as an authority; and in the next seven years through the educational effect of independent judgment. The influence we have lies not in our outer physical being. What we carry in us as educators will only acquire a physical form in our next incarnation, for all the qualities we have in us that are worthy of being imitated or that lend us authority are in a germinal state and will shape our next incarnation. Our own future incarnation as an educator communicates with the children's earlier incarnations. It is an illusion to think that our present selves are talking to the present children. We will only develop the right feeling for this if we realize that the best in us—what our mind can think and what our soul can feel, what prepares in us the person we can be in a future incarnation—can have an effect on that in the children which, coming from a long-gone past, strives to take form in them. Our musical qualities are the part of us that can have an educational effect. And the plastic forces within the child are what we can reach with our education.

Think of everything I have said in the past days about the musical element and how, in its highest manifestation, it comes close to an initiation experience. The musical element relates to development, to the future, while the plastic-architectural element relates to the past. Children are the most wonderful examples of sculptural art. We as educators must have the musical mood that can live in us as a mood of the future. Feeling this really deeply—in the way I have just described for education—will lend a special nuance to the way we approach the children as teachers, because it will lead us to have the highest expectations of ourselves and to gain the greatest understanding for any problems the children may confront us with. This mood is a real force in education.

In: Rudolf Steiner (GA 275) (1990): *Kunst im Lichte der Mysterienweisheit.* 1914–1915. Third edition. Dornach: Rudolf Steiner Verlag, p. 122ff., Lecture 6, January 2, 1915

5.12 Sources of education

S 29 Pedagogical intuition (1920)

S 30 Moral intuition, moral imagination, and moral technique (1894/1918)

In an anecdote that is both amusing and serious Steiner describes three teachers and their individual ways of preparing for the new school year. It could easily apply to three early childhood educators, too. While two of these teachers prepare for the next school year by reviewing their work of the previous year, the third does little in terms of preparation, focusing instead on the children and their needs and relying on having the right inspiration in the right moment (Steiner GA 166, p. 60ff; Wiehl 2015, p. 164ff.). But that is not a reliable method. Pedagogical intuition is not just a spontaneous idea; it requires intensive preparation. In his work Steiner presents various methods for achieving intuition, such as meditative anthropology (S 29) and the observation of intuitive thinking (S 30). For teachers he proposes a three-stage study method that involves the meditating on anthropological contents: taking them in, understanding them through meditation, and remembering them creatively (S 29; for more ways of working with this cf. Chapter 6). Steiner developed a way of observing one's thinking in his early work *The Philosophy of Freedom* (Steiner GA 4)—as a basis of "ethical individualism," an attitude and ability that can be particularly effective in education once one has acquired it. Ethical individualism is based on moral intuition, moral imagination, and moral technique, all of which enable us to act out of freedom and responsibility (S 30). If we bear these aspects in mind, "pedagogical intuition"—a much-cited principle in education today—assumes concrete practical meaning. Christoph Hueck (2016) has composed a comprehensive documentation on "intuitive cognition in Rudolf Steiner's written work;" a scientific study of pedagogical intuition by Shozan Shimoda is expected in 2019 (Wiehl 2017b).

S 29 Pedagogical intuition (1920)

If you bring all these things together and form mental images of them in active meditation, you can be sure that the vigorous power of ingenuity you need when facing the children you are educating will be kindled in you.

Ideas like these, stemming from a spiritual-scientific method of education, have as their aim a more intimate knowledge of the human being. When you meditate on them, you cannot halt their continued effect within yourself. When you eat a piece of bread and butter, you are first aware of a conscious action; but what takes place when the bread and butter pass through the complicated process of digestion is something you can affect very little, yet this process takes its course and your general wellbeing is closely bound up with it. Now if you study anthropology as we have done you experience it consciously to start with, but if you meditate upon it afterward, an inner process of digestion goes on in your soul and spirit, and that is what makes you an educator and teacher. A healthy metabolic process makes an active human being out of you, and in the same way this meditative digestion of a true knowledge of the human being makes you an educator. You simply face the children as their teacher in an entirely different way if you have experienced what results from a genuine, spiritual-scientific anthropology. What makes us into educators actually grows out of the meditative work of acquiring such knowledge. Such observations as we have made today, if we keep returning to them if only for five minutes a day, will bring our inner soul life into movement. We will produce so many thoughts and feelings that they will just pour out of us. Meditate in the evening upon such knowledge of the human being and in the morning you will know in a flash, "Of course, this or that is what I must do with Johnnie Miller," or, "This girl needs this or that," and so on. In short, you will know what to do in every case.

In our human life it is important to bring about this sort of cooperation between inner and outer experiences. You do not even need much time for it. Once you have got the knack, in three seconds you can get an inner grasp of things that will keep you going for a whole day's teaching. Time loses its significance when it is a matter of bringing the supersensible to life. The spirit simply has different laws. Just as everything contracts in a dream, things we receive from the spirit can expand. In the same way, on waking up you can have a thought whose time-content could fill weeks but shoots through your mind in no time at all: so permeating yourself through meditation with this spiritual-scientific knowledge of the human being can bring you to the point when you have reached your fortieth or forty-fifth year to carrying out in five minutes the whole inner transformation that you need for your teaching. You will be quite different then in ordinary life from what you were before.

One can read about such things in the writings of those who have experienced them. You can begin to understand them, but you must also understand that what is experienced by a few individuals to an especially high degree, in a way that can then throw light upon the whole of life, must take place on a smaller scale in the teacher's case.

As teachers we must take up for ourselves the study of the human being; we must come to comprehend human nature through meditation and keep it in our memory—then the memory will become vigorous life. It is not the usual kind of remembering, but one that gives new inner impulses.

In this instance memory surges up from the life of the spirit and carries initiatives over into our external work. This is the third stage. Meditative comprehension is followed by active, creative remembering, which is at the same time a receiving of what emanates from the spiritual world. We start with an acceptance or perception of knowledge of the human being; then comes comprehension, a meditative comprehension of this knowledge that becomes inward and is received by the whole of our rhythmic system; finally, we have a remembering of the knowledge of the human being out of the spirit. In other words, we must teach creatively out of the spirit, become artists of education. This must become inner conviction; a state of soul.

In: Rudolf Steiner (GA 302a) (2007): *Balance in Teaching*. Great Barrington: Anthroposophic Press/SteinerBooks, tr. Ruth Pusch. Lecture 3, September 21, 1920. Translation adapted.

S 30 Moral intuition, moral imagination, and moral technique (1894/1918)

Free spirits act out of their impulses—that is, from intuitions chosen by thinking from the totality of their world of ideas. The reason that unfree spirits separate particular intuitions from their world of ideas, to make them the basis of an action, lies in what the perceptual world has given them—that is, in their previous experiences. Before coming to a decision, unfree spirits remember what someone did, or recommended, or what God commanded in such a case, and so forth. Then they act accordingly. Free spirits have other sources of action than these preconditions. They make absolutely original decisions. They worry neither about what others have done in their situation, nor about what they have been commanded to do. Purely conceptual reasons move them to select a particular concept from the sum of their concepts and translate it into action. Their action, however, belongs to perceptible reality. What they perform there will thus be identical to a quite specific perceptual content. The concept will have to realize itself in a concrete, individual event. But, as a concept, it cannot contain that event. It can relate to it only as any concept relates to a percept—for example, as the concept of "lion" relates to an individual lion. The link mediating between a concept and a percept is the mental picture. For an unfree spirit, this link is given in advance—motives are present in advance as mental pictures in consciousness. When unfree spirits want to do something, they do it as they have seen it done, or as they have been told to do in this particular case. Authority, therefore, works best through examples, that is, through the transmission of quite specific, individual acts to the consciousness of unfree spirits. A Christian acts less in accordance with the teachings than with the model of the Redeemer. With regard to positive action, rules have less value than they do for the restraint of particular actions. Only when they forbid actions, and not when they command them to be done, do laws take on universal conceptual form. Laws concerning what unfree spirits should do must be given to them in quite concrete form: Clean the street in front of your doorway! Pay your taxes at just this rate at tax-office X! and so forth. The laws forbidding actions take the conceptual form: Thou shalt not steal! Thou shalt not commit adultery! But these laws, too, affect unfree spirits only by their appeal to concrete mental pictures, such as that of the corresponding secular punishment, torments of conscience, eternal damnation, and so forth.

As soon as an impulse to action is present in the form of a general concept—for example, thou shalt do good to thy neighbor, or thou shalt live so as best to further thy well-being—then a concrete mental picture of the action (the relation of the concept to a perceptual content) must first be found in each individual case. This translation of concept into mental picture is always necessary for a free spirit, who is driven neither by a model nor by fear of punishment.

Imagination is the chief means by which human beings produce concrete mental pictures from the sum of their ideas. Free spirits need moral imagination to realize their ideas and make them effective. Moral imagination is the source of a free spirit's actions. Therefore, only people who have moral imagination are really morally productive. Simple moral preachers—that is, people who spin out codes of ethics without being able to condense them into concrete mental pictures—are morally unproductive. They are like critics who can rationally discuss what works of art should be like, but cannot themselves produce anything at all.

To turn a mental picture into a reality, moral imagination must set to work in a specific field of percepts. Human action does not create percepts, it recasts already existing percepts and gives them a new form. To be able to transform a specific perceptual object or group of objects in accordance with a moral mental picture, one must have understood the laws of the perceptual picture to which one wants to give new form or new direction—that is, one must have understood how it has worked until now. Further, one must find the method by which those laws can be transformed. This part of moral efficacy depends on knowledge of the phenomenal world with which one is dealing. This knowledge must therefore be sought in a branch of general scientific knowledge. Hence, along with the faculty for moral ideas and imagination, moral action presupposes the capacity to transform the world of percepts without interrupting its coherence in natural law. The capacity to transform the world of percepts is moral technique. It is learnable in the sense that any knowledge is learnable. Generally, people are better equipped to find concepts for the world that is already finished than to determine productively, out of their imagination, future, not-yet-existent actions. Therefore, those without moral imagination may well receive the moral mental pictures of other people and skillfully work them into reality. The reverse can also occur: people with moral imagination can lack technical skill and may have to make use of others to realize their mental pictures.

Insofar as knowledge of the objects within our field of action is necessary for moral action, our actions are based upon this kind of knowledge. What is relevant here are natural laws. We are dealing with natural science, not with ethics.

Moral imagination and the moral capacity for ideas can become objects of knowledge only after an individual has produced them. By then, they no longer regulate life; they have already regulated it. They can be regarded as effective causes like any others—they are purposes only for the subject. Hence, we deal with them as with a natural history of moral ideas.

Apart from this, there can be no science of ethical norms.

In: Rudolf Steiner (GA 4) (1995): *Intuitive Thinking as a Spiritual Path. A Philosophy of Freedom*. Hudson NY: Anthroposophic Press. Tr. Michael Lipson (Chapter 12: Moral Imagination).

5.13 Exercises for self-education

S 31 Six exercises for developing perception and thinking (1909)

S 32 The six "subsidiary" exercises (1906)

S 33 Attention to detail (1924)

S 34 Developing inner peace (1904)

S 35 Recall exercise (1907)

Meditation and mindfulness have become popular ways of taking oneself out of the hustle and bustle of everyday life and of escaping the ubiquitous media influences above all. Meditation exercises make us aware of ourselves and freer in the way we meet the world; they help us look at life from a higher perspective, strengthened by the forces of our higher self. The source texts contain selected exercises for meditative spiritual development, strengthening, and moral-ethical self-education that can enable us to become a positive force in our spheres of activity. Meditative reflection is something we take on for self-development out of our own free will, and it changes the way we experience ourselves and the world.

The meditative exercises Steiner recommended are based on the conscious, self-guided thinking that can be achieved with the "cloud exercise," for instance (S 31). This is one of six exercises he gave for the "practical training of thinking" (Steiner 1909, p. 256ff.; Steiner 1928) that can enhance perception and thinking and enable us to act and educate out of deeper insight.

The six "subsidiary" exercises are well suited for self-education and the harmonization of soul forces, but they also support a good pedagogical attitude (S 32). Steiner developed them to be used in preparation for, but also alongside, meditative spiritual training. Similarly to the mindfulness exercises often recommended today to adults, children and adolescents for personal strengthening, they support the unfolding of the soul forces of thinking, feeling, and will and promote positivity, open-mindedness, and balance of soul.

The "attention to detail" meditation (S 33) helps us to become more aware of our connection with the spirit—a mood in which young children are at home and from which they draw the forces for their development (S 3 and Chapter 2). Steiner recommended this exercise above all to special needs teachers, as a way of gaining insight into the inner dynamics of the human bodily organization (Steiner GA 317, S. 152ff.; Selg 2013).

Finding moments of "inner peace" (S 34) creates the space in spirit and soul that we need for self-reflection and meditation. Experience has shown, however, that endless activities and distractions, or a dreamy "letting go of stress" prevent the necessary inner presence. Becoming aware of the connection of "I" and body and finding inner calm therefore requires certain techniques in the form of movement, touch, or breathing exercises. Loosening the shoulders, feeling the surface of the skin down into the soles of the feet and observing the breathing as it becomes calmer are ways of drawing a protective line between I-imbued body experience and the events of the external world.

The daily recall in the evening (S 35) does not only create distance and a free and open view of the events and encounters of the day, it also allows for a conscious entering into the stream of time and evolution and should accompany any striving for self-knowledge. It helps us focus on the essence of past or future actions so that we can become aware of their consequences. As a result the soul feels integrated in the biography and the stream of world events, for the impulses for the future lie in the recollection or "presencing" of the past—a fact that is particularly relevant to teachers, because they need to reestablish their presence anew every day.

Recommended reading on this topic includes Heinz Zimmermann and Robin Schmidt's introduction to anthroposophical meditation (2016) and Steiner's own contributions on the theme across his work (Steiner 1928, 2010, 2014, 2017).

S 31 Six exercises for developing perception and thinking (1909)

True practice of thought requires us in the first place to have the right attitude of mind, the right feeling about thinking. How can we gain this? No one can come to a right feeling about thinking who imagines that thinking is something which merely takes place within us, inside the head, or in our mind or soul. Anyone who starts with this idea will have a wrong feeling, and will continually be diverted from the search for a truly practical way of thinking. They will fail to make the necessary demands on their thinking activity. To acquire the right feeling towards thinking, we must rather say to ourselves: "If I am able to have thoughts about the things, if I am able to get at the things through thoughts, then the things must already contain the thoughts within them. The thoughts must be there in the very plan and structure of the things. Only so can I draw the thoughts out of them."

We must realize that it is the same with the things in the world outside as with a watch. The comparison of the human organism to a watch is frequently used, but people often forget the most important thing. They forget the watchmaker. The cogs and wheels did not run together and join up of their own accord and set the watch in motion, but there was a watchmaker there first, to construct the watch. We must not forget the watchmaker. It is through thoughts that the watch has come into being. The thoughts have, as it were, flowed out into the watch, into the external object. And this is the way we must think of all the works of nature and of all natural processes. It can easily be illustrated with things that are human creations, with things in nature it is not quite so easy to perceive. And yet they too are works of the spirit; behind them are *spiritual beings*. When we think about things, we merely reflect on what has gone into them before. We must believe that the world has been created by thought and is still in continual process of creation by thought. This belief, and this alone, can give birth to a really fruitful inner practice of thought. [...]

Before we can speak of genuine thinking practice, we must first know that thoughts can only be drawn from a world that already contains thoughts. Just as you can only draw water from a glass that does really contain water, you can only draw thoughts from things that already contain thoughts. The world is built up by thoughts, and it is only for that reason that we can gain thoughts from the world. If that was not the case, then there could be no such thing as a practice of thought. If we really feel through and through what has been said here, we will easily be able to overcome abstract thinking. If we fully trust that there are thoughts behind things, that life really unfolds on the basis of thoughts, we will readily be converted to a practice of thinking that is founded on reality.

I will now describe the practice of thinking that is particularly relevant to anthroposophy. If you are penetrated by the belief that the world of facts unfolds on the basis of thoughts, you will understand how important it is to develop true thinking. If you strive to strengthen your thinking so that it will find its true bearings at every point in life, you must take guidance from what will now be said. The indications that will now be given are to be taken as real practical principles, that is to say principles that, if you try again and again and again to guide your thought accordingly, will lead to definite results. Your thinking will become practical, even though it may not appear so at first sight. Indeed, if you carry out these principles, you will have altogether fresh experiences in your thinking life.

Assume someone makes the following experiment: on a certain day he carefully observes some process in the world which is accessible to him, which he can observe quite accurately—say, for example, the appearance of the sky. He observes the cloud formations in the evening, the way in which the sun went down. And now he makes a distinct and accurate mental image of what he has observed. He tries to hold on to this image in all its details. He holds on to as much of it as he can, and tries to keep it till the following day. At about the same time on the following day, or maybe even at another time of day, he again observes the appearance of the sky and the weather, and he tries once more to form an exact mental image of it.

If in this way he forms clear mental images of successive conditions, he will soon perceive with extraordinary distinctness how his thinking grows ever richer and more intense. For what makes our thinking unpractical is the fact that in observing successive processes in the world we are generally too much inclined to leave out the actual details and to retain only a vague and confused picture in our mind. What is essential and most valuable in strengthening our thinking is that we form exact pictures, above all in the case of successive processes, and then say to ourselves, "Yesterday it was like that and today it is like this." And in doing this we must bring before our minds the two pictures which are separated in the real world, as graphically, as vividly as possible.

To begin with, this exercise is simply a particular expression of our belief that the thoughts are there in reality. We are not immediately to draw conclusions from what we have observed today to what the weather and the sky will be like tomorrow. That would only corrupt our thinking. No, we must have faith that outside in the reality of things they have their connection, and that tomorrow's process is somehow connected with today's. We are not to speculate about it, but first of all to think, in mental images as clear as possible, the scenes which in the external world are separated in time. We place the two pictures side by side before our minds, and then let the one gradually change into the other.

In: Rudolf Steiner (1928): *Practical Training in Thought*. Anthroposophical Publishing Co 1928, tr. George Kaufmann, translation adapted.

EXERCISE	METHOD	CONTENT	EFFECT
1	Precise observation; recalling, comparing and bringing together memorized images	Cloud formations and movements	Trust in thoughts; the experience that the world is born from thinking
2	Forming precise mental images	Observing someone's behaviors; imagining what your next meeting with them will be like	Strengthening and awareness of the forces of thoughts; trust in the inner necessity of things and events
3	Gaining insight into causes	Asking about the causes for a person's particular behavior	Observant thinking or having the impression of being within the things with one's thinking
4	Consciously directing one's thoughts	Becoming inwardly detached from inner impressions and associations that we are not in control of	Resourcefulness, having ideas at the right time
5	Precise remembering	Remembering a person precisely, picturing every detail clearly	Strong memory as a result of precise observation and remembering
6	Thinking possibilities	Not be hasty in one's thinking; taking time with making decisions	Activating the forces of thinking

Table by A. Wiehl, based on Rudolf Steiner (1909).

S 32 The six "subsidiary" exercises (1906)

1. Thought control – for the development of thinking

This means preventing, at least for a short time every day, all sorts of thoughts from drifting through the mind, and bringing a certain ordered tranquility into the course of thinking. You must take a definite idea, set it in the centre of your thinking, and then logically arrange your further thoughts so that they are all closely linked with the original idea. Even if you do this for only a minute, it can be of great importance for the rhythm of the physical body and the life body.

2. Initiative in action – for the development of will

You must compel yourself to some action, however trivial, which owes its origin to your own initiative, to some task you have laid on yourself. Most actions derive not from your own initiative but from your family circumstances, your education, your calling and so on. You must therefore give up a little time to performing actions which derive from yourself alone. They need not be important; quite insignificant actions fulfil the same purpose.

3. Tranquility – for the development of feeling

Here you learn to regulate your emotions so that you are not at one moment up in the skies and at the next down in the dumps. If you refuse to do this for fear of losing your originality in action or your artistic sensibility you can never go through esoteric development. Tranquility means that you are master of yourself in the most intense pleasure and in the deepest grief. Indeed, we become truly receptive to the joys and sorrows of the world only when we do not give ourselves over egotistically to them. The greatest artists owe their greatest achievements precisely to this tranquility, because through it they have opened their eyes to subtle and inwardly significant impressions.

4. Freedom from prejudice – to develop positivity (thinking and feeling)

This, the fourth characteristic, sees good in everything and looks for the positive element in all things. Relevant to this is a Persian legend told of Christ Jesus. One day Christ Jesus saw a dead dog lying by the wayside; he stopped to look at the animal while those around him turned away in disgust. Then Jesus said, "What beautiful teeth the dog has!" In that hideous corpse he saw not what was ugly or evil but the beauty of the white teeth. If you can acquire this mood, you will look everywhere for the good and the positive, and you will find it everywhere. This has a powerful effect on the physical body and the life body.

5. Faith – to develop open-mindedness

Next comes faith, which in its esoteric sense implies something rather different from its ordinary meaning. During esoteric development you must never allow your judgment of the future to be influenced by the past. Under certain circumstances you must exclude all that you have experienced so far, so that you can meet every new experience with new faith. The esoteric student must do this quite consciously. For instance, if someone comes up to you and tells you that the church steeple is crooked and at an angle of 45 degrees, most people would say that is impossible. The esoteric student must always leave a way open to believe. You must go so far as to have faith in everything that happens in the world; otherwise you bar the way to new experiences. You must always be open to new experiences; by this means your physical body and your life body will be brought into a condition which may be compared with the contented mood of a broody hen.

6. Inner Balance – for the development of harmoniousness

This is a natural outcome of the other five qualities. As esoteric pupils you must keep the six qualities in mind, take your life in hand, and be prepared to progress slowly in the sense of the proverb about drops of water wearing away a stone.

In: Rudolf Steiner (GA 95) (2012): *Founding a Science of the Spirit.* Forest Row: Rudolf Steiner Press, p. 107ff., Lecture 12, September 2, 1906. Tr. unknown. Translation adapted.

S 33 Attention to detail (1924)

People generally don't achieve much in education because they don't earnestly awaken within themselves one particular truth. It can be done like this: In the evening, create consciously within yourself the mood, "In me is God"—In me is God, or the divine spirit, or whatever you would like to call it. Don't just repeat it to yourself like some theory; for most people meditating means repeating theories to themselves. And in the morning, so that it shines out over your whole day: "I am in God." Consider what you are actually doing by bringing these two mental images to life within yourself, by letting them permeate your feeling life and even become will impulses. You have this image before you of "In me is God," and the next morning you have the image, "I am in

God." [...]² You must simply understand that this is a circle and this is a point. It just doesn't become apparent in the evening, only in the morning. In the morning you must think, "This is a circle, this is a point." You must understand, deep inside you, that a circle is a point and a point a circle.

Only then will you come closer to human nature. If you remember the drawing I did for you of the metabolism-and-limb person and the head person in us—that drawing is nothing other than an elaboration and realization of the simplified meditative symbol I have put before you here. Within the human being is realized that the I-point of the head becomes a circle in the limb-person, a circle which has, of course, been configured. By approaching it in this way, by trying to understand this deep inside you, you will come to understand the whole human being. But first you must understand that the two figures, the two mental images, are one and the same, they only differ from each other when seen from the outside. Here is a yellow circle, and there it is too. Here is a blue point, and there it is too. Why? Because this figure represents the head and this one represents the body. But when the point asserts itself into the body it turns into spinal marrow. What the point is meant to be in the head organization will continue into the spinal marrow when it enters into here. There you have the inner dynamics of morphology. [...]

In meditation, the prevailing mood must, however, not be: I want to snuggle down in a cozy nest inwardly where I feel nice and warm. Instead we should feel that we enter into and take hold of reality. Attention to detail, to the very smallest detail!

In: Rudolf Steiner GA 317 (1995): *Heilpädagogischer Kurs.* 1924 Eighth edition. Dornach: Rudolf Steiner Verlag, p. 152ff. (Lecture 10, July 5, 1924).

S 34 Developing inner peace (1904)

As students of the spirit, we must set aside a brief period of time in daily life in which to focus on things that are quite different from the objects of our daily activity. The kind of activity we engage in must also differ from what occupies the rest of our day. This is not to say, however, that what we do in the minutes we have set aside is unconnected with the content of our daily work. On the contrary, we soon realize that, if approached in the right way, such moments give

---

2 Steiner draws a blue circle on the blackboard with a yellow point in the middle, and below that a yellow circle with a blue point in the middle.

us the full strength for completing our daily tasks. We need not fear that following this rule will actually take time away from our duties. *If someone really cannot spare any more time, five minutes a day are sufficient.* What matters is how those five minutes are used.

In these moments we should tear ourselves completely out of everyday life. Our thinking and feeling lives should have a quite different coloring than they usually have. We should allow our joys, sorrows, worries, experiences, and actions to pass before our soul. But our attitude toward these should be one of looking at everything we have experienced from a higher point of view. Consider, in ordinary life, how differently we perceive what other people have experienced or done from the way we perceive what we ourselves have experienced or done. This must be so. We are still interwoven with what we experience or do, but we are only *onlookers* of other people's experiences or acts. In the time we have set aside for ourselves, then, we must strive to view and judge our own experiences and actions as though they belonged to another person.

For example, imagine you have had a serious misfortune. You naturally regard your own misfortune differently than you would that of another person. This attitude is quite justified; it is simply human nature. Indeed, it comes into play not only in exceptional circumstances but also in the events of everyday life.

As students of higher knowledge we must find the strength to view ourselves as we would view strangers. We must face ourselves with the *inner tranquility* of a judge. If we achieve this, our own experiences will reveal themselves in a new light. As long as we are still woven into our experiences, and stand within them, we will remain as attached to the nonessential as to the essential. But once we have attained the *inner peace* of the overview, the nonessential separates itself from the essential. Sorrow and joy, every thought, every decision will look different when we stand over against ourselves in this way.

It is as if we spent the whole day somewhere and saw everything, small and large, at close range, and then in the evening climbed a neighboring hill and enjoyed an overview of the whole place at once. Then the various parts of the town and their relationships to each other appear very different from when we stood among them. Of course, one cannot succeed in achieving such a transcendent perspective toward whatever experience destiny daily brings us—nor is it necessary to do so. However, as students of the spiritual life, we must strive to develop this attitude toward events that occurred in the past. The value of such inner, peace-filled self-contemplation depends less upon *what* one contemplates and more upon finding the inner *strength* that such inner calm develops.

For all human beings, in addition to what we may call the ordinary, everyday self, also bear within themselves a higher self or *higher human being*. This higher human being remains concealed until it is awakened. And it can be awakened only as each of us, individually, awakens it within ourselves. Until then, the higher faculties that are latent within each one of us and that lead to supersensible knowledge remain hidden.

In: Rudolf Steiner (GA 10) (2010): *How To Know Higher Worlds. A Modern Path of Initiation.* Hudson NY: Anthroposophic Press, p. 26ff., tr. Christopher Bamford. (Chapter: Inner Peace)

S 35 Recall exercise (1907)

Every evening before you go to sleep, review the events of the day in reverse sequence. The day should pass before us in images. An important aspect of this is that we ought never to let a sense of remorse arise. Remorse is always egotistic. Someone who regrets or is remorseful wishes he had been better, an entirely egotistic wish. We should not wish we had been better but should instead desire to become better. We should learn from our daily life. If we have done something badly, we should not regret it but think: at the time I was unable to act differently, but now I can and will do it better in future. In relation to every experience of the day we should ask ourselves: Did I do it right, couldn't I have done it better. Another thing is very important here also: to learn to observe ourselves as if we were someone else; as if we see and criticize ourselves from outside. Overall we should form as clear a picture of the day as possible. It is much more important to be able to remember small details than important circumstances. A military commander who was involved in a fierce battle will have the picture of the battle in his mind in the evening. It will engrave itself into his soul by itself. But all the small details of the day—for instance how he put on and took off his boots—have faded from his mind. And this is what is important: to form as complete a picture of the day as possible. For example, we can observe ourselves crossing the road and try to recall how the rows of houses looked, which shop windows we passed, who we encountered on the way and what they looked like; and what we ourselves looked like. Then we might see ourselves entering a shop and recall who the shopkeeper or sales attendant was who came to serve us—what she was wearing, how she spoke and moved, and so forth. To recall such little details we have to exert ourselves considerably, and this strengthens the powers of the soul.

Don't imagine that this will take a whole hour. Initially you will recall only a few things, and then gradually, with increasing effort, more and more. By practicing you will eventually be able to let the whole day with all its details pass before your soul in five minutes like a series of tableaux. But patience is needed to achieve this. This exercise will be of no use at all to you if you go over the day's events quickly and mechanically, merely registering them in a colorless kind of way.

The aim of this exercise is as follows. If someone goes for a long walk and at the end of his journey wishes to gain a sense of the path he has travelled, he can do this in one of two ways. Firstly, he can keep his back turned to the path and try to recall what lies behind him. Or he can turn round and gain an overview of the path he has taken. Now when we have completed a journey through time we can only initially recall it in memory rather than actually *looking* back over what we experienced. Yet this looking back, as we know it only in spatial terms, is also possible in the temporal realm, and we can learn this by trying to let the past day pas again before us in a clear, vivid, pictorial way. No past event has passed entirely: it is all still there, inscribed in what we call the Akashic record. Only by this means can we learn to read it. Initially, by doing so, we only perceive there what relates to ourselves; but gradually other things come into view too. This is why the evening review is such an important and indispensable exercise.

In: Rudolf Steiner (GA 266/1) (1995): *Aus den Inhalten der esoterischen Stunden. Gedächtnisaufzeichnungen von Teilnehmern. Band I: 1904–1909.* Dornach: Rudolf Steiner Verlag, p. 199ff. (Esoteric Lesson of January 29, 1907).

English translation in: Rudolf Steiner (2010), *Strengthening the Will. The Review Exercises.* Selected and compiled by Martina Maria Sam, Forest Row: Rudolf Steiner Press, p. 17 ff. Tr. Matthew Barton

6 The study and practice of Waldorf education

ANGELIKA WIEHL

6.1 Introduction

Aside from everyday duties and activities, the main task of parents, educators, and teachers is to perceive and accompany the developing child. Acquiring practical care and educational skills as well as being aware of the responsibility one has in the first phase of childhood used to be an intrinsic part of living family traditions. Given that, in the course of the twentieth and twenty-first centuries, due to modern Western lifestyles, these traditions have moved increasingly into the background, and that daughters and sons no longer learn from their parents how to nurture and educate young children, this task falls increasingly to the educational specialists working in kindergartens, day-care centers, homes, and schools. Today's living conditions demand from all of us that we become conscious of the responsibility we have for children and adolescence, for it is no longer just a matter of mastering the practical task of bringing up children but modern life requires us to develop sensitivity for children's developmental needs, a clear inner educational orientation, and a healthy personal understanding of what it means to be human. The following sections are devoted to this requirement. The ideas for the study and practice of Waldorf education are addressed at student teachers and educators, as well as at parents and anyone, in whose loving care children like to feel safe and protected even if they have to adjust at an ever earlier age to changing attachment figures in part- and full-time childcare situations. They are also meant as an encouragement for parents who would like to share the responsibility involved in bringing up children with educators and teachers.

6.2 How to observe children

In addition to studying childhood and its anthropology and pedagogy scientifically and analyzing the outcomes of these studies, personal practice research can help to develop sensitivity for the constitution and developmental needs of children. It allows us to observe children and reflect on our observations, deriving from them our own anthropological insights. After completing his university studies, Rudolf Steiner had the chance to work as a private tutor for several years. He did this in the family of the Jewish merchant Ladislaus Specht (Lindenberg 1988, p. 71; id. 1997, p. 114). At the time it was a typical way of starting a professional career and he shared it with renowned personalities such as the German philosophers Johann Gottlieb Fichte, Immanuel Kant, and Johann Friedrich Herbart (Wiehl 2015, p. 89ff.). Steiner's teaching experiences, in particular his reflections on the effective, development-enhancing education of Hans, the younger son of the Specht family who had special needs, already reflect the individual way he had of interpreting the anthropological insights he later on developed further in connection with the Waldorf school. The biographical account below casts light on the anthropology of Waldorf education as well as on its practical application:

> Destiny brought me a special educational task. I was recommended as tutor to a family with four boys. Three of them required no more than preparatory instruction for elementary school and, later, additional tutoring for middle school. But the fourth boy, who was about ten years old, was entrusted to me for his entire education. He was a problem for his parents, particularly for his mother. When I came into the family, he had barely acquired the rudiments of reading, writing, and arithmetic. He was considered so abnormal in his physical and mental development that the family doubted that he could be educated at all. His thinking was slow and sluggish, and even slight mental exertion caused a headache, lowered vitality, pallor, as well as alarming emotional behavior.
>
> After I had gotten to know the child, I felt certain that an education adapted to this particular soul and bodily constitution would awak-

en his dormant capacities, and I proposed to the parents that they leave his education in my hands. The boy's mother met my proposal with confidence, and thus I was able to face this task of a special education.

I had to find access to a soul that was dormant, as it were, and had to be gradually brought to master the bodily expressions. First, the soul had to be helped to enter the body. I was convinced that the boy had great intellectual capacities. But this was not apparent, and it made my task deeply satisfying. After a short time, I succeeded in gaining the child's love. Merely being with him and communicating with him had the effect of awakening his sleeping soul faculties. I had to devise special methods for teaching him. Even a quarter of an hour over the specified length of time for lessons adversely affected his health. The boy found a relationship to some subjects only with great difficulty.

This educational task became a rich source of learning for me. The educational methods I had to adopt gave me insight into how the soul and spirit are connected with the human bodily nature. In fact, it became my training in physiology and psychology. I came to realize that education and teaching must become an art based on true knowledge of the human being. I had to adhere to a carefully planned, economical program. In order to take the greatest advantage of the boy's intellectual capacities in the shortest possible time and with the least strain on his mental and physical forces, I often had to spend as much as two hours preparing the material I would teach for half an hour. The sequence of the subjects I taught had to be carefully arranged, and the whole day's schedule properly determined.

Within two years, I had the satisfaction of seeing the boy catch up with the primary school curriculum. He successfully passed the entrance examination for the *Gymnasium* [secondary school], and his health had improved considerably. His hydrocephalic condition was diminishing quickly. I was able to advise the parents to send the boy to the public school, because I thought it was essential that he grow up with other children. I remained with the family as tutor for several more years and devoted myself particularly to this boy, whose successful progress through school depended entirely on the fact that at home his activities continued in the same spirit in which they had begun. This was the occasion to which I referred earlier, when I continued my study of Greek and Latin, for I had to help this boy and one other in the family with those subjects, because they were required for the *Gymnasium* curriculum.

I am grateful that destiny brought me such a circumstance in life. I gained an understanding of human nature in a living, practical way that otherwise would have been barely possible. The family accepted me with exceptional kindness; we came to share a beautiful life together. The boys' father was an agent for Indian and American cotton, and I was able to gain some understanding of the operation of that business and much that was related to it. This was again a great source of learning for me. I looked into the activities of a very interesting branch of the importation business and could observe transactions between business associates and the connections between various commercial and industrial activities.

My "charge" was successfully helped through the *Gymnasium*; I remained with him until the eighth year. By then he had progressed to the degree that he no longer needed my help. After graduating from *Gymnasium*, he entered a school of medicine and became a physician. Serving in that capacity, he was killed in the [first] World War. The mother, who became a close friend through my work with her son and who always clung to this "problem child" with deep love, died soon after he did. The father had died earlier.

Much of my life as a young man was related to this task. For several years, each summer I went with the family to Attersee in Salzkammergut, where I became familiar with the wonderful alpine nature of Upper Austria. I had continued to give private lessons after assuming this educational task but was gradually able to pass them on to others, thus allowing me time to pursue my own studies.

Before I came to this family, my opportunities to participate in children's games had been limited. Consequently, finally, during my twenties I had time to *play*, since I had to learn how to play and direct the games. I did this with great satisfaction. I think that during my life I have played as much as anyone, but it was not until I was between twenty-two and twenty-eight that I did what is usually accomplished before the age of ten.

(from GA 28, p. 102ff.)[1]

---

1 English translation in Rudolf Steiner, *Autobiography. Chapters in the Course of my Life 1861-1907.* SteinerBooks 2005, p. 73f. (Kindle edition), tr. R. Stebbing (revised)

¹n summary, there are several important aspects to consider:

A child with special needs who tired after even "slight mental exertion" was entrusted to Steiner: an indication of the necessarily individualized nature of education.

Steiner gains access to the soul of the child. The child becomes fond of him and his dormant faculties awaken: an indication of the educational relationship between the child and the adult.

The educational task becomes the source of the future teaching practice; the study of physiology, psychology, and "true knowledge of the human being" point to possibilities of a life- and practice-related anthropological research.

The child develops well—a reflection of the individualized teaching efforts.

Finally, Steiner learned "to play" thanks to the educational tasks he had within the family—in other words he could enter childhood again as a learner.

These experiences show us a basic educational attitude that is not guided by prescribed pedagogy but a "true knowledge of the human being" gained in the observation of individual children and their destiny that can then evolve into the art of teaching. This biographical account is therefore a key, not only to the specific anthropology of Waldorf education but also to the art of the individualized child study or child conference (Chapter 6.6). It is, in turn, also the source of an educational anthropology devoted to the child's inner being and the knowledge of this being (Chapter 2). Steiner's biographical account encourages us to reflect on and observe children in depth and can therefore serve as a source text for studying in faculty meetings or in teacher training.

6.3 The teacher's attitude

When the first Waldorf school was founded in 1919, Rudolf Steiner emphasized how important it was to study anthropological and psychological questions. It was essential, he said, that teachers were not only competent educators but that they "reflect on the evolving human being" (GA 293, p. 27f.) because then they would have "a different effect on their students than those who know nothing about it and are not interested" (ibid.).

Steiner pointed out repeatedly how reflection on ideal-typical aspects of being human informs the teacher's attitude: "What happens when you think such thoughts, when you begin to understand the importance of the breathing process and its transformation through education, or the cosmic significance of the rhythm between sleeping and waking? As soon as you think such thoughts, something in you begins to overcome your self-centeredness. Something of what lives in you because you are physical beings is eliminated [...]" (ibid.).

Self-centered behaviors and actions are on the one hand those that are directly reactive and driven by subjective judgments or moods, but on the other hand also those based on habits or on instructions imposed from the outside. Being able to leave behind personal feelings and habitual behaviors is not only professional but reflects above all one's conscious inner approach to the work of the teacher. It is important that, as you enter the kindergarten, home, or school where you work, you leave your own private worries or concerns outside in the parking lot and only pick them up again on your way home. In other words, carry as little as possible of your "self-centeredness" into the classroom. Steiner speaks of "eliminating what lives in you because you are physical beings" so that "inner forces" can arise in you that help you to establish a suprapersonal relationship with the children (GA 293, p. 28).

Working with children, if it is not to be restricted to pragmatic aspects alone, requires the teacher to be mindful and present in the moment. Steiner provides a wealth of exercises (S 31–35) that can help teachers to approach everyday occurrences in a more relaxed and less impulsive manner. This capacity of being present in the moment, mindful, and serene is enhanced by suprapersonal "reflections on the evolving human being" that are not only concerned with everyday life.

6.4 Reading source texts like an "orchestral score"

As a way of deepening the "anthroposophical knowledge of the human being," of which most of the source texts in this book are a part, Steiner proposes a method of study that can be practiced both in individual meditation and in groups. This method serves to build up in teachers an inner source of strength, a process that unfolds in the following stages:

1. Studying the human being
2. Coming to a comprehension of the human being through meditation
3. Active creative remembering
4. Teaching out of the "power of ingenuity" (GA 302a, p. 52;[2] S 29)

Steiner used the language of his time, which can make his writings difficult to access when one comes across them for the first time. The same

---

2 English in Rudolf Steiner, *Balance in Teaching*, Great Barrington: Anthroposophic Press, 2007, tr. R. Pusch (revised), p. 39f.

is true for his lectures, which were usually noted down in shorthand and then transcribed. Both these sources deal, moreover, with challenging topics, covering all kinds of areas. Reading these sources is a question of practice and also of ingenuity. The following is a description of the study method proposed by Rudolf Steiner.

In a first step one should "merely" read the texts and register their content. Following the way Steiner develops his thoughts can be a challenge in itself due to his unconventional way of thinking and his remarkable erudition. Using vibrant characterizations and pictorial presentation, he takes his readers and listeners on an inner journey that inspires creative thinking and invites them to look at the issues presented from many different perspectives. We recommend to first read through the texts so as to get an idea of their content and to note down some key thoughts and questions that can then be the starting point for further deepening. It is important not to finish reading with a feeling of being "well informed" but to feel the need to explore the contents further, taking note of anything that is still open or unclear, cryptic or even questionable, and therefore worth pursuing in greater depth. The source texts can, for instance, be used as a basis for exploring themes such as "the essence of human nature" (S 1), "the child's first three years" (S 3), "imitation in childhood" (S 7-10), "the development of imagination" (S 13-15), "child play" (S 19-21), or for discussing any questions that have been inspired by reading the texts and relating them to practical teaching experiences. For a deeper understanding we recommend to focus on short text passages, work out the main thoughts expressed in them, and if necessary consult the secondary literature available on them.

Once the text has been read through once—either individually or in groups—students should try to rephrase the content in their own words, either by writing down a summary or outline and then presenting it to their fellow students, by discussing it in conversation groups, or in "dialog walks," that is, during a seven-minute walk in groups of three. This interactive method not only enhances the comprehension and retention of contents, but also inspires spontaneous ideas that should, however, be held back at first. When studying the texts students can formulate key sentences for each paragraph that can serve as triggers for recalling the entire content in conversation or in personal study and for new thoughts and perspectives to arise. The key thoughts can then be made visible in a diagram. The whole experience can be deepened further by including specialist fields such as anthropology, psychology, and education, or examples from the teaching practice.

Steiner uses the example of music to illustrate how "comprehending meditation" is followed by "active, creative remembering" that "gives new inner impulses" (ibid.).[3]

He likens this method to the reading of an "orchestral score" (GA 301, p. 115f.), in which the separate thoughts or trains of thought can be perceived, like the parts of the individual instruments, but these parts only unfold their artistic power when they interact and sound together: "We shall produce so many thoughts and feelings that they will pour out of us. Meditate in the evening upon such knowledge of the human being and in the morning you will know in a flash, 'Of course, this or that is what I must do [with a particular child]' (GA 302a, p. 51f.; S 29); […] returning to them if only for five minutes a day, will bring our inner soul life into movement" (ibid., p. 51).[4]

As students work on the source texts in this book, they can focus on particular, manageable themes and deepen them in meditative contemplation. Because the source texts have been arranged according to topics and are separately introduced they provide many starting points for further reading and discussion. Repeated deepening of the source texts will inspire diverse ideas for practice and so enliven the group work and provide impulses for the "power of ingenuity" we need as teachers.

6.5 Invisible friends

Children often have invisible friends or companions. While they would not necessarily mention them to others, they live in close companionship with them (S 16). It requires mindfulness and empathy to find out more about these beings who are described as angels or gnomes, humans or animals. For children they tend to be more natural than for adults, who often don't even notice them or deny their existence because they don't believe in them. Children, if left to themselves, are open to these beings, as we can see from the following personal experience.

For several years, when I was a child, I took the train on my way to school and happened to share this train journey with a boy who was always accompanied by an "invisible friend." He called his friend "little fox" and, especially in winter when the windows on the train were steamed up, it became visible to all of us because, the boy, as soon as he had stepped onto the train, would draw his little fox on the window pane as if it was

---

3 English translation in Rudolf Steiner, *Renewal of Education,* Anthroposophic Press 2001, p. 130, tr. R. Lathe, N. Whittaker
4 English translation in Rudolf Steiner, *Balance in Teaching,* SteinerBooks 2007, p. 40f., tr. R. Pusch (revised)

another traveler, and then he would chat with him throughout the journey. What exactly they were talking about remained a mystery, but the little fox seemed to have a lively interest in the boy's life. Both would look at each other smilingly. The boy drew the little fox often and always in a similar way, so that it became recognizable, but he always removed the drawing before getting off the train. We fellow-students were so familiar with the fox that in the end no one questioned its presence or meaning. One day the boy's sister told me, "He always has his little fox with him and speaks with it, at home too." The fox continued to be the boy's faithful companion until puberty. Then it disappeared.

Some children live happily with such invisible beings if adults don't try to convince them that they don't exist or express doubts about them. They appear in many folktales, too, both as friends and as mischief-makers. "The Tale of the Toad" reflects on the sad effects parental interference can have (S 16). Here is the story as related by the Brothers Grimm:

> There was once a little girl whose mother gave her a small bowl of milk and bread every afternoon, and the child seated herself in the yard with it. But when she began to eat, a toad came creeping out of a crevice in the wall, dipped its little head in the dish, and ate with her. The child took pleasure in this, and when she was sitting there with her little dish and the toad did not come at once, she cried:

> *Toad, o toad, you little dear,*
> *Do come hither, never fear,*
> *You shall have some bread and milk,*
> *Fresh and cool and smooth as silk.*

> Then the toad came in haste, and enjoyed its food. It even showed gratitude, for it brought the child all kinds of pretty things from its hidden treasures, bright stones, pearls, and golden playthings. The toad, however, drank only the milk and left the bread-crumbs alone. Then one day the child took its little spoon and struck the toad gently on its head, and said, 'Eat the bread-crumbs as well, little toad.'

> The mother, who was standing in the kitchen, heard the child talking to someone, and when she saw that she was striking a toad with her spoon, ran out with a log of wood, and killed the good little creature.

> From that time forth, a change came over the child. As long as the toad had eaten with her, she had grown tall and strong, but now she lost her pretty rosy cheeks and wasted away. It was not long before the funeral bird began to cry in the night, and the robin to collect

little branches and leaves for a funeral wreath and soon afterwards the child lay on her bier. (Grimm 1975, p. 209ff.).[5]

Invisible beings often appear in folktales and seem to be as real as anything else in ordinary life. For children they are images of soul processes and at the same time a part of themselves that they trust, consult with, and feel supported by. These invisible friends could be an indication of the sensitivity and disposition in children that Lisa Miller (Miller/Barker 2016) found evidence of in her numerous studies (see Introduction). Children long to share their spiritual experiences with others, but grown-ups often don't know how to deal with these intimations. Many, even if they are religious, doubt the reality and significance of spiritual or soul experiences. Children then feel misunderstood, rejected, and cut off from their own "higher" soul being—as if the invisible "toad" had been killed or the "little fox" been called into question. In the end they keep their secrets to themselves and, if they are lucky, are able to cherish them for a while longer.

Lisa Miller now travels internationally, trying to motivate parents and educators to make use of their children's natural spirituality, which is such an essential resource, and to allow them to transform their spiritual disposition into qualities that can enhance development. The worldwide research carried out by Miller proves that there is no better prophylaxis against drugs and addiction than the fostering of spiritual dispositions that can facilitate meaningful and significant experiences in later life. Parents and educators can strengthen this spiritual potential by "trusting heart knowledge and validating direct transcendent experience; encouraging natural love of nature, of spiritual ritual and prayer and right action, and the sense of family as special" (ibid., p. 178).

If we sensitively acknowledge the invisible friends that our children are as deeply connected with as they are to close relatives, this can open a door to the spiritual experiences that resonate in the child's soul and that the child may sometimes like to share with us.

6.6 The child study or child conference

In his book *Solving the Riddle of the Child* Christof Wiechert writes about the child study used in Waldorf education, describing on the one hand its origin, in 1919, in the Faculty Meetings of the first Waldorf school and presenting on the other hand examples of how educators and teachers can

---

5 English translation by Margaret Hunt (revised and adapted) in *The Brothers Grimm: The Complete Fairy Tales*. Ware, Hertfortshire, UK (1997): Wordsworth Editions, p. 480f.

consult on individual children in such a child study or child conference (Wiechert 2014). Ideally, the child study forms the heart of the collegial work and is a source for bringing the anthroposophical view of the human being to life, so that teachers learn to understand the children's different constitutions, talents and abilities, and, above, are enabled to form a loving professional teacher-child relationship.

The motto goes back to a lecture by Rudolf Steiner in which he outlines the ideal teacher's attitude:

> If your attitude to children is that they have come down to you from the spiritual world and that you must solve each child's riddle every day, every hour—then you are filled with the loving inner devotion to child development that is required for you to be a child's companion whatever unexpected situation may arise. And one often meets such unexpected situations in teaching and education (GA 297a, p. 150).

That a child is entrusted to a particular educator or teacher and that they have the task to "solve the riddle of this child" may not be coincidence. We have seen from Steiner's account of teaching the young Specht boy that it needs loving, selfless affection for and interest in children if one is to gain an insight into their individual life intentions and recognize the talents one needs to awaken in them. When teachers had questions about individual children in the Faculty meetings, Steiner's recommendations used to be pragmatic, if unconventional. For him, teaching was not about getting children to adapt to outer circumstances but about helping them to unfold their individual potential. When asked whether a boy in fifth grade, who was good at languages but did not work well in other subjects, should be sent to a remedial class, Rudolf Steiner replied that the boy "loves being different" and recommended he should "make a pair of shoes," that he would enjoy making "real boots for someone else" (GA 300a, p. 281f.)[6] Steiner did not recommend correcting a weakness or sending the boy to remedial lessons, but promoting the strengths needed for self-development.

From these impulses given by Steiner, various child study and child observation methods have emerged, alongside diagnostic, therapeutic and educational recommendations which are put into practice in Waldorf kindergartens and schools (Seydel 2009; Ruhrmann/Henke 2017). We will briefly introduce some tried and tested methods below. Important further information can be found in the publications mentioned.

---

6 English in *Faculty Meetings with Rudolf Steiner, Volume 1: 1919-1922*, Hudson NY, Anthroposophic Press, p. 305, tr. R. Lathe, N. Parsons Whittaker

Often, child studies are convened when a problematic situation arises because a child causes difficulties in kindergarten or grade school. It is therefore the more important to make the decision to devote particular attention to each child once in the course of two or three years and to talk about them with the parents and colleagues, in other words, to not only consult on children when there is a problem but to consciously accompany all the children. This can be simply and effectively done by using a "child diary" to note down special occurrences and personal impressions. This is more than is required by the often formalized documentation sheets or files. The teacher's personal impressions are important and teachers should therefore consider the following questions when preparing for a child study:

1. What is my motivation for this child study?
2. What was my first impression of this child?
3. How would I like to proceed?
4. How can I find the way from my observation of this child to anthropological and psychological considerations?

In addition to personal notes and preliminary conversations with parents and colleagues that serve to gather information about the child's development, a "mood picture" can be used to start the child study. Colored chalks are used to express moods that evoke memories of the child in question. It often happens surprisingly in this process that feelings of love and affection arise in the teachers for this child, however great the disruption caused by him or her in class. As personal characterizations and particular experiences of the child are added, such a mood picture can lead over into a child study, for instance as part of a faculty meeting. Child studies should be carried out in a particular order, as shown below, although the idea is not to go through the list and tick off the individual items, because these items must be given different weight depending on the individual child:

1. Describing the child
- *name, age, family, general situation*
- *physical aspects: body shape, proportions, head/face, trunk, limbs, health*
- *gait, movements, habits, temperament, social behavior*
- *learning, memory, concentration, perceptive and cognitive abilities*
- *strengths, weaknesses, inclinations, talents*
- *work, ability, performance, plans*
2. Environment: kindergarten, school, home, other
3. Biography (information from the child and the parents)

7 The future of childhood

DAVID MARTIN AND SILKE SCHWARZ

7.1 Introduction

"Hypotheses are nets; only those who cast will catch." (Novalis 2001)

One often hears demands for an evidence-based education today, a request that can only be supported from the medical standpoint: any measures introduced to education should be evaluated in trials. However, if we conducted trial after trial before doing anything in education, we would be like chefs who refuse to use a particular recipe unless it has been subjected to blind testing. The entire process would take far too long, with many inedible and unpalatable dishes being produced along the way. No chef can afford this waiting for evidence, nor can we when the wellbeing of our children is at stake. Chefs can also rely on and be guided by their experience, taste, expertise, and intuition. And in education we can, *in addition* to evidence-based research, let ourselves be guided by the children themselves and rely on the ideas, feelings, and impulses that arise from a gradually deepening observation and understanding of children. In this chapter we will introduce some thoughts that can be fruitful for both future education and research.

7.2 Childhood in the past

When one hears how children were treated in the past it is quite clear that our approach to childhood today is very different. Looking back in history we realize that the concept of childhood as an independent period in life that needs to be protected is quite a recent one. In his book *The Disappearance of Childhood* Neil Postman points out that there was no clear concept of child development in the Middle Ages (Postman 1982). Lloyd de Mause, in his work *History of Childhood,* describes the sad destinies of children in the distant past when infanticide, child labor, and child exploitation were widespread because the specific needs of children were not understood (Mause/Langer 1974). De Mause takes his readers back to a time when, due to poverty or starvation, people would throw newborn babies over the garden wall and leave them to die. There were no accepted moral or legal restrictions to infanticide, although it was usually girls who were affected by it. Even Aristotle, while deploring infanticide and proposing restrictions to unlimited reproduction considering that so many newborn children had to be killed, raised no categorical objections against this and even demanded the killing of malformed children (Dunn 2006). In his writings on education Plato suggested disciplinary measures that we would today describe as child abuse. It was only during the Roman Empire that children were for the first time legally protected when, in 374 CE, the first law against infanticide was passed.

This historical background is sufficient justification for us to ask how clear we are today when it comes to the needs and rights of children. In Germany the rights of children are still not established by law and a coalition is working actively to remedy this situation (*Aktionsbündnis Kinderrechte ins Grundgesetz 2018*). While it is true to say that in many respects, including when it comes to their rights, children were never as well cared for as today, it is not that long ago that, even in our Western culture, children could, for instance, be violently punished or left alone in hospital. In medicine, the idea that children are basically little adults is only just beginning to be overcome.

7.3 Children today—what we will look back on uneasily

There is still a real danger that we fail to understand children and their bodily, emotional, and spiritual needs. Children today are still at risk, if in different ways from before, of not having their needs and rights acknowledged.

The question we could ask is what future generations will find shocking in the way we think about childhood and treat children today. We could imagine that the subtle, often covert unease we feel today will in future turn into the same experience of shock we have today when we read about the violent treatment of children by past generations. We must try to become more sensitive and find solutions by imagining a world that we will not have to look back on uneasily from the future.

We will start by briefly outlining some such feelings of unease. The list below is meant as a basis to work on. It gives insight into topics that are also addressed by our *Future of Childhood* initiative.[1]

Readers are encouraged, before looking at our list, to reflect for a moment and note down what they feel apprehensive about. Additions to our list are also welcome.

YOUR LIST:

_____

_____

_____

_____

_____

_____

_____

_____

_____

_____

_____

_____

_____

_____

1 www.lebens-weise.org/index.php/projekte/future-of-childhood/ Translator's note: this website is mainly in German but has references to English-language publications under "Research"

OUR LIST OF SHORTCOMINGS:

• The topic is not internationally discussed yet
• Girls and boys are not treated equally
• Child poverty. This has been acknowledged as a serious problem worldwide for many decades (Seils/Höhne 2015a). One of the most recent studies on child poverty in Germany—the Child Poverty Report 8, composed on behalf of the German Institute of Economic and Social Research (WSI)—noted a marked rise in the number of poor children in Germany: in 2015, for instance, their number rose by 77,000 (0.7 percentage points) to 2.55 million (19.7 per cent).

Education:
• Children spend too much time sitting in schools
• The average square meter to child ratio in schools restricts movement
• Compulsory schooling with insufficient consideration of individual needs
• Assessment based on grades given for performance
• Low admission criteria and insufficient assessment of teachers, most of whom have civil servant status[2] (and therefore little extrinsic motivation)
• Inartistic, one-sidedly intellectual learning that fails to address the whole person
• Starting school too early: the fact that younger children are more often diagnosed with ADHD than older children in the same grade prompts many questions

Medicine:
• Medicalization: the tendency today is to treat primarily the symptoms of behavioral problems with drugs (for instance Ritalin, a drug that requires a narcotic prescription), without establishing a differential diagnosis based on underlying causes
• Hospitals that don't offer parent-child rooms up to the age of 18. Even with adults we need to ask whether the care provided in hospital is more effective when a partner or friend stays with them in hospital—an option that is already widely available in hospices.

Time:
• Scientific research into healthy rhythms and the use of time in childhood is only just starting.
• Physiologically non-optimal school hours (starting time, length of school day, and other factors).

---

2 State school teachers in many parts of Germany have civil servant status and cannot normally not be dismissed.

• After-school stress due to rise in extracurricular learning paid for by parents; multiple afternoon activities such as music lessons, creative pursuits or sports, which, although each of them is meaningful in itself, limit children's free time.
• Not enough time for just being and playing freely; burnout symptoms in children are on the rise.
• Loss of community and of children educating each other because they no longer meet to spend time together in the street, in playgrounds or in the woods.

Religion:
• Fundamentalist-religious or strictly atheist upbringing that leaves children too little scope for inner development

Institutions:
• Direction of kindergartens, schools, and hospitals as purely profit-oriented enterprises

Family:
• Financial insecurity of single parents

Environment:
• Pollution, exploitation of natural resources, maltreatment of animals, factory farming, species extinction. Young children suffer with nature.

Nutrition:
• Advertising of sugary foods, fast food, cigarettes, alcohol, and so on
• Pesticides
• Inferior quality
• Lack of rhythm, reverence, and mindfulness in the production and consumption of food

Digitization:
• Uncritical introduction of modern media in schools although their effect has not been investigated in independent controlled trials
• Release of potentially addictive media devices without legal age restrictions

Architecture, town planning:
• Bleak and soulless school campuses, communal institutions, and residential areas

Before we explain some of these points in more detail, we will look at evolution as a basis for developing more precise criteria of future viability.

7.4 Future viability

We observe two different developments: one is that the world is becoming ever more child-friendly and more conscious of the needs of children; the other is that the space and time granted to childhood is as threatened as never before by our modern lifestyles. Given that creating and maintaining a more child-friendly world takes some effort, it can be assumed that there are certain forces or factors driving these positive developments. Finding out what these factors are could make us future-viable and teach us to become more intuitive when it comes to ensuring that childhood will be a positive experience in the future.

If we start by asking about basic childhood experiences we can identify a state of person-to-person, loving, playful movement and warmth. The experience of a loving person, a child, or moments of creativity when we love what we are doing, often stand out as particularly meaningful and enjoyable. For such moments to be possible at all a long evolutionary process was required. Exploring this process both conceptually and intuitively reveals many evolutionary factors that go beyond reproduction, mutation, and selection. Maybe these additional factors can guide us toward a future understanding and realization of childhood.

As we try to trace these factors it can help to look back on the history of humanity and of life and consult diverse evolutionary theories. Darwin's evolutionary theory, for instance, constituted a quantum leap in the organic sciences of his time. While his followers focused too one-sidedly on the notion of the "egoistical survival of the fittest" and Darwin himself neglected the phenomenon that animals help each other, Darwinism has contributed much to explaining the evolution of species. Yet neither Darwin's original studies nor evolutionary theory as it is taught in most schools around the globe today, with their focus on mutation, recombination, selection, and genetic drift, can offer much that can help us to understand childhood. These ideas that have become so deeply rooted in our culture cannot be driving forces for a social, child-friendly world— neither in the way they affect our thinking (adults and children) nor with regard to their social implications (if distorted by social Darwinism). This means we have to look elsewhere for the factors and forces that have driven more child-friendly developments in the past, for once we have found them, we will be able to foster them for a better future.

Rudolf Steiner mentioned the Goethean approach as a second theory after Darwin's: "Darwinism considers physical evolution from the physical side: external impulses, struggle for survival, selection, and so on, and in this way outlines an evolution which is dying down—everything you can discover about organic life if you give yourself up to impulses which came up in earlier times. To understand Darwin, one merely has to make a synthesis of all the laws discovered in the past. To understand Goethe, one has to rise above this to laws which are ever new in earth existence. Both are necessary. It is not Darwinism which is the problem, nor Goetheanism, but the fact that people want to follow one or the other rather than one *and* the other. That is what really matters" (Steiner GA 177, p. 209).[3]

It seems that Goethe saw something in children that brings human evolution forward. At a time when higher education was mostly the prerogative of men,[4] he postulated that education would only be whole once women were included and considered equal (a goal we are still striving to achieve today all over the world) and once children were included (something we still have to discover). This explains the following words by Goethe that seem unusual at first glance: "What even women leave uneducated in us, children will develop if we engage with them" (Goethe 1989, p. 469).

What Goethe is saying is that children bring with them forces and qualities that can promote education if we are open to them. Our hypothesis is that these as yet unidentified forces are important motors of human evolution that will become freer and more apparent with every new generation. With every new generation humanity will "rise [...] to laws which are ever new in earth existence" (Steiner, GA 177, p. 210). If we are to understand the riddle of childhood and do justice to the future of children, we must focus much more on forces than on heredity or the functional adaptation to our environment.

We will now consider other conditions and factors—let's call them "principles"—that will facilitate the "visibility and new creation" of childhood and capacity for development, starting with biology and the anatomy of a very "down-to-earth" part of the body: the heel.

Bernd Rosslenbroich and his co-workers have established that in the course of evolution the heel—along with many other developments—appeared simultaneously in various groups of animals, as if there was a kind of superordinate impulse for the forming of heels. But the various groups developed very distinct, partly adventurous strategies for forming a heel. If we then look at the groups that formed the kind of heels that would

---

3 English in Rudolf Steiner, *The Fall of the Spirits of Darkness*, Forest Row: Rudolf Steiner Press, 1995, p. 189. Tr. A. Meuss
4 Anna Maria von Schürmann attended university lectures in Utrecht in the 17th century, but had to sit behind a latticed partition so as not to distract the male students. In the 18th century, Luise Adelgunde Victorie Gottsched heard her husband's lectures at Leipzig University, standing behind a door that was left ajar (Niemeyer 1996).

persist in the long term, we find that the heel-forming in those particular groups proceeded particularly slowly. Due to their slow, one could almost say "prudent" evolution, these animals were able to develop a particularly adaptable heel, which was in turn the precondition for the next evolutionary step toward greater autonomy (Rosslenbroich 2014b). This gives us another principle of child development: *Deceleration can promote future viability*.

We should know that the children who—from our modern, often somewhat functional perspective—are seen as "slow developers" might be the ones who will later make crucial contributions to the development of society.

Of course, being quick can also promote future viability: that is the better known principle, which we sometimes fail to consider, however, when we meet impetuous, hyperactive children.

Another principle, related to the former one, is that of the morphological and functional "rejuvenation" that occurs in the course of evolution. Homo sapiens, for instance, had a more childlike appearance (the forehead more pronounced than the jaws) and was functionally more universal (more embryonic looking hands) than Neanderthal man (Verhulst 1999; Rosslenbroich 2009). This trend toward a "rejuvenation of humanity" was also observed by scientists in the 1970s (Neugarten 1974) and referred to as the new "generation of the young-old," who are also behaviorally younger than their ancestors, a fact that, in turn, has an influence on the following generation. This brings us to the next principle: *Future viability means "being closer to children" in the widest sense*.

"At the same time came the disciples unto Jesus, saying, Who is the greatest in the kingdom of heaven? And Jesus called a little child unto him, and set him in the midst of them, and said, Verily I say unto you, Except you be converted and become as little children, you shall not enter into the kingdom of heaven."[5] (Sand/Eckert/Wikenhauser 1986).

Or, in Goethe's words (Goethe 1998a, p. 384):

Let all things be where thou art, childlike ever,
Thus thou'lt be all, thus thou'lt be vanquished never.[6]

Humans live this principle biologically more thoroughly than any other creatures in that they give more time to childhood and adolescence, for instance by actively suppressing pubertal hormones. In addition, humans don't specialize early, neither physically (hoofs, wings, and fins all derive

---

5 King James Bible, Matthew 18:1-3
6 English by Edgar Alfred Bowring, source en.wikisource.org/wiki/The_Works_of_J._W._von_Goethe/Volume_9/Trilogy_of_Passion

from the same original embryonic form, to which the human hand has remained closest) nor behaviorally. Most animal behaviors become quite specific with puberty. Humans only just begin at that point to ask themselves what they want to be in life and what profession they might like to practice in the future. The principle in this case could be described as: *Protection from premature specialization promotes universality and the ability to learn.*

A further principle can be found in play: one of life's most mysterious and wonderful phenomena. Even primitive dinosaurs displayed rudiments of playfulness, a behavior that seems to be experienced as pleasant but that has no purpose. The ability to play continually increased through evolution, reaching a first climax in birds who have developed quite enchanting ways of playing (Rosslenbroich 2014a). The young of a species tend to play more than older specimens, with puberty constituting something of a threshold after which playfulness decreases, although it never ceases altogether in higher animals. Evolutionary biologists have discovered that the most playful sub-groups are the ones capable of taking the next evolutionary steps. This brings us to another principle of evolution: *The future finds and forms itself in play*

We can see this reflected in human evolution, which began on the African continent around 7.5 million years ago. Neanderthal man, who developed faster than Homo sapiens and reached puberty earlier, appears to have played less according to modern estimations—and was unable to survive in the long term.

Evolutionary biology can therefore confirm what Friedrich Schiller meant when he said, "We only play when we are human in the fullest sense of the word, and we are only fully human when we play." (Schiller 1875/2004, p. 93.)

When we look at qualities that are typically human (self-determined actions, upright gait, speech, thinking, love; freedom, gratitude, modesty, and so on), we realize that we can only develop and retain these qualities as long as we live in human communities. We are consequently, strictly speaking, never fully human, but always in a process of helping each other to become human. From which we can conclude that *Human evolution and individual development are emergent and occur in dialog with nature, other humans and oneself.*

In young children this happens initially through creative imitation—a principle we don't find developed to the same degree in any other creatures (Chapter 4). The question we need to ask is if humanity has not, in the course of evolution, always imitated some "higher" principle? This kind of "top-down" thinking is unusual and somewhat daring in the "bottom-up" mood that prevails in the sciences today. But it is nevertheless a thought we can play with as a hypothesis, in the sense of what has been said earlier. There are, after all, no known ancient peoples or high cultures who did not assume the existence of higher beings. This gives us another principle of future viability: *Does a sense of the existence of "higher" beings promote future viability?*

Scientific studies as well as our own experience teach us that a sense of "awe" or reverence promotes human well-being (Rudd/Vohs/Aaker 2012), as do the qualities of generosity and selflessness we see in so many people who happily and voluntarily, day in day out, nurture the social fabric of our society. Interestingly, Rudolf Steiner begins his instructions for future viability (Steiner GA 10, p. 8) with the intense practice of reverence for higher beings and devotion to truth and knowledge.

One could ask why, if this is the case, we do not, or rarely, perceive this assumed "top-down" effect or these alleged "higher" beings? The answer is that young children have a natural feeling for this higher spirituality and that this feeling is increasingly lost as they grow up (Chapter 2.2).

This gradual loss of a paradise-like, direct connection with a "higher" entity could, however, be prerequisite to the most important principle of future viability there is: our inner autonomy. The concept of free will may be controversially discussed by the sciences, but it forms the foundation of our culture and of our laws. *Autonomy is the basis of human freedom.*

When children play freely they practice autonomy. This requires imagination and is therefore a wonderful preparation for the tasks in life that require imagination and the realization of ideals. The feeling and freedom of contributing to shaping one's own life creatively engender self-efficacy and resilience. *Being creative—being an artist—fosters future viability.*

Future viability and artistic creativity begin with the ability to nurture warm thoughts and feelings playfully and energetically. For this we need to recognize feelings and thoughts as real forces. Using these forces freely and responsibly enables us to turn our will impulses into actions.

"Genuine art will not only take hold of soul and spirit, but it will also enhance health and growth. Genuine art has always had healing powers." (Steiner GA 304a, p. 28)[7]

Readers may have noticed that we have moved from an approach that focuses on biological evolutionary aspects of the past to one that looks to the future and is guided by aspects of soul and spirit. If we look for faculties that are seen as future-viable today by institutions and enterprises, we will find that flexibility, leadership, creativity, empathy, communication and team skills, selflessness, innovativeness, and resilience are in first

---

7 English in Rudolf Steiner, *Waldorf Education and Anthroposophy Vol. 2*, Hudson: Anthroposophic Press 1996, tr. R. Everett.

place (rightmanagement.co.uk 2018b; Forbes Coaches Council 2018). Just like the arts, all these skills are not developed sufficiently in schools today; and yet they constitute precisely the faculties that children bring with them as potential. We need an education that is prepared to learn from the deepest childhood impulses, that nurtures and promotes them in order to enable their "resonant, creative emergence" through practice.

Following these contemplations, we will now turn our attention to practical life situations.

7.5 Ensouled movement, use of time, nutrition

That children and young people have to sit so much in schools and at their work places is seen as a definite health risk today. Lack of exercise has been shown to be linked to a higher risk of cardio-vascular disease (Dunstan et. al. 2012), while people who exercise regularly have fewer phases of depression (Chekroud et. al. 2018). But that is not all: most recent trials show a correlation between children's mental and social development and the time they spend playing outside in their preschool years (Ulse et.al. 2017).

Of course, many adults spend much time sitting too and remain healthy in spite of this. But what are the implications? Are they inwardly mobile? There are no studies on this to our knowledge. Today's trend of working out in sport and fitness studios, on the other hand, has not been proven to be linked to longer life expectancy. The city with the longest life expectancy in the German state of Baden Wurttemberg (Baden Wurttemberg Statistical Office, Tübingen 2016) does not excel because of the opportunities for physical exercise it offers, but because of its rich educational and cultural program.

Children move most when they can play freely. Maybe it will be understood in the future that movement is healthiest when it is truly ensouled and not just physical, particularly with young children. Steiner recommended that parents and educators should use nursery rhymes, songs, and music to dance with three- to four-year-olds because this would enhance the wellbeing of everyone involved. Eurythmy is also a rewarding, holistic way of moving for young children.

What is the healthiest ensouled movement for the various age groups today? Yoga instructor is the fastest growing choice of profession. Many people experience this movement art as helpful and attempts are being made increasingly to introduce yoga for children in schools or at home. This should be done with caution, however. Based on the experience the authors have with yoga and eurythmy and their understanding of the developing human being, one needs to ask which of these movement arts is better suited to children and promotes child development more naturally.

Careful scientific studies are required, starting for instance with comparisons of the effects of both yoga and eurythmy in adults. Aside from yoga and eurythmy there are other forms of movement that need to be investigated in more depths, such as Tai Chi, Spacial Dynamics, Bothmer Gymnastics, and Chi Gong. Several trials to this effect are presently being carried out by Witten-Herdecke University in Germany[8] (Büssing et. al. 2018).

If we look at our attitude to time today we notice a general trend toward acceleration. "Time is money!" What would Momo, the kind heroine of the eponymous book by Michael Ende, say to this? Let's remind ourselves: Momo owns nothing apart from what she finds or what is given to her. She is free, lives in the present and has an extraordinary gift: she always has time and is a wonderful listener. One day certain strange "grey gentlemen" appear in town. They are time thieves who are after people's valuable living time. Only Momo can stop them. In offering friendship and listening to people she displays a rare quality that connects her with others at a deeper level. She speaks of "riches that will kill us if we can't share them with others" (Ende 2005). We would add that there are riches that only reveal themselves if one devotes time to them, and love. Our children can teach us to live in the moment and devote ourselves to the minutest details, such as the flutter of a butterfly's wing: a crucial ability in times when one in six children suffers from stress.

Looking at nutrition, it needs to be pointed out that not only the quantity and quality of our food is important but also the time we devote to eating it. There is no research as yet into the immediate and long-term effect rhythmic and harmonious mealtimes have on children.

"But we will be less exposed to the dangers of egotism in later life, if we are taught about nutrition and hygiene in the last years of middle school [age 10 to 12], when such lessons don't appeal to our egotism but to what still lives naturally in us" (Steiner GA 294, p. 188).

The way we feed our children at home and above all in schools is lagging far behind our scientific and intuitive knowledge. Everyone knows that school kitchens almost everywhere, across the world, don't serve good food. And yet, nothing changes. We know that a school garden can improve health, food choices, the relationship with nature, even self-efficacy. So why does not every school have a school garden? We know now that our children's diet affects their future eating behavior, food preferences, microbiomes, and lifelong health. Because of the problems with obesity and malnutrition in our society, preventative action is increasing-

---

8 Faculty of Medical Theory, Integrative Medicine, and Anthroposophic Medicine

ly aimed at children and their mealtimes. Trying to change one's eating habits later requires a conscious effort. The same is true for habits in connection with the sustainable use of resources.

Ancient shamanic wisdom demands that, with all decisions involving humankind, both the past and the future seven generations must be considered. Whether or not seven generations are really enough is another question, but this is a worthwhile exercise to play through in one's mind before reading on.

Taking this demand seriously would mean weighing up every social or political decision with a view to children and childhood and with future generations in mind. A consciousness of humanity is needed that does justice to the present but is at the same time formed out of the past and directed toward the future. It is true that we are borrowing the earth from our children and that it belongs to future generations. Sustainability is a key aspect, for without the effective protection of climate and biodiversity the survival and existence of our children and grandchildren is in danger. Sustainability requires us to use resources in accordance with the natural regeneration of systems in all areas of human development, including town planning, financial politics, economics, the extraction of raw materials, and food production. Biodynamic farming and the Demeter movement lead the way when it comes to high ethical standards and respect for nature.

7.6 The child's environment

This section looks at institutions, environments, architecture, and their importance for the growing child.

Is it really acceptable that institutions that are there to serve humanity, such as schools, homes, and hospitals, are run as profit-making enterprises? The children's hospital of Tübingen University in southern Germany has launched a campaign calling attention to the implications of looking at patients primarily in economic terms: it leads to surgery being carried out unnecessarily in order to keep patient numbers at a required level, while in other cases necessary interventions are left undone. Even if we personally try to live as ethically and socially aware as possible, we often don't notice that as members of particular collectives we support and participate in actions that are not primarily concerned with the individual or common good. The problem is addressed in the following hypothesis by Rudolf Steiner: "The wellbeing of a community of people working together will be the greater the less the individuals in this community claim the proceeds from their work for themselves, in other words, the more of these proceeds they give to their co-workers, and the more their individual needs are met not by the proceeds from their own but from others' work" (Steiner GA 34, p. 213).

So much for the economic aspects. When it comes to culture, we may ask how meaningful it is for the state, in addition to ensuring equality before the law, to also insist that all schools have the same curriculum? According to Rudolf Steiner, there is a connection between the two problem areas mentioned: "Anyone who fails to believe that a free spiritual life generates this kind of love is unaware that it is the dependence of spiritual and cultural life upon the state and the economy that creates desire for personal profit—this desire for profit is not a fundamental aspect of human nature" (Steiner GA 24, p. 51).[9]

We have not found any scientific study that goes into this hypothesis by Rudolf Steiner.

There is no law at present that would protect enterprises and institutions from short-sighted and unethical profit-seeking, a shortcoming that also applies to architectural firms and the aesthetic and social aspects of town planning and buildings. We know so much today about the effect of architecture on children that it is truly irresponsible to ignore this knowledge. And yet, it is still ignored. The color and shape of rooms, the height of ceilings, the form of windows, the furniture and plants, even a building's exterior—they all affect children's feelings, behavior, even appetite: how happily children enter a building, how easily they can get into playing together, how much they fight or argue, how well they sleep, and so on (Fricke et. al. 2018).

Town or city planners have a significant influence on the social life, the quality of life, criminality, and directly and indirectly on children's lives. One can only hope that cities will not only become greener, cleaner, and more sustainable, but that they will become real gardens. Since, according to the prognoses, more and more of us will move into the cities, we will have to bring nature closer to us. Nature has a crucial impact on air quality and health. Recent research has revealed that terpenes—substances released into the air by trees—have a positive, stimulating effect on the human immune system (Arvay 2015). And not only that, seeing green trees and fields alone reduces stress, relaxes, and enhances wound healing. There are studies that show how often students underestimate how good a walk in nature can be for their wellbeing (Mayer et. al. 2009). "Biophilia" is the subject of many books and was defined by Erich Fromm as "the passionate love of life and of all that is alive; it is the wish to enhance growth, whether this is in humans, plants, ideas, or social groups" (Fromm 1964, p. 331).

9 English translation in Rudolf Steiner, *The Renewal of the Social Organism*, GA 24, London: Rudolf Steiner Press 1998, tr. E. Bowen-Wedgewood and R. Mariott, p. 82

7.7 Dealing with digital media

It is possible today for us to—almost always and unrestrictedly—access knowledge without thinking for ourselves. Many pioneers of education tend to agree with Andreas Schleicher, the director of education at OECD who said that "The world no longer rewards people for their knowledge—Google knows everything—but for what they can do with their knowledge" (EduAction Summit 2018).

But what are the creative, social, and practical skills we need in order to become self-effective, healthy, and successful human beings without losing our capacity for independent thinking? How do we adults acquire the skills that are needed in the future? And how can we convey these to our children at the right time and in the right way?[10] Although the potential for addiction is widely known, many babies, children, and adolescents have unlimited access to digital devices, because there are no official regulations to protect them. Parents and professionals struggle to find practicable, healthy, and future-oriented concepts because they are concerned about the findings that relate child media usage (BLIKK Study 2017) to health problems. People of all backgrounds—managers, young social-media users, bloggers—talk about the stress of being continuously available on digital media, the absence of real sensory experiences, and the ensuing lack of an interpersonal relationship culture. Temporary media abstinence can help to find one's healthy center again and establish a new approach to the media. Try spending a few days without your cell phone or computer. Try driving without a GPS, walking in nature without a plant app, stargazing without a stars app. Instead, use paper and crayons to capture in detail what you have observed. When children use their own hands to make dough and bake bread, they have sensory experiences that they miss out on and that fade away if bread or cake always comes wrapped in plastic from the supermarket. We are in the process of working with students and experts on preparing a large-scale media-fast for everyone, with recommendations on how to regain self-experiences. Periods of media abstinence will allow us to become more sensitive again to how much media use is tenable. While there is much to appreciate in the technological achievements of our time and one would not want to do without them, it is important to learn to use them in healthy and age-appropriate ways.

---

10 For more information visit www.lebens-weise.org (website in German only)

7.8 What is important in life?

A professor once introduced a lecture by saying, "Today will be about time management and I would like to do a little experiment with you!" The students were excited by this unusual opening and they watched with interest how the professor picked up a glass jar and placed it on the desk. Slowly, he placed rocks into the glass jar until it was full and no more rocks fitted in. He looked at the students and asked, "Is the jar full now?" The students thought for a moment and then replied unanimously that yes, the jar was full. "Really full?" asked the professor and took out a small container filled with tiny pebbles. He poured the pebbles into the jar so that they filled up all the space in between the pieces of rock. The professor then looked at the students again and asked, "Is the jar full now?" The students, who had learned their lesson, replied, "No, probably not."

"Very good," said the professor. He pulled out a bag of sand and poured the sand slowly into the jar, so that it gradually filled the gaps in between the rocks and pebbles. He looked at the students and asked, "What do we learn from this experiment?"

One of the students thought for a while and then said, "It proves that, even if one thinks one has no time left for a particular task, one can still always do more and fit more into one's day if one goes about it intelligently."

"Yes," said the professor, "but it means something else, too. What we also learn from this experiment is that if we don't put the big rocks into the jar first, they won't fit in later."

The students thought about this. The professor then asked, "Which are the big rocks in your life? What is really important to you? Health, family, self-realization? Always make sure that they come first in your life and that they are not eclipsed by the many small and much less important things!" (adapted from Covey 2014)

What are the big, important rocks in a child's life? We adults need to ask ourselves this, because we decide on our children's priorities and time structure when they are young.

There are many general but nonetheless important aspects we think of first, such as the child's environment, nutrition, rhythm, and so on. But then there are also very individual needs. What is most important for this child right here and right now? And how can we make sure that it is provided? If we ask ourselves this question in a quiet moment, we might be surprised at the ideas we suddenly come up with. They can be quite simple: putting a home-made cookie on the pillow of a fourteen-year old who's had bad results in a math test; spending a day at home with no plans other than just being together; or playing a trick by knotting a child's shoe laces together: small but important ways of creating laughter, confidence and togetherness. Children have a special sense for the greatness in small things. They speak of angels, play with fairies, create root caves with gnomes, and pray to God with touching devotion. Sometimes they have visits from relatives who passed away; after the funeral their beloved grandpa has become a guardian angel, and the adored family dog who died is now playing with other dogs up on the starry meadow.

Children live in spiritual worlds that are often closed to us adults and that don't correspond to the experiences we have (Chapter 2). They also experience religious and annual festivals in a deep and existential way.

There is no doubt that the life of adults changes tremendously once a child enters it. And it does not only change outwardly: if we look carefully we realize that life becomes more spiritual for the adults. People who have more than one child are astounded at their individual characters. Sometimes they detect gifts in their children that go far beyond what lives within the family. The thought of reincarnation and karma is ubiquitous again and for many of us it is a real possibility that our children have acquired their gifts in a previous incarnation. This leads to a deeper respect for children because they may, after all, have been much more advanced in their previous life than we are now and bring with them more pertinent impulses from the spiritual world or from "heaven."

This attitude in parents, as long as they are cautious and modest about it, can help children—because children believe in a life before birth, as N. Emmons and D. Kelemen, both psychologists at Boston University, found out in a representative survey. The belief in a pre-existence of the soul is most widespread in children of around seven or eight, and no less than 50 percent of eleven- and twelve-year-olds still believe in preconceptional existence or "prelife." A religious context for this belief could be excluded, and the scientists assume that children have the innate faculty of imagining an immortal human essence (Emmons und Kelemen 2014). Research into near-death experiences and how they affect those who have them also brings up the question of an existence that is independent of our present body (Van Lommel et. al. 2001).

Independently of the thought of reincarnation or pre-existence, children have a kind of nondenominational religiosity that makes them susceptible for the religiousness that lives in the culture they are born into. Bearing in mind the principles of future viability described earlier, it has to be the task of any "church" to ensure that children are not restricted to a particular religious practice.

What should future relationships be like? At present we are witnessing a breaking up of our relationship culture at all levels. Life communities such as marriage, big families, villages, church congregations, permanent work places, social hierarchies that used to be the norm are losing their former importance. Instead we see same-sex marriages, open relationships, and all forms of loose or narrow, long- or short-term community-building. As the overarching structures disappear, more and more people seek free, socially responsible life communities. We can expect this searching to continue in the future as ways of life emerge that allow for individual development in a society that is growing ever healthier due to the contributions each individual makes to it.

More than anything, children need reliable, loving adults who are aware of their responsibility and who are present in a continuous rhythm. In order to find a modern, free, responsible relationship culture it will be particularly important for adolescents that the adults develop a deeper spiritual interest in new, modern ways of living. In such an environment the growing children and adolescents can feel protected and grow into free and future-viable individuals.

7.9 How do we ourselves become future-viable?

Looking back on our journey through this chapter, we can hypothesize that there is something that, in the course of human evolution, has brought us closer and closer to children and to the forces of childhood. In the widest sense, there seem to be "forces" (for change always relies on forces) that have caused us to become more child-friendly and less violent, more empathetic, flexible, playful, and more understanding of children. Where do these forces come from? Can we activate them consciously within us?

The answer is Yes! We can definitely make sure that we become more susceptible to the needs of children, everywhere in the world. Studies on attachment confirm this: the absence of attachment between mother and baby results in clearly definable and diagnosable symptoms in infants (looking away from the mother during contact; the gaze rigid as if absent; turning to the side, regulation movements such as clenching hands, yawning, and so on). If mothers are taught to perceive and make contact with their babies, these symptoms improve measurably, as does the attachment quality and the baby's health along with the mother's stress levels and life quality (Wright/Edginton 2016).

How can parents, teachers, therapists, people who work for and with children, prepare themselves for the future of childhood? There are already many evaluated, evidence-based studies on this question (Collins/Fetsch 2012). Rudolf Steiner's anthroposophy and its further developments (Köhler 2014) offer much inspiration, with explicit recommendations on how we make ourselves more intuitive for our everyday life with children by meditating on the anthroposophical understanding of the human being (Wember 2017; Chapter 6) and deciding on a path of inner development (S 31–35).

Deciding consciously and in freedom to embark on such a journey of inner development is one of the things we can do as parents in order to become role-models for our children and gain a better understanding of childhood.

7.10 Looking ahead

We don't know much about the future needs of our children. Much of this we will probably have to learn from them. Such learning will have to become ever more subtle and situation-related. We will learn from each child anew because the needs of children will become increasingly individual. It will be our task to make ourselves more susceptible and capable of learning even if we meet challenges and feel stretched to our limits. This requires unconditional openness and "positive anticipation" (Köhler 2018).

A documentary about the incumbent pope, quite unprecedented in its form, was recently shown in cinemas all over the world. We will conclude this chapter with some quotations from this film:

"Parents, remember to play with your children!"
"Have you whiled away some time playing with your children today?"
"Let us pray daily for love and a sense of humor."
"There is so much to do—and we must do it together!"

(Quoted from memory from *Pope Francis - A Man of his Word*, film documentary, Wim Wenders, 2018)

Bibliography

Rudolf Steiner's works cited in the text are referenced with their GA numbers (*Gesamt-ausgabe* or complete works), special editions with the year of publication.

Adorno, Theodor W. (1990): *Über Walter Benjamin. Aufsätze, Artikel, Brief.* Hrsg. und mit Anmerkungen versehen von R. Tiedemann. First revised edition. Frankfurt am Main: Suhrkamp.

Adorno, Theodor W. (1972): *Ästhetische Theorie.* Frankfurt am Main: Suhrkamp.

Aeppli, Willi (2013): *The Care and Development of the Human Senses. Rudolf Steiner's work on the significance of the senses in education.* Tr. V. Freilich. Edinburgh: Floris Books.

Agte, Vaishali V., Shashi A. Chiplonkar (2007): Linkage of concepts of good nutrition in yoga and modern science. *Current Science*, 956–961.

Aktionsbündnis Kinderrechte ins Grundgesetz (2018): Kinderrechte ins Grundgesetz | Deutsches Kinderhilfswerk. Aktionsbündnis Kinderrechte ins Grundgesetz. 2018. Online: www.dkhw.de/unsere-arbeit/schwerpunkte/kinderrechte/buendnisarbeit-fuer-die-kinderrechte/kinderrechte-ins-grundgesetz/.

Antonowsky, Aaron (1997): *Salutogenese: Zur Entmystifizierung der Gesundheit.* Erweiterte deutsche Ausgabe von A. Franke, Tübingen: dgvt.

Ariès, Philipp (1975/2014): *Geschichte der Kindheit.* Mit einem Vorwort von Hartmut von Hentig. 18th edition. Munich: Deutscher Taschenbuch Verlag.

Aristoteles (2018): *Über die Seele. De anima.* Greek-German edition. Edited, translated, introduced, and with commentary by Klaus Corcilius. Hamburg: Meiner.

Arvay, Clemens G. (2016): *Der Biophilia-Effekt: Heilung aus dem Wald.* Berlin: Ullstein.

Auer, Wolfgang-M. (2007): *Sinnes-Welten. Die Sinne entwickeln, Wahrnehmung schulen, mit Freude lernen.* 4. Auflage. Munich: Kösel.

Auer, Wolfgang-M. (2008): *Praxisbuch Sinne wecken: Sinne wecken: Spiele und Gestaltungsmöglichkeiten für Kindergarten und Vorschule.* Westermann.

Auer, Wolfgang-M. (2015): *Praxisbuch Sinne wecken.* 2nd edition, Schubi, Schaffhausen

Auer, Wolfgang-M. (eds) (2015): *Trau deinen Augen. Kunstbetrachtung an Waldorfschulen.* 2. Aufl. Stuttgart: Pädagogische Forschungsstelle beim Bund der Freien Waldorfschulen (edition waldorf).

Auer, Wolfgang-M. (2017): *Das Bochumer Modell des Bewegten Klassenzimmers.* Stuttgart: Pädagogische Forschungsstelle beim Bund der Freien Waldorfschulen (edition waldorf).

Ayres, A. Jean (1992): *Bausteine der kindlichen Entwicklung.* 2nd edition. Wiesbaden: Springer. English original: *Sensory Integration and the Child. Understanding Hidden Sensory Challenges.* Los Angeles (2005): Western Psychological Services.

Bandura, Albert (1976): *Lernen am Modell. Ansätze zu einer sozial-kognitiven Lerntheorie.* Stuttgart: Klett-Cotta.

Bandura, Albert/Walters, Richard Haig (1963/70): *Social Learning und Personality Development.* London, New York, Sydney, Toronto: Holt.

Bauby, Jean-Dominique (2004): *The Diving Bell and the Butterfly.* London: Harper Perennial.

Bauer, Joachim (2006): *Warum ich fühle, was du fühlst. Intuitive Kommunikation und das Geheimnis der Spiegelneurone.* 17th edition. Hamburg: Heyne.

Bauer, Joachim (2016): *Das Gedächtnis des Körpers. Wie Beziehungen und Lebensstile unsere Gene steuern.* Revised and extended edition. 7th edition. Frankfurt: Pieper.

Benedikter, Roland. (2017). Homo deus? Das Zusammenwachsen von Mensch und Maschine. Konrad Adenauer Stiftung. *Analysen & Argumente.* 270. p. 1–14.

Benjamin, Walter (1974): *Denkbilder.* Frankfurt: Suhrkamp.

Bintener, Véroniqe (2017): *Embodiment als Wirkmechanismus des Waldorfunterrichts. Die Sinneslehre Rudolf Steiners in ihrem Bezug zur physischen, sozial-emotionalen und kognitiven Entwicklung des Menschen.* Baden-Baden: Tectum.

Birnthaler, Michael (ed.) (2010): *Praxisbuch Erlebnispädagogik.* Stuttgart: Freies Geistesleben.

Bischof-Köhler, Doris (2011): *Soziale Entwicklung in Kindheit und Jugend. Bindung, Empathie, Theory of Mind.* Stuttgart: Kohlhammer.

BLIKK Studie - Stiftung Kind und Jugend (. o. J.). Online: www.stiftung-kind-und-jugend.de/projekte/blikk-studie/ (Accessed on 12.08. 2018).

Bockemühl, Almut (2010): *... das Herz eine Weile in den Kopf hinauffahren lassen: Rudolf Steiners Märchendichtung.* Dornach: Verlag am Goetheanum.

Bockemühl, Jochen (ed.) (1977): *Erscheinungsformen des Ätherischen. Wege zum Erfahren des Lebendigen in Natur und Mensch.* Stuttgart: Freies Geistesleben.

Bruland, Hansjörg (2008): *Wilde Kinder in der Frühen Neuzeit. Geschichte von der Natur des Menschen.* Stuttgart: Franz Steiner.

Bühler, Charlotte (1930): *Kindheit und Jugend. Genese des Bewusstseins.* 2nd edition. Leipzig: Hirzel.

Büssing, Arndt/Poier, Désirèe/Ostermann, Thomas/Kröz, Matthias/ Michalsen, Andreas (2018): Treatment of Chronic Lower Back Pain: Study Protocol of a Comparative Effectiveness Study on Yoga, Eurythmy Therapy, and Physiotherapeutic Exercises. *Complementary Medicine Research* 25 (1): 24–29. Online: doi.org/10.1159/000471801.

Campenhausen, Christoph von (1993): *Die Sinne des Menschen. Einführung in die Psychophysik der Wahrnehmung.*2nd edition. Stuttgart: Thieme.

Chekroud, Sammi R./Gueorguieva, Ralitza/ Zheutlin, Amanda B./ Paulus, Martin/ Krumholz, Harlan M./ Krystal, John H./ Chekroud, Adam M. (2018): Association between Physical Exercise and Mental Health in 1·2 Million Individuals in the USA between 2011 and 2015: A Cross-Sectional Study. *The Lancet Psychiatry* 0 (0). Online: doi. org/10.1016/S2215-0366(18)30227-X.

Collins, Christina L./ Fetsch, Robert J. (2012): A Review and Critique of 16 Major Parent Education Programs. *Journal of Extension* 50 (4). Online: www.joe.org/joe/2012august/a8.php.

Conard, Nicholas/Kind, Claus-Joachim (2017): *Als der Mensch die Kunst erfand. Eiszeithöhlen der Schwäbischen Alb.* Darmstadt: Theiss.

Covey, Stephen R. (2014): *The 7 habits of highly effective families.* London: St. Martin's Press.

Demisch, Hans-Christian/Greshake-Ebding, Christa/Kiersch, Johannes/ Schlüter, Martin/Stocker, Gerhard (eds) (2014): *Steiner neu lesen. Perspektiven für den Umgang mit Grundlagentexten der Waldorfpädagogik.* Frankfurt am Main: Peter Lang.

Dühnfort, Erika/Kranich, Ernst-Michael (1996)): *Der Anfangsunterricht im Schreiben und Lesen.* 5th edition. Stuttgart: Freies Geistesleben.

Dunn, Peter. M. (2006): Aristotle (384–322 Bc): Philosopher and Scientist of Ancient Greece. *Archives of Disease in Childhood – Fetal and Neonatal Edition* 91 (1): F75–77. Online: doi.org/10.1136/adc.2005.074534.

Dunstan, David W./ Howard, Bethany/ Healy, Genevieve N./ Owen, Neville (2012): Too much sitting–a health hazard. *Diabetes research and clinical practice* 97 (3): 368–376.

EduAction-Bildungsgipfel (2018): Den Weg für Zukunftskompetenzen ebnen. metropolregion.rhein.neckar. 2018. Online: www.m-r-n.com/pressemeldung-details/100287/.

Ekman, Paul (2004): *Gefühle lesen. Wie Sie Emotionen erkennen und richtig interpretieren.* München: Spektrum.English original: *Emotions revealed. Understanding Faces and Feelings.* London (2003): Phoenix.

Eller, Helmut (2018): *The Four Temperaments: Suggestions for Teachers.* Hudson NY: Waldorf Publications. Tr. C. Eller.

Eliot, Lise (2001): *Was geht darinnen vor? Die Gehirnentwicklung in den ersten fünf Lebensjahren.* Berlin: Berlin Verlag. English original: *What's Going on in There? How the Brain and Mind Develop in the First Five Years of Life.* New York (1999): Bantam Books.

Emmons, Natalie A./ Kelemen, Deborah (2014): The development of children's prelife reasoning: Evidence from two cultures. *Child development* 85 (4): 1617–1633.

Ende, Michael (2005): *Momo.* Neuausgabe. Esslingen: Thienemann.

Eric Seils, Eric/Höhne, Jutta (2015): III. WSI-KINDERARMUTSBERICHT. Online: www.boeckler.de/pdf/wsi_vm_kinderarmut_2015.pdf.

Erikson, Erik H. (1966/2013): *Identität und Lebenszyklus. Drei Aufsätze.* 26th edition. Frankfurt am Main: Suhrkamp.

Faraday, Michael (1964): *Naturgeschichte einer Kerze.* Stuttgart: Reclam.

Fichtner, Bernd (2008): *Lernen und Lerntätigkeit. Ontogenetische, phylogenetische und epistemologische Studien.* 2nd edition. Berlin: Lehmanns.

Flammer, August (2010): Psychologische Entwicklungstheorien. In: Krüger, Heinz-Hermann/Grunert, Cathleen (eds) (2010): *Handbuch Kindheits- und Jugendforschung.* 2nd revised and extended edition. Wiesbaden: VS, p. 43–64.

Föller-Mancini, Axel/Berger, Bettina (2016): Der Rubikon als Entwicklungsphänomen in der mittleren Kindheit. In: Schieren, Jost (ed.) (2016): *Handbuch Waldorfpädagogik und Erziehungswissenschaft. Standortbestimmung und Entwicklungsperspektiven.* Weinheim, Basel: Beltz Juventa, p. 272–299.

Forbes Coaches Council (2018): 16 Essential Leadership Skills For The Workplace Of Tomorrow. Forbes. 2018. Online: www.forbes.com/sites/forbescoachescouncil/2017/12/27/16-essential-leadership-skills-for-the-workplace-of-tomorrow/.

Fricke, Oliver/Halswick, Daniel/Längler, Alfred/ Martin, David D. (2018): Architecture for Sick Kids – Concepts of Environmental and Architectural Factors in Child and Adolescent Psychiatry. *Kinder- und Jugendpsychiatrie.*

Fromm, Erich (1977): *Anatomie der menschlichen Destruktivität.* 26th edition. Reinbek: Rowohlt.

Fromm, Erich (2016): *Die Seele des Menschen. Ihre Fähigkeit zum Guten und zum Bösen.* München: dtv.

Friedrich Fröbel (1823): Fortgesetzte Nachricht von der allgemeinen deutschen Erziehungsanstalt in Keilhau. In: id. (1914): *Fröbels kleinere Schriften zur Pädagogik. Mit bisher unveröffentlichtem Material.* Koehlers Lehrerbibliothek Vol. 6. Edited by H. Zimmermann, Leipzig: Köhler, p. 236ff.

Fuchs, Thomas (2008): *Leib und Lebenswelt. Neue philosophische psychiatrische Essays.* Kusterdingen: Graue Edition.

Fuchs, Thomas (2013): *Das Gehirn – ein Beziehungsorgan: Eine phänomenologisch-ökologische Konzeption.* 4th, revised and extended, edition. Stuttgart: Kohlhammer.

Fuchs, Thomas (2016): *Das Gehirn – ein Beziehungsorgan: Eine phänomenologisch-ökologische Konzeption.* 5th, revised and extended edition. Stuttgart: Kohlhammer.

Gebauer, Gunter/Wulf, Christoph (1992): *Mimesis. Kultur – Kunst – Gesellschaft.* Reinbek: Rowohlt.

Gebauer, Gunter/Wulf, Christoph (1998): *Spiel, Ritual, Geste. Mimetisches Handeln in der sozialen Welt.* Reinbek: Rowohlt.

Gebauer, Gunter/Wulf, Christoph (2003): *Mimetische Weltzugänge: Soziales Handeln - Rituale und Spiele - ästhetische Produktionen.* Stuttgart: Kohlhammer.

Gelitz, Philipp/Strehlow, Almuth (2018): *Die sieben Lebensprozesse: Grundlagen und pädagogische Bedeutung in Elternhaus, Kindergarten und Schule.* 2nd edition. Stuttgart: Freies Geistesleben. English translation: *The Seven Life Processes: Understanding and Supporting Them in Home, Kindergarten and School.* Spring Valley, NY: Waldorf Early Childhood Association of North America (2016), tr. N. Kuettel.

Glas, Alexander/Heinen, Ulrich/Krautz, Jochen/Lieber, Gabriele/Sowa, Hubert/Uhlig, Beate ((eds) (2017): *Mimesis. Imago. Zeitschrift für Kunstpädagogik.* Munich: kopaed.

Gläser-Zikuda, Michaela (ed.) (2007): *Lerntagebuch und Portfolio auf dem Prüfstand. Landau: Empirische Pädagogik.* Bad Heilbrunn: Klinkhardt.

Gläser-Zikuda, Michaela/Hascher, Tina (eds.) (2007): *Lernprozesse dokumentieren, reflektieren und beurteilen. Lerntagebuch und Portfolio in Bildungsforschung und Bildungspraxis.* Bad Heilbrunn: Klinkhardt.

Glöckler, Michaela (ed) (1992): *Das Schulkind – Gemeinsame Aufgabe von Arzt und Lehrer. Konstitutionsfragen, Unterrichtsschwierigkeiten, Therapeutische Lehrplanprinzipien.* Dornach: Verlag am Goetheanum.

Göhlich, Michael/Zirfas, Jörg /2007): *Lernen. Ein pädagogischer Grundbegriff.* Stuttgart: Kohlhammer.

Goethe, Johann Wolfgang (1998a): *Trilogie der Leidenschaft. An Werther.* In: ders.: Werke. Band 1. Gedichte und Epen I. Critically revised and commented by E. Trunz. 12th revised edition. Munich: Beck S. 380–386.

Goethe, Johann Wolfgang (1998b): *Wilhelm Meisters Lehrjahre.* In: ders.: Werke. Band 7. Romane und Novellen II. Critically revised and commented by E. Trunz. 12th revised edition. Munich: Beck.

Gopnik, Alison/Kuhl, Patricia; Meltzoff, Andrew (2000): *Forschergeist in Windeln.* Kreuzlingen: Ariston.

English original: *The Scientist in the Crib. What Early Learning Tells Us About the Mind.* New York (2001): Perennial.

Grimm, Jacob/Grimm, Wilhelm (1852 – 1960): Deutsches Wörterbuch. Online unter: woerterbuchnetz.de/cgi-bin/WBNetz/wbgui_py?sigle=DWB (Abruf: Oktober 2018).

[Grimm] (1975): *Kinder und Hausmärchen* gesammelt durch die Brüder Grimm mit den Zeichnungen von Otto Ubbelohde und einem Vorwort von I. Weber-Kellermann. Part 2. Frankfurt am Main: Insel.

Grossmann, Karin/Grossmann, Klaus E. (2017): *Bindungen – das Gefüge psychischer Sicherheit.* 7th edition. Stuttgart: Klett-Cotta.

Grunelius, Elisabeth/Kügelgen, Helmut von (1071): *Das Wesen des kleinen Kindes.* Studienmaterial der Vereinigung der Waldorfkindergärten. H. 3. Zusammenstellung von Texten Rudolf Steiners. Stuttgart: Vereinigung der Waldorfkindergärten und Pädagogische Forschungsstelle beim Bund der Freien Waldorfschulen.

Grunwald, Martin (2017): *Homo hapticus. Warum wir ohne Tastsinn nicht leben können.* Munich: Droemer.

Hadot, Pierre (2011): *Philosophie als Lebensform. Antike und moderne Exerzitien der Weisheit.* 3. Auflage. Frankfurt a. M.: Fischer.

Hannaford, Carla (2013): *Bewegung, das Tor zum Lernen.* VAK, Kirchzarten. English original: *Smart Moves. Why Learning is not all in the Head.* Great Ocean Publishers U.S., 2005.

Hatt, Hanns (1997): Der Geschmackssinn. In: Schmidt, Robert F./Thews, Gerhard (1997): *Physiologie des Menschen.* P. 318ff. 27th edition. Wiesbaden: Springer.

Hatt, Hanns/Dee, Regine (2008): *Das Maiglöckchen-Phänomen.* Piper, Munich

Hübner, Edwin (2008): *Imagination im virtuellen Raum. Technik und Spiritualität – Chancen eines neuen Jahrhunderts.* Frankfurt am Main: Clavis.

Humboldt, Wilhelm von (1792/2015): *Ideen zu einem Versuch, die Grenzen der Wirksamkeit des Staates zu bestimmen.* Stuttgart: Reclam.

Hobson, Peter (2003): *Wie wir denken lernen. Gehirnentwicklung und die Rolle der Gefühle.* Ostfildern: Patmos.

Hueck, Christoph (2016): *Intuition – das Auge der Seele: Die Darstellung des intuitiven Erkennens im schriftlichen Werk Rudolf Steiners.* 3th edition. Books on Demand.

Ich bin keine Fallpauschale. Universitätsklinik für Kinder- und Jugendmedizin Tübingen. www.ichbinkeinefallpauschale.de/portfolio/universitatsklinik-fur-kinder-und-jugendmedizin-tubingen/ (Accessed on 12.08.2018).

Jochem, Carmen/Leitzmann, Michael (2018): *Sitzstreik. Tipps und Tricks gegen die Risiken und Nebenwirkungen des Sitzens.* Freiburg: Herder.

Keller, Helen (2016): *The Story of my life,* New York: Quarto Publishing.

Kiersch, Johannes (2011): Waldorfpädagogik als Erziehungskunst. In: Uhlenhoff, Rahel (ed.) (2011): *Anthroposophie in Geschichte und Gegenwart.* Berlin: BWV, p. 423–476.

Kiersch, Johannes (2014): Einleitung. In: Demisch, Hans-Christian/Greshake-Ebding, Christa/Kiersch, Johannes/Schlüter, Martin/Stocker, Gerhard (Hrsg.) (2014): *Steiner neu lesen. Perspektiven für den Umgang mit Grundlagentexten der Waldorfpädagogik.* Frankfurt am Main: Peter Lang, p. 9–18.

Kiese-Himmel, Christiane (2001): Sprachentwicklung und haptische Wahrnehmung. In: Grunwald, Martin/Beyer, Lothar (eds): *Der bewegte Sinn. Grundlagen und Anwendungen zur haptischen Wahrnehmung.* Basel: Birkhäuser, p. 109–124.

Kluge, Norbert (2003): *Anthropologie der Kindheit. Zugänge zu einem modernen Verständnis von Kindsein in pädagogischer Betrachtungsweise.* Bad Heilbrunn: Klinkhardt.

Köhler, Henning (1998): *Vom Ursprung der Sehnsucht. Die Heilkraft von Kreativität und Zärtlichkeit.* Stuttgart: Freies Geistesleben.

Köhler, Henning (1999): *Schwierige Kinder gibt es nicht. Plädoyer für eine Umwandlung des pädagogischen Denkens.* 4th edition. Stuttgart: Freies Geistesleben.

Köhler, Henning (2003): *Vom Wunder des Kindseins. Kinder vertrauen sich uns an.* Stuttgart: Freies Geistesleben.

Köhler, Henning (2014): *Von ängstlichen, traurigen und unruhigen Kindern: Grundlagen einer spirituellen Erziehungspraxis.* Stuttgart: Freies Geistesleben.

Köhler, Henning (2018): Schritte für eine Bewusstseinswandel im Hinblick auf so genannte schwierige Kinder. Unpublished.

König, Karl (1971/1986): *Sinnesentwicklung und Leibeserfahrung.* 3rd edition. Stuttgart: Freies Geistesleben.

König, Karl/Soldner, Georg (2017): *Die ersten drei Jahre des Kindes: Erwerb des aufrechten Ganges, Erlernen der Muttersprache, Erwachen des Denkens.* Stuttgart: Freies Geistesleben.

Koepke, Hermann (1989a): *Das neunte Lebensjahr. Seine Bedeutung in der Entwicklung des Kindes.* 3rd edition. Dornach: Verlag am Goetheanum.

Kranich, Ernst Michael (1999): *Anthropologischen Grundlagen der Waldorfpädagogik.* Stuttgart: Freies Geistesleben.

Krautz, Jochen/Schieren, Jost (2013a): Persönlichkeit und Beziehung als Grundlage der Pädagogik. Zur Einführung. In: eadem. (ed.) (2013): *Persönlichkeit und Beziehung als Grundlage der Pädagogik.* Weinheim, Basel, p. 7–28.

Krüger, Heinz-Hermann/Grunert, Cathleen (Hrsg.) (2010): *Handbuch Kindheits- und Jugendforschung.* 2nd, revised edition. Wiesbaden: VS.

Kuckenburg, Martin (2001): *Als der Mensch zum Schöpfer wurde. An den Wurzeln der Kultur.* Stuttgart: KlettCotta.

Kühlewind, Georg (2001): *Sternkinder. Kinder, die uns besondere Aufgaben stellen.* Stuttgart: Freies Geistesleben.

Kühlewind, Georg (2006): *Das Leben der Seele zwischen Überbewusstsein und Unterbewusstsein. Elemente einer spirituellen Psychologie.* New edition (3rd overall edition), Stuttgart: Freies Geistesleben.

Kutik, Christiane (2012): *Entscheidende Kinderjahre: Ein Handbuch zur Erziehung von 0 bis 7.* 5th edition. Stuttgart: Freies Geistesleben.

Kutik, Christiane (2013): *Spielen macht Kinder stark.* Stuttgart: Freies Geistesleben.

Landau, Gerd/Sobczyk, Barbara (2001): Das mobile Klassenzimmer – ein Konzept, Unterricht in Bewegung zu bringen. In: Zimmer, Renate/Hunger, Ina (ed.): *Kindheit in Bewegung.* Schorndorf: Karl Hofmann, p. 226–231.

Lane, Harlan (1985): *Das wilde Kind von Aveyron. Der Fall des Wolfsjungen.* Frankfurt, Berlin, Vienna.

Lang, Thomas (1995): *Kinder brauchen Abenteuer.* 2nd edition. Munich: Ernst Reinhardt.

Largo, Remo (2010): *Lernen geht anders: Bildung und Erziehung vom Kind her denken.* Hamburg: edition Körber-Stiftung.

Largo, Remo (2019): *The Right Life. Human individuality and its role in our development, health and happiness.* Penguin Random House UK.

Leber, Stefan (1992): Zur Biographie und Pädagogik Rudolf Steiners. In: Leber, Stefan (1992): *Die Pädagogik der Waldorfschule und ihre Grundlagen.* Einleitung. 3rd edition. Darmstadt: Wissenschaftliche Buchgesellschaft.

Leber, Stefan (2002): *Kommentare zu Rudolf Steiners Vorträgen über Allgemeine Menschenkunde als Grundlage der Pädagogik.* 3 volumes. Stuttgart: Freies Geisteleben.

Lehrs, Ernst (1973/1982): *Vom Geist der Sinne. Zur Diätetik des Wahrnehmens.* 2nd edition. Frankfurt am Main: Klostermann.

Leonhardt, Wolfgang (2016): *Temperament und Lebenswirklichkeit. Zur Erneuerung der Temperamentenlehre in Pädagogik und Selbsterkenntnis.* Berlin: Pro Business.

Lievegoed, Bernard C. J. (1981): *Lebenskrisen – Lebenschancen. Die Entwicklung des Menschen zwischen Kindheit und Alter.* 2nd edition. Munich: Kösel.

Lievegoed, Bernard C. J. (2016): *Entwicklungsphasen des Kindes.* 10th edition. Stuttgart: Mellinger.

Lindenberg, Christoph (1988): *Rudolf Steiner: Eine Chronik; 1861–1925.* Stuttgart: Freies Geistesleben.

Lindenberg, Christoph (1997): *Rudolf Steiner. Eine Biographie.* Vol. 1: 1861–1914; Vol. 2: 1915–1925. Stuttgart: Freies Geistesleben.

Loebell, Peter (2004): *Ich bin, der ich werde: Individualisierung in der Waldorfpädagogik.* Stuttgart: Freies Geistesleben.

Loebell, P. (2016): Begründungsansätze für das Konzept der Jahrsiebte in der Waldorfpädagogik. In: Schieren, J.: *Handbuch Waldorfpädagogik und Erziehungswissenschaft. Standortbestimmung und Entwicklungsperspektiven.* Weinheim/Basel: Belz Juventa, p. 228–253.

Löffler, Thomas (2017): Erfahrungen mit dem Parcours. In: Auer, Wolfgang-M. (2017): *Das Bochumer Modell des Bewegten Klassenzimmers.* Stuttgart: Pädagogische Forschungsstelle beim Bund der Freien Waldorfschulen (edition waldorf), p.111–121.

Lukács, Georg (1963): *Eigenart des Ästhetischen.* 1. Halbband. Munich: Luchterhand.

Lumley, Henry de/Lumley, Marie Antoinette de (2011): *Les premiers peuplements de la Côte d'Azur et de la Ligurie.* Colomars: Melis.

Lutzker, Peter (1996): Der Sprachsinn. Sprachwahrnehmung als Sinnesvorgang. Stuttgart: Freies Geistesleben.

Magin, Renate (2017): Unterricht im Bewegungsspiel. In: Auer, Wolfgang-M. (2017): *Das Bochumer Modell des Bewegten Klassenzimmers.* Stuttgart: Pädagogische Forschungsstelle beim Bund der Freien Waldorfschulen (edition waldorf), p. 84–111.

Malson, Lucien/Itard, Jean/Mannoni, Octave (1972: *Die wilden Kinder.* Frankfurt am Main: Suhrkamp.

Mause, Lloyd de (ed.)/Langer, William L. (1974): *The History of Childhood.* New York: Psychohistory Press.

Mayer, F. Stephan/ McPherson Frantz, Cynthia/ Bruehlman-Senecal, Emma/ Dolliver, Kyffin (2009): Why is nature beneficial? The role of connectedness to nature. *Environment and behavior* 41 (5): 607–643.

Merleau-Ponty, Maurice (1966): *Phänomenologie der Wahrnehmung.* Berlin: Gruyter.

Mescerjakov, Alexander (2001): *Helen Keller war nicht allein.* Berlon: Spiess.

Metscher, Thomas (2004): *Mimesis.* 2nd revised edition. Bielefeld: transcript.

Meyer-Drawe, Käte (2012): *Diskurse des Lernens.* 2nd, revised edition. Munich: Fink.

Miller, Lisa/Barker, Teresa (2015): *The Spiritual Child. The New Science on Parenting for Health and Lifelong Thriving.* New York, St. Martin's Press.

Mietzel, G. (2002): *Wege in die Entwicklungspsychologie. Kindheit und Jugend.* 4th edition. Weinheim: Beltz.

Moritz, Karl Philipp (ed.) (1783/1986): *ΓΝΩΘΙ ΣΑΥΤΟΝ oder Magazin zur Erfahrungsseelenkunde als ein Lesebuch für Gelehrte und Ungelehrte.* First volume. Nördlingen: Greno.

Moritz, Karl Philipp (1999): Anton Reiser. *Ein psychologischer Roman.* In: Moritz, Karl Philipp (1999): Werke. Vol. I. Edited by H. Hollmer and A. Meier. Frankfurt a. M.: Deutscher Klassiker Verlag, p. 85-518.

Müller-Wiedemann, Hans (2015): *Mitte der Kindheit. Das neunte bis zwölfte Lebensjahr. Eine biographische Phänomenologie der kindlichen Entwicklung.* Stuttgart: Freies Geistesleben.

Neider, Andreas (2012): *Der Mensch zwischen Über- und Unternatur. Das Erwachen des Bewusstseins im Ätherischen und die Gefährdung der freien Kräfte.* Stuttgart: Freies Geistesleben.

Neider, Andreas (2014a): *Die Evolution von Gedächtnis und Erinnerung. Lesen in der Akasha-Chronik.* Stuttgart: Freies Geistesleben.

Neider, Andreas (ed.) (2014b): *Wo steckt unser Ich? Beiträge zu einer sphärischen Anthropologie.* Stuttgart: Freies Geistesleben.

Neugarten, Bernice L. (1974): Age groups in American society and the rise of the young-old. *The annals of the American academy of political and social science* 415 (1): 187–198.

Nielsen, Thomas William (2004): *Rudolf Steiner's Pedagogy of Imagination.* Bern: Peter Lang.

Niemeyer, Beatrix (1996): Ausschluss oder Ausgrenzung?: Frauen im Umkreis der Universitäten im 18. Jahrhundert. In: Kleinau, Elke/ Opitz, Claudia (eds): *Geschichte der Mädchen- und Frauenbildung.* Vol. 1: Vom Mittelalter bis zur Aufklärung. Frankfurt am Main: Campus.

Novalis (2001): *Werke.* Herausgegeben und kommentiert von Gerhard Schulz. Munich: Beck.

Oesterdiekhoff, Georg W. (2013): *Die Entwicklung der Menschheit von der Kindheitsphase zur Erwachsenenreife.* Wiesbaden: Springer VS.

Patzlaff, Rainer (2014): Pädagogische Grundlagen und Zielsetzungen. In: Patzlaff, Rainer/McKeen, Claudia/von Mackensen, Ina/Grah-Wittich, Claudia (2014): *Leitlinien der Waldorfpädagogik für die Kindheit von der Geburt bis zum dritten Lebensjahr.* 4th edition. Stuttgart: Pädagogische Forschungsstelle beim Bund der Freien Waldorfschulen, p. 7–24.

Patzlaff, Rainer/McKeen, Claudia/von Mackensen, Ina/Grah-Wittich, Claudia (2014): *Leitlinien der Waldorfpädagogik für die Kindheit von der Geburt bis zum dritten Lebensjahr.* Auflage. Stuttgart: Pädagogische Forschungsstelle beim Bund der Freien Waldorfschulen.

Pestalozzi, Heinrich (2009): *Wie Gertrud ihre Kinder lehrt. Ein Versuch, den Müttern Anleitung zu geben, ihre Kinder selbst zu unterrichten, in Briefen.* 2nd edition. Bad Schwartau: WFB.

Piaget, Jean (1945/2003): *Nachahmung, Spiel und Traum. Die Entwicklung der Symbolfunktion beim Kind.* 5th edition. Stuttgart: Klett-Cotta.

Piaget, Jean/Inhelder, Bärbel (1977/2002): *Von der Logik des Kindes zur Logik des Heranwachsenden. Essay über die Ausformung der formalen operativen Strukturen.* Olten, Freiburg: Walter.

Pikler, Emmi (2001): *Lasst mir Zeit: Die selbständige Bewegungsentwicklung des Kindes bis zum freien Gehen.* Untersuchungsergebnisse, Aufsätze und Vorträge aus dem Nachlass zusammengestellt und überarbeitet von Anna Tardos. 4th edition. Munich: Richard Pflaum.

Pleger, Wolfgang (2013): *Handbuch der Anthropologie. Die wichtigsten Konzepte von Homer bis Sartre.* Darmstadt: Wissenschaftliche Buchgesellschaft.

Pollmann, Stefan (2008): *Allgemeine Psychologie.* Munich, Basel: Reinhardt.

Parzinger, Hermann (2015): *Die Kinder des Prometheus. Eine Geschichte der Menschheit vor der Erfindung der Schrift.* Munich: Beck.

Postman, Neil (1982): *The Disappearance of Childhood.* New York: Delacorte Press.

Prahl, Hans-Werner (2002): *Soziologie der Freizeit.* Paderborn: Ferdinand Schöningh.

Prange, Klaus (1985/2000): *Erziehung zur Anthroposophie. Darstellung und Kritik der Waldorfpädagogik.* 3rd, extended edition, Bad Heilbrunn: Klinkhardt.

rightmanagement.co.uk. 2018. Online: www.rightmanagement.co.uk/ wps/wcm/connect/350a18c6-6b19-470d-adba-88c9e0394d0b/ Right+Management+Flux+Report+Spread.pdf?MOD=AJPERES.

Rittelmeyer, Christian (2010): Die Temperamente in der Waldorfpädagogik. Ein Modell zur Überprüfung ihrer Wissenschaftlichkeit. In: *RoSE*, Januar 2010, V 1, No. 1, p. 60–64. Online: www.rosejourn.com/index.php/rose/article/view/9/52.

Rizzolatti, Giacomo/ Sinigaglia, Corrado. (2014): *Empathie und Spiegelneurone. Die biologische Basis des Mitgefühls.* 5th edition. Frankfurt a. M.: Suhrkamp.

Rohen, Johannes W. (2009): *Eine funktionelle und spirituelle Anthropologie unter Einbeziehung der Menschenkunde Rudolf Steiners.* Mit Illustrationen von Jörg Pekarsky. Stuttgart: Freies Geistesleben.

Rosa, Hartmut (2016): *Resonanz. Eine Soziologie der Weltbeziehung.* Berlin: Suhrkamp.

Rosslenbroich, Bernd (1994): *Die rhythmische Organisation des Menschen. Aus der chronobiologischen Forschung.* Mit einem Vorwort von W. Schad. Stuttgart: Freies Geistesleben.

Rosslenbroich, Bernd (2009): *The theory of increasing autonomy in evolution: a proposal for understanding macroevolutionary innovations.* Biology & Philosophy 24 (5): 623–644.

Rosslenbroich, Bernd (2014a): *Die evolutionäre Bedeutung des Spiels. Jahrbuch für Goetheanismus.* Niefern-Öschelbronn: Tycho Brahe.

Rosslenbroich, Bernd (2014b): *On the origin of autonomy: a new look at the major transitions in evolution.* Vol. 5. Wiesbaden: Springer.

Rousseau, Jean-Jacques (2009): *Émile oder Über die Erziehung.* Hrsg. und mit Anmerkungen versehen von M. Rang. Stuttgart: Reclam.

Rudd, Melanie/Vohs, Kathleen D./Aaker, Jennifer (2012): Awe expands people's perception of time, alters decision making, and enhances well-being. *Psychological science* 23 (10): 1130 – 1136.

Ruhrmann, Bettina/Henke, Ingrid (2017): *Die Kinderkonferenz: Übungen und Methoden zur Entwicklungsdiagnostik.* 3rd edition. Stuttgart: Freies Geistesleben.

Sacks, Oliver (2006): *The Man Who Mistook his Wife for a Hat.* London: Picador.

Sand, Alexander/Eckert, Jost/Wikenhauser, Alfred (1986): *Das Evangelium nach Matthäus.* Vol. 1. Regensburg: Pustet.

Scheer-Krüger, Gerda (1996): *Das offenbare Geheimnis der Temperamente: Studien zu einem vertieften Verständnis der Temperamentskunde.* 2nd edition. Dornach: Verlag am Goetheanum.

Scheler, Max (1931): *Wesen und Formen der Sympathie. Eine Phänomenologie der Sympathiegefühle.* 3rd edition. Bonn: Friedrich Cohen.

Scheurle, Hans Jürgen (1984): *Die Gesamtsinnesorganisation. Überwindung der Subjekt-Objekt-Spaltung in der Sinneslehre.* 2nd edition. Stuttgart: Thieme.

Scheurle, Hans Jürgen (2016): *Das Gehirn ist nicht einsam: Resonanzen zwischen Gehirn, Leib und Umwelt.* 2nd, revised edition. Stuttgart: Kohlhammer.

Schiller, Friedrich (1795/2004): *Über die ästhetische Erziehung des Menschen in einer Reihe von Briefen*. Mit Ausführungen Rudolf Steiners und einer Einführung und einem Nachwort von Heinz Zimmermann. 3rd extended edition. Stuttgart: Freies Geistesleben.

Schneider, Wolfgang/Lindenberger, Ulman (eds) (2012): *Entwicklungspsychologie*. 7th fully revised edition. Weinheim, Basel: Beltz.

Selg, Peter (2011): *I am Different from You: How Children Experience Themselves and the World in the Middle of Childhood*. Tr. M. Saar. Great Barrington: SteinerPress.

Selg, Peter (2013): *Die Punkt-Umkreis-Meditation des Heilpädagogischen Kurses. Vom werdenden Ich des Menschen*. Arlesheim: Ita Wegman Institut.

Selg, Peter (2015a): *Anthroposophische Pädagogik. Rudolf Steiners Kurs im Berner Rathaus*. Arlesheim: Ita Wegmann Institut.

Selg, Peter (2015b): *Kindheit und Christus-Wesen. Von der therapeutischen Haltung im Angesicht der Bedrohung*. Arlesheim: Verlag des Ita Wegmann Instituts.

Selg, Peter (2017): *The Child as Sense Organ. An Anthroposophic Understanding of Imitation Processes*. Tr. C. Creeger. Great Barrington: SteinerPress.

Seydel, Anna (2009): *Ich bin Du, Kindererkenntnis in pädagogischer Verantwortung*. 4. Auflage. Stuttgart: Pädagogische Forschungsstelle beim Bund der Freien Waldorfschulen (edition waldorf).

Sherrington, Charles (1906): *The Integrative Action of the Nervous Systems*. Cambridge: Yale University Press.

Singh, Josef Amrito Lal (1942): *Wolf-Children and Feral Man*, New York: Harper & Brothers.

Smit, Jörgen (1996): *Lighting Fires. Deepening Education Through Meditation*. Tr. S. Blaxland-de Lange. Stroud, UK: Hawthorn Press.

Soesman, Albert (2017): *Our Twelve Senses: How Healthy Senses Refresh the Soul*. Stroud UK: Hawthorn Press.

Statistisches Landesamt Baden-Württemberg (2016): Höchste Lebenserwartung der Frauen und Männer im Landkreis Breisgau-Hochschwarzwald. Online: www.statistik-bw.de/Presse/Pressemitteilungen/2016326.

Stern, William (1920): *Die Intelligenz der Kinder und Jugendlichen und die Methoden ihrer Untersuchung. An Stelle einer dritten Auflage des Buches: Die Intelligenzprüfung an Kindern und Jugendlichen.* 3rd edition. Leipzig: Barth.

Steiner, Rudolf (GA 4) (1995): *Philosophie der Freiheit. Grundzüge einer modernen Weltanschauung. Seelische Beobachtungsresultate nach naturwissenschaftlicher Methode.* 1894/1918. 16th edition. Dornach: Rudolf Steiner Verlag.

Steiner, Rudolf: (GA 9) (2013): *Theosophie. Einführung in übersinnliche Weltanschauung und Menschenbestimmung.* 1904/1924. 33th edition. Dornach: Rudolf Steiner Verlag

Steiner, Rudolf (GA 10) (1992): *Wie erlangt man Erkenntnisse der höheren Welten?* 1904–1905. 24th edition. Dornach: Rudolf Steiner Verlag.

Steiner, Rudolf (GA 12) (1993): *Die Stufen der höheren Erkenntnis.* 1905–1908. 7th edition. Dornach: Rudolf Steiner Verlag.

Steiner, Rudolf (GA 13) (1989): *Die Geheimwissenschaft im Umriss.* 1910/1923. 30th edition. Dornach: Rudolf Steiner Verlag.

Steiner, Rudolf (GA 14) (2007): *Four Mystery Dramas. I. The Portal of Initiation. II. The Soul's Probation. III. The Guardian of the Threshold. IV. The Soul's Awakening.* Great Barrington: SteinerBooks/Anthroposophic Press. Tr. R. and H. Pusch.

Steiner, Rudolf (GA 15) (1987): *Die geistige Führung des Menschen und der Menschheit. Geisteswissenschaftliche Ergebnisse über die Menschheits-Entwicklung.* 1911. 10th edition. Dornach: Rudolf Steiner Verlag.

Steiner, Rudolf (GA 21) (1983): *Von Seelenrätseln. Anthropologie und Anthroposophie, Max Dessoir über Anthroposophie, Franz Brentano (Ein Nachruf). Skizzenhafte Erweiterungen.* 1917. 5th edition. Dornach: Rudolf Steiner Verlag.

Steiner, Rudolf (GA 24) (1982): *Aufsätze über die Dreigliederung des sozialen Organismus und zur Zeitlage.* 1915 – 1921. 2nd edition. Dornach: Rudolf Steiner Verlag.

Steiner, Rudolf (GA 28) (2000): *Mein Lebensgang.* 1925. 9th edition. Dornach: Rudolf Steiner Verlag.

Steiner, Rudolf (GA 34) (1987): *Lucifer – Gnosis. Grundlegende Aufsätze zur Anthroposophie und Berichte aus Zeitschriften «Luzifer» und «Lucifer – Gnosis» 1903–1908.* 2nd, newly revised edition. Dornach: Rudolf Steiner Verlag.

Steiner, Rudolf (GA 45) (2009): *Anthroposophie. Ein Fragment aus dem Jahre 1910.* 5th edition. Dornach: Rudolf Steiner Verlag.

Steiner, Rudolf (GA 53) (19841): *Ursprung und Ziel des Menschen. Grundbegriffe der Geisteswissenschaft.* 2nd extended edition. Dornach: Rudolf Steiner Verlag.

Steiner, Rudolf (GA 55) (1983): *Die Erkenntnis des Übersinnlichen in unserer Zeit und deren Bedeutung für das heutige Leben.* 2nd edition. Dornach: Rudolf Steiner Verlag.

Steiner, Rudolf (GA 57) (1984): *Wo und wie finden wir den Geist?* 1908–1909. 2nd revised and improved edition. Dornach: Rudolf Steiner Verlag.

Steiner, Rudolf (GA 59) (1984): *Metamorphosen des Seelenlebens. Pfade der Seelenerlebnisse. Zweiter Teil.* 1910. 1st edition in this combination. Dornach: Rudolf Steiner Verlag.

Steiner, Rudolf (GA 61) (1983a): *Menschengeschichte im Lichte der Geistesforschung.* 1909–1912. 2nd edition. Dornach: Rudolf Steiner Verlag.

Steiner, Rudolf (GA 62) (1988): *Ergebnisse der Geistesforschung.* 1912–1913. Dornach: Rudolf Steiner Verlag.

Steiner, Rudolf (GA 81) (1994): *Erneuerungsimpulse für Kultur und Wissenschaft. Berliner Hochschulkurs.* Dornach: Rudolf Steiner Verlag.

Steiner, Rudolf (GA 84) (1986): *Was wollte das Goetheanum und was soll die Anthroposophie?* 1923–1924. 2nd edition. Dornach: Rudolf Steiner Verlag.

Steiner, Rudolf (GA 95) (1990): *Vor dem Tore der Theosophie.* 4th, improved edition. Dornach: Rudolf Steiner Verlag.

Steiner, Rudolf (GA 107) (2013): *Disease, Karma, and Healing. Spiritual-Scientific Enquiries into the Nature of the Human Being,* Forest Row: Rudolf Steiner Press, tr. M. Barton

Steiner, Rudolf (GA 108) (1986): *Die Beantwortung von Welt- und Lebensfragen durch Anthroposophie.* 1908–1909. 2nd edition. Dornach: Rudolf Steiner Verlag.

Steiner, Rudolf (GA 115) (2001): *Anthroposophie, Psychosophie, Pneumatosophie.* 1909–1911. 4th, newly revised edition. Dornach: Rudolf Steiner Verlag.

Steiner, Rudolf (GA 124) (1995): *Exkurse in das Gebiet des Markus-Evangeliums.* 1910–1911 4th, newly revised edition. Dornach: Rudolf Steiner Verlag.

Steiner, Rudolf (GA 127) (1989): *Die Mission der neuen Geistesoffenbarung. Das Christus-Ereignis als Mittelpunktsgeschehen der Erdenevolution.* 1911. Dornach: Rudolf Steiner Verlag.

Steiner, Rudolf (GA 154) (1985): *Wie erwirbt man sich Verständnis für die geistige Welt? Das Einfließen geistiger Impulse aus der Welt der Verstorbenen.* 1914. Rudolf Steiner Verlag.

Steiner, Rudolf (GA 166) (1982): *Notwendigkeit und Freiheit im Weltgeschehen und im menschlichen Handeln.* 1916. 3rd, newly revised edition. Dornach: Rudolf Steiner Verlag.

Steiner, Rudolf (GA 169) (1998): *Weltwesen und Ichheit.* 1916. 3rd edition. Dornach: Rudolf Steiner Verlag.

Steiner, Rudolf (GA 170) (1992): *Das Rätsel des Menschen. Die geistigen Hintergründe der menschlichen Geschichte.* Vol. 1. 1916. 3rd edition. Dornach: Rudolf Steiner Verlag.

Steiner, Rudolf (GA 177) (1996): *Die spirituellen Hintergründe der äußeren Welt. Der Sturz der Geister der Finsternis.* 1917. 6th edition. Dornach: Rudolf Steiner Verlag.

Steiner, Rudolf (GA 179) (1993): *Geschichtliche Notwendigkeit und Freiheit. Schicksalseinwirkungen aus der Welt der Toten.* 1917. 4th edition. Dornach: Rudolf Steiner Verlag.

Steiner, Rudolf (GA 224) (2015): *Die menschliche Seele in ihrem Zusammenhang mit göttlich-geistigen Individualitäten.* 1923. 4th edition. Dornach: Rudolf Steiner Verlag.

Steiner, Rudolf (GA 266a) (1995): *Aus den Inhalten der esoterischen Stunden. Gedächtnisaufzeichnungen von Teilnehmern.* Band I: 1904–1909. Dornach: Rudolf Steiner Verlag.

Steiner, Rudolf (GA 269) (1997): *Ritualtexte für die Feiern des freien christlichen Religionsunterrichtes und das Spruchgut für Lehrer und Schüler der Waldorfschule.* Dornach: Rudolf Steiner Verlag.

Steiner, Rudolf (GA 271) (1985): *Kunst und Kunsterkenntnis. Grundlagen einer neuen Ästhetik.* 1888–1921. 3rd edition, with four added essays 1890 and 1898. Dornach: Rudolf Steiner Verlag.

Steiner, Rudolf (GA 275) (1990): *Kunst im Lichte der Mysterienweisheit.* 1914–1915. 3rd edition. Dornach: Rudolf Steiner Verlag.

Steiner, Rudolf (GA 276) (2002): *Das Künstlerische in seiner Weltmission. Der Genius der Sprache. Die Welt des sich offenbarenden strahlenden Scheines. Anthroposophie und Kunst Anthroposophie und Dichtung.* 1923. 4th edition. Dornach: Rudolf Steiner Verlag.

Steiner, Rudolf (GA 277a) (1998): *Die Entstehung und Entwicklung der Eurythmie.* 3rd edition. Dornach: Rudolf Steiner Verlag.

Steiner, Rudolf (GA 291a) (1990): *Farbenerkenntnis. Ergänzungen zu dem Band «Das Wesen der Farben». Schriftliche und mündliche Darstellungen von Rudolf Steiner und Anderen Abbildungen, Handschriftenwiedergaben und Dokumente.* 1889–1925. Dornach: Rudolf Steiner Verlag.

Steiner, Rudolf (GA 293) (1992): *Allgemeine Menschenkunde als Grundlage der Pädagogik, Teil I.* 1919. 9th, newly revised and extended edition. Dornach: Rudolf Steiner Verlag.

Steiner, Rudolf (GA 294) (1990): *Erziehungskunst. Methodisch-Didaktisches (II).* 1919. 6th edition. Dornach: Rudolf Steiner Verlag.

Steiner, Rudolf (GA 295) (1984): *Erziehungskunst. Seminarbesprechungen und Lehrplanvorträge (III).* 1919. 4th edition. Dornach: Rudolf Steiner Verlag.

Steiner, Rudolf (GA 297) (1998): *Idee und Praxis der Waldorfschule.* 1919–1920. Dornach: Rudolf Steiner Verlag.

Steiner, Rudolf (GA 297a) (1998): *Erziehung zum Leben. Selbsterziehung und pädagogische Praxis.* 1921–1924. Dornach: Rudolf Steiner Verlag.

Steiner, Rudolf (GA 300a, b, c) (1995): *Konferenzen mit den Lehrern der Freien Waldorfschule 1919–1924.* Bd. I: Ausführliche Einleitung von E. Gabert. Konferenzen 1919–1921; Bd. II: Konferenzen 1921–1923; Bd. III: Konferenzen 1923–1924. Register. Unveränderter Nachdruck der 1. Auflage. Dornach: Rudolf Steiner Verlag.

Steiner, Rudolf (GA 301) (1991): *Die Erneuerung der pädagogisch-didaktischen Kunst durch Geisteswissenschaft.* 1920. 4th edition. Dornach: Rudolf Steiner Verlag.

Steiner, Rudolf (GA 302) (1986): *Menschenerkenntnis und Unterrichtsgestaltung.* 1921. 5th edition. Dornach: Rudolf Steiner Verlag.

Steiner, Rudolf (GA 302a) (1993): *Erziehung und Unterricht aus Menschenerkenntnis.* 1920–1923. 4th edition. Dornach: Rudolf Steiner Verlag.

Steiner, Rudolf (GA 303) (1987): *Die gesunde Entwicklung des Menschenwesens. Eine Einführung in die anthroposophische Pädagogik und Didaktik.* 1921–1922. 4th edition. Dornach: Rudolf Steiner Verlag.

Steiner, Rudolf (GA 304) (1979): *Erziehungs- und Unterrichtsmethoden auf anthroposophischer Grundlage.* 1921–1922. Dornach: Rudolf Steiner Verlag.

Steiner, Rudolf (GA 304a) (1979): *Anthroposophische Menschenkunde und Pädagogik.* 1923–1924. Dornach: Rudolf Steiner Verlag.

Steiner, Rudolf (GA 305) (1991): *Die geistig-seelischen Grundkräfte der Erziehungskunst. Spirituelle Werte in Erziehung und sozialem Leben.* 1922. 3rd edition. Dornach: Rudolf Steiner Verlag.

Steiner, Rudolf (GA 306) (1989): *Die pädagogische Praxis vom Gesichtspunkt geisteswissenschaftlicher Menschenerkenntnis.* 1923. 4th edition. Dornach: Rudolf Steiner Verlag.

Steiner, Rudolf (GA 307) (1986): *Gegenwärtiges Geistesleben und Erziehung.* 1923. 5th edition. Dornach: Rudolf Steiner Verlag.

Steiner, Rudolf (GA 308) (1986): *Die Methodik des Lehrens und die Lebensbedingungen des Erziehens.* 1924. 5th edition. Dornach: Rudolf Steiner Verlag.

Steiner, Rudolf (GA 310) (1989): *Der pädagogische Wert der Menschenerkenntnis und der Kulturwert der Pädagogik.* 1924. 4th edition. Dornach: Rudolf Steiner Verlag.

Steiner, Rudolf (GA 311) (1989): *Die Kunst des Erziehens aus dem Erfassen der Menschenwesenheit.* 1924. 5th edition. Dornach: Rudolf Steiner Verlag.

Steiner, Rudolf (GA 317) (1995): *Heilpädagogischer Kurs.* 1924. 8th edition. Dornach: Rudolf Steiner Verlag.

Steiner, Rudolf (1907): Die Erziehung des Kindes vom Gesichtspunkte der Geisteswissenschaft. In: Steiner, Rudolf (1987): *Lucifer – Gnosis. Grundlegende Aufsätze zur Anthroposophie und Berichte aus Zeitschriften «Luzifer» und «Lucifer – Gnosis» 1903–1908.* GA 34. Dornach: Rudolf Steiner Verlag, p. 309–348.

Steiner, Rudolf (1909): Praktische Ausbildung des Denkens. In: id. (GA 108) (1986): *Die Beantwortung von Welt- und Lebensfragen durch Anthroposophie, 1908–1909.* 2nd edition. Dornach: Rudolf Steiner Verlag, p. 256–278.

Steiner, Rudolf (1984): *Wege der Übung.* Vorträge, ausgewählt und hrsg. von St. 3rd edition. Stuttgart: Freies Geistesleben.

Steiner, Rudolf (2004a): *Ich bin. Meditationen für den Alltag.* Ausgewählt und hrsg. von T. Gut. Dornach: Rudolf Steiner Verlag.

Steiner, Rudolf (2004b): *Texte zur Pädagogik. Anthroposophie und Erziehungswissenschaft. Quellentexte für die Wissenschaften.* Vol. 2. Ed. J. Kiersch. Dornach: Rudolf Steiner Verlag.

Steiner, Rudolf (2006): *Die Welt der Märchen: Ausgewählte Texte.* Edited by A. Bockemühl. Dornach: Rudolf Steiner Verlag.

Steiner, Rudolf (2007): *Das gespiegelte Ich. Der Bologna-Vortrag – die philosophischen Grundlagen der Anthroposophie.* 1911. Edited and introduced by A. Neider. Dornach.

Steiner, Rudolf (2008): *Die Welt der Pädagogik. Ausgewählte Texte.* Edited by U. Dietler. Dornach: Rudolf Steiner Verlag.

Steiner, Rudolf (2009a): *Die praktische Ausbildung des Denkens. Drei Vorträge.* Edited by J.-C. Lin. 4th edition. Stuttgart: Freies Geistesleben.

Steiner, Rudolf (2009b): *Rückschau. Übungen zur Willensstärkung.* Edited and introduced by M. M. Sam. Dornach: Rudolf Steiner Verlag.

Steiner, Rudolf (2012): *Sich selbst erziehen. Das Geheimnis der Gesundheit.* Edited and introduced by H. Haas. Basel: Futurum.

Steiner, Rudolf (2013a): *Die Erziehung des Kindes vom Gesichtspunkte der Geisteswissenschaft.* With an introduction by Cornelius Bohlen. 2nd edition. Basel: Futurum.

Steiner, Rudolf (2013b): *Die praktische Ausbildung des Denkens. Drei Vorträge.* Edited by W. Kugler and J.-C. Lin. 5th edition. Stuttgart: Freies Geistesleben.

Steiner, Rudolf (2014): *Andacht und Achtsamkeit: Stufen des Wahrnehmens.* Edited by A. Neider. Dornach: Rudolf Steiner Verlag.

Steiner, Rudolf (2015a): *Die Chakren: Sinnesorgane der Seele.* Edited by A. Neider. Dornach: Rudolf Steiner Verlag.

Steiner, Rudolf (2015b): *Nervosität und Ichheit. Stressbewältigung von innen.* Mit einem Vorwort von Frank Meyer. Dornach: Rudolf Steiner Verlag.

Stoltz, Tania/Wiehl, Angelika (2019): Das Menschenbild als Rätsel für jeden. Anthropologische Konzeptionen von Jean Piaget und Rudolf Steiner im Vergleich. In: *Pädagogische Rundschau* 2019 (in preparation)

Storch, Maja/Cantiene, Benita/Hüther, Gerald/Tschacher, Wolfgang (2017): *Embodiment. Die Wechselwirkung von Körper und Psyche verstehen und nutzen.* Göttingen: Hogrefe.

Taylor, Charles (2012): *Quellen des Selbst. Die Entstehung der neuzeitlichen Identität.* 8th edition. Frankfurt am Main: Suhrkamp.

Thiel, Ansgar/Teubert, Hilke/Kleindienst-Cachay (2006): *Die Bewegte Schule auf dem Weg in die Praxis. Theoretische und empirische Analysen einer pädagogischen Innovation.* 3rd, revised edition. Baltmannsweiler: Schneider.

Tomasello, Michael (2006): *Die kulturelle Entwicklung des menschlichen Denkens.* Frankfurt am Main: Suhrkamp.

Tomasello, Michael (2010): *Warum wir kooperieren.* Berlin: Suhrkamp.

Tomasello, Michael (2016): *Naturgeschichte der menschlichen Moral.* Berlin: Suhrkamp.

Treichler, Rudolf (2015): *Die Entwicklung der Seele im Lebenslauf. Stufen, Störungen und Erkrankungen des Seelenlebens.* 7th edition. Stuttgart: Freies Geistesleben.

Ullrich, Heiner (1986/1991): *Waldorfpädagogik und okkulte Weltanschauung. Eine bildungs- philosophische und geistesgeschichtliche Auseinandersetzung mit der Anthropologie Rudolf Steiners.* 3rd edition. Weinheim, Munich: Juventa.

Ullrich, Heiner (2015): *Waldorfpädagogik: Eine kritische Einführung.* Weinheim: Beltz.

Ulset, Vidar/Vitaro, Frank/Brendgen, Mara/Bekkhus, Mona/Borge, Anne (2017): Time spent outdoors during preschool: Links with children's cognitive and behavioral development. *Journal of Environmental Psychology* 52: 69 – 80.

Van Lommel, Pim/Van Wees, Ruud/Meyers, Vincent/ Elfferich, Ingrid (2001): Near-death experience in survivors of cardiac arrest: a prospective study in the Netherlands. *The Lancet* 358 (9298): 2039–2045.

Verhulst, Jos (1999): *Der erstgeborene: Mensch und höhere Tiere in der Evolution.* Stuttgart: Freies Geistesleben.

Vinzens, Albert (2013): *Spiel-Zeuge: Hommage an das Spiel.* Klein Jasedow: thinkOya.

Vinzens, Albert/Denger, Johannes/Guttenhöfer, Peter/Kuhfuss, Werner/ Schulze, Manfred (2011): *Lasst die Kinder spielen: Wie das Spiel den Menschen bildet.* Stuttgart: Verlag Freies Geistesleben.

Wagemann, Johannes (2010): *Gehirn und menschliches Bewusstsein. Neuromythos und Strukturphänomenologie.* Aachen: Shaker.

Wember, Valentin (2017): *Menschenkunde Meditieren.* Tübingen: Stratos.

Wenders, Wim (2018): *Pope Francis – A Man of his Word.* Film documentary.

Wiechert, Christof (2014): *Solving the Riddle of the Child. The Art of Child Study.* Dornach: Verlag am Goetheanum.

Wiehl, Angelika (2015): *Propädeutik der Unterrichtsmethoden in der Waldorfpädagogik.* Frankfurt a. M.: Peter Lang.

Wiehl, Angelika (2016a): Bilderfahrung als pädagogisches Paradigma. Anschauungsunterricht versus bildhafte Unterrichtsmethoden in der Waldorfpädagogik. In: *Research on Steiner Education* (RoSE). Vol 7, No 1 (2016), p. 31–41 (Online at: www. rosejourn.com).

Wiehl, Angelika (2016b): Das propädeutische Methodenkonzept der Waldorfpädagogik. In: Schieren, Jost (Hrsg.): *Handbuch Waldorfpädagogik und Erziehungswissenschaft. Standortbestimmung und Entwicklungsperspektiven.* Weinheim, Basel: Beltz Juventa. p. 538–576.

Wiehl, Angelika (2017a): Erzählen – eine grundlegende Methode der Waldorfpädagogik. In: *Lehrerrundbrief* 106, p. 86–104.

Wiehl, Angelika (2017b): „Pädagogische Intuition" – ein Forschungsprojekt am Graduiertenkolleg Waldorfpädagogik. Dr. Angelika Wiehl im Gespräch mit Prof. Dr. Wolfgang Nieke, Universität Rostock, und Shozan Shimoda, Stipendiat des Graduiertenkollegs Waldorfpädagogik. In: *RoSE* 2017, V 8, No. 1, S. 15–21. Online: www.rosejourn.com/index.php/rose/article/view/391/365.

Wiersing, Erhard (2015): *Theorie der Bildung. Eine humanwissenschaftliche Grundlegung*. Paderborn: Schöningh.

Winckelmann, Johann Joachim (1756/2013): *Gedancken über die Nachahmung der Griechischen Wercke in der Mahlerey und Bildhauer-Kunst. Sendschreiben. Erläuterung*. Edited by M. Kunze. Stuttgart: Reclam.

Woitinas, Siegfried (2003): *Wer sind die Indigo-Kinder? Herausforderungen einer neuen Zeit*. Stuttgart: Urachhaus.

Wright, Barry, und Elizabeth Edginton (2016): Evidence-based parenting interventions to promote secure attachment: findings from a systematic review and meta-analysis. *Global pediatric health* 3: 2333794X16661888.

Wulf, Christoph (no year): Mimesis. In: Online: www.ewi-psy.fu-berlin.de/einrichtungen/arbeitsbereiche/antewi/media/buecher_historische_anthropologie/historische_anthropologie/historische_anthropologie_04.pdf (Accessed on 25.8.2017).

Wulf, Christoph (2005): *Zur Genese des Sozialen. Mimesis, Performativität, Ritual*. Bielefeld: transcript.

Wulf, Christoph (2014a): *Bilder des Menschen. Imaginäre und performative Grundlagen der Kultur*. Bielefeld: transcript.

Wulf, Christoph (2014b): Mimesis. In: Wulf, Christoph/Zirfas, Jörg (eds) (2014): *Handbuch Pädagogische Anthropologie*. Wiesbaden: Springer VS, p. 247–257.

Wulf, Christoph (2017): Mimesis. In: Glas, Alexander/Heinen, Ulrich/Krautz, Jochen/Lieber, Gabriele/Sowa, Hubert/Uhlig, Beate ((eds) (2017): *Mimesis. Imago. Zeitschrift für Kunstpädagogik*. Munich: kopaed, p. 14–26.

Wulf, Christoph/Zirfas, Jörg (eds) (2014): *Handbuch Pädagogische Anthropologie*. Wiesbaden: Springer VS.

Wundts, Wilhelm (1911): *Einführung in die Psychologie*. Leipzig: Dürr'sche Buchhandlung.

Zech, M. Michael (2011): „Jahrsiebte" als heuristisches Instrumentarium – oder: weshalb Waldorfpädagogik wirksam ist. Ein Essay zu Steiners Entwicklungskonzept. In: *Rundbrief der pädagogischen Sektion am Goetheanum* 42. Michaeli 2011, p. 17–21.

Zech, M. Michael (2018): Anthroposophische Jugendpädagogik und die Herausforderungen des frühen 21. Jahrhunderts. In: Wiehl, Angelika/ Zech, M. Michael (eds.): *Jugendpädagogik in der Waldorfschule. Studienbuch*. 2nd, improved edition. Kassel: Pädagogische Forschungsstelle beim Bund der Freien Waldorfschulen (edition waldorf).

Ziegler, Renatus (2015): *Intuition und Ich-Erfahrung. Erkenntnis und Freiheit zwischen Gegenwart und Ewigkeit*. 2nd, revised edition. Stuttgart: Freies Geistesleben.

Zimmer, Renate (2002): *Schafft die Stühle ab! Was Kinder durch Bewegung lernen*. Freiburg: Herder.

Zimmer, Renate (2012): *Handbuch Sinneswahrnehmung*. 22. Auflage. Freiburg: Herder.

Zimmermann, Heinz/Schmidt, Robin (2016): *Meditation. An Introduction to the Anthroposophical Practice of Meditation*. Tr. M. Rommelt, H. Vukovich, B. Knaack. Quebec: Perceval.

English-language editions of source texts by Rudolf Steiner

The following is not an exhaustive list, but is intended as an aid to further research for the English-speaking reader. Books by Rudolf Steiner are frequently published with new translations, altered titles, or in different combinations, and there may be alternate or newer versions of the ones listed here. The GA number, referring to the number given to each work in the German *Gesamtausgabe* (catalog of collected works) is a reliable means of identification. The term CW is sometimes used in English editions.

For the particular edition used in preparing the source texts in this volume, see the notes after each entry. When no English edition is given there, the text was newly translated from the German.

GA 4: *Intuitive Thinking as a Spiritual Path. A Philosophy of Freedom.* Hudson NY 1995. Tr. Michael Lipson.

GA 9: *Theosophy. An Introduction to the Spiritual Processes in Human Life and in the Cosmos.* Hudson NY 1994, tr. Catherine E. Creeger.

GA 10: *How To Know Higher Worlds. A Modern Path of Initiation.* Hudson NY 2010, tr. Christopher Bamford.

GA 15: *The Spiritual Guidance of the Individual and Humanity,* Hudson NY 1992, tr. Samuel Desch.

GA 24: *The Renewal of the Social Organism,* London 1998, tr. E. Bowen-Wedgewood and R. Mariott.

from GA 34: "The Education of the Child in the Light of Spiritual Science," in *The Education of the Child and Early Lectures on Education,* Great Barrington 1996, tr. George and Mary Adams.

from GA 57: *The Four Temperaments.* Forest Row 2008. Tr. Brian Kelly. Also in *Anthroposophy in Everyday Life,* Great Barrington 1996.

GA 61: Human History in the Light of Spiritual Research. Not published in English.

from GA 62 and 108: *The Poetry and Meaning of Fairy Tales.* Spring Valley 1989. Tr. Ruth Pusch.

GA 95: *Founding a Science of the Spirit.* Forest Row 2012. Tr. not credited.

from GA 108: "Practical Training in Thought," Anthroposophical Publishing Co 1928, tr. George Kaufmann. Also in *Anthroposophy in Everyday Life,* Great Barrington 1996.

GA 127: The Mission of the New Spiritual Revelation. Not published in English.

GA 154: *The Presence of the Dead on the Spiritual Path.* Hudson NY 1990. Tr. Christian von Arnim.

GA 169: *Toward Imagination. Culture and the Individual.* Hudson NY 1990, tr. Sabine Seiler.

GA 170: *The Riddle of Humanity. The Spiritual Background of Human History.* Forest Row 1990, tr. John Logan.

GA 179: *The Influence of the Dead on Destiny.* Great Barrington 2007. Translator not credited. Translation updated by Marsha Post.

GA 266: *Esoteric Lessons Part I: 1904–1909,* Great Barrington 2011.

GA 271: Art and Knowledge of Art. Not published in English.

GA 276: *The Arts and Their Mission.* Anthroposophic Press, 1964.

GA 293: *Study of Man,* translated by A C Harwood, London 1995. Also available as *The Foundations of Human Experience,* Great Barrington 1996.

GA 294: *Practical Advice to Teachers,* Great Barrington 2000, tr. Johanna Collis.

GA 295: *Discussions with Teachers,* Great Barrington 1997, tr. Helen Fox, Catherine Creeger and Maisie Jones.

GA 302a: *Balance in Teaching.* Great Barrington 2007. Tr. Ruth Pusch.

GA 303: *Soul Economy: Body, Mind, and Spirit in Waldorf Education,* Great Barrington 2003.

GA 304a: *Waldorf Education and Anthroposophy 2,* Hudson NY 1996, tr. Roland Everett.

GA 305: *The Spiritual Ground of Education,* Great Barrington 2004.

GA 306: *The Child's Changing Consciousness as the Basis of Pedagogical Practice,* Hudson NY 1996, tr. R. Everett.

GA 307: *A Modern Art of Education.* Great Barrington 2004, tr. R. Lathe, N. Whittaker.

GA 311: *The Kingdom of Childhood,* Hudson NY 1995, tr. Helen Fox.

GA 317: *Education for Special Needs,* London 2015.

About the authors and translator

WOLFGANG-M. AUER, PH.D., born 1943; doctorate in art history; 30 years' experience as Steiner Waldorf grade and high school teacher; lecturer in Waldorf school and Kindergarten trainings; author of the *Moving Classroom* concept in Waldorf schools; publications on art observation, Waldorf education, and the World of the Senses; presently lecturing worldwide on Waldorf education with specific focus on anthropology and the education and development of the senses.

DAVID MARTIN, M.D., born 1973, university professor, pediatrician, pediatric endocrinologist and oncologist; since 2011 qualified university lecturer in pediatrics; since 2014 adjunct professor of pediatrics at Tuebingen University (Germany); senior physician for general pediatrics and acute psychosomatics, head of endocrinology and oncology at Filderklinik, Filderstadt (Germany); since 2017 holder of the Gerhard Kienle Chair for Medical Theory, Integrative and Anthroposophic Medicine at Witten-Herdecke University (Germany).

SILKE ALMA SCHWARZ, M.D., born 1971; studied special needs education, art therapy, and medicine at Cologne University (DE); doctorate in neonatology; medical resident at Cologne University Pediatric Clinic and in private pediatric practice. Public health officer for pediatrics; anthroposophic kindergarten and school doctor; director of *Kindgerecht*, a medical-educational advice center; and research fellow at Witten-Herdecke University (Germany).

ANGELIKA WIEHL, PH.D., born 1956; studied German and Romance philology and art history; co-founder of the Wolfsburg Waldorf school (DE); many years' experience as grade and high school teacher; lecturer in Waldorf teacher seminars; doctorate on the "Propaedeutics of Teaching Methods in Waldorf Education;" publications on Waldorf education, anthropology, and art; now lecturer in education sciences and Waldorf education at the Institute for Waldorf Education, Inclusion and Interculturality at Alanus University, Mannheim (Germany).

MARGOT M. SAAR has a degree in linguistics, translating and interpreting from Saarbrücken University (Germany), and studied Waldorf Education at Witten-Annen (Germany) and Philosophy of Mind at the Open University (United Kingdom). She taught at Waldorf Schools in the UK for twenty years, has translated many books, mostly in philosophy, anthroposophy, education, complementary medicine and the history of medicine, and is now working as a full time translator and conference interpreter.

CPSIA information can be obtained
at www.ICGtesting.com
Printed in the USA
BVHW041652270120
570628BV00009B/85